# The Kabbalah of Intimacy

# The Kabbalah of Intimacy

## A Modern Implication of
## a Primordial Wisdom

### Limor Blockman, PhD

Waterside Productions

Printed in the United States of America

First Printing, 2020

ISBN-13: 978-1-947637-04-7 print edition
ISBN-13: 978-1-947637-05-4 ebook edition

**Waterside Productions**
2055 Oxford Ave
Cardiff, CA 92007
www.waterside.com

When I was scheming to write this book, I was in the midst of a vast research. Yes, it was comprised of reading, collecting, and analyzing the resources around Kabbalah, but it was also a very deep dive into the very core of my soul.

This book is a collection of thoughts and practices that formulated the path toward my own personal healing and enlightenment.

# Table of Contents

# Chapter 1
## Knowledge Is Power

You would think one would begin with the question of "What is Kabbalah?" but before I embark on that long journey, I would like to propose a preliminary question: What is intimacy?

In Western upbringing, we are exposed to certain ideas around love, relationship, and the bond of a conventional coupledom, but looking back at my own very conventional young adult life, I do not think the word or the concept of intimacy ever reared its beautiful head. Think back to your experience. Was the idea of intimacy a part of it? And if so, what did it look like?

I was raised in a functional two-parent home where no mighty expressions of fondness were exhibited, but they weren't reserved either. I believe that the concept of true intimacy (no, we haven't defined it yet. You're following along sensationally!) is a very private notion, one that forms with the onset of a supportive relationship and continues to grow and evolve as we acquire further experiences, relational mistakes, and disappointments. But wait, don't we need to arrive at a relationship equipped with the skill of intimacy in order to make it a successful one? I chose to start small and optimistic, so I consulted the common dictionary, which defines intimacy as *close familiarity or friendship*, as *sexual intercourse* or as *closeness of observation or knowledge of a subject*.

You may say, "Sure, sexual exchange, that is intimacy, over and out!" But if intimacy is simply the act of fornication, it wouldn't be a solely human ability (is it?). And no, I am not referring to nonreproductive sexual engagements that certain mammals do enjoy and practice,[1] bear with me as we create our own definition here.

So, in lieu, we are left with *close familiarity or closeness and knowledge of a subject*.

Let's put this to the test. If I develop intimacy with my partner, does it mean we are close? Likely, yes. Check.

If we are indulging in the act of love together, does it mean we have a "firm knowledge of one another"? Hopefully so. Check!

Here's where the connection between intimacy and the wisdom of Kabbalah merges: knowledge; or rather, knowingness.

As promised, I will explore and define Kabbalah (as much as possible, giving the fact that no one has been successful of truly defining this ancient wisdom per se), but for now, let me throw you back in a dream and land you in the middle of the beautiful Garden of Eden.

## Quickstep Meditation

Close your eyes and take a deep breath through your mouth, all the way up to the top of your lungs. Now, purse your lips and let your breath out slowly, as if you're whistling through them. Repeat this three times, and keep a comfortable posture while reverting to normal breathing.

The imagery: you are now in the presence of creation par excellence. There has never been nor will there be a more refined outcome in this material world of ours. Yes, I'm relating to this place and its inhabitants. With your eyes closed, I'd like you to imagine the sound of dew on the ground; waterfalls running peacefully in all directions of

---

1   DeWaal, Frans B. M. 2006. "Bonobo Sex and Society." *Scientific American* 16 (2): 14–21. https://doi.org/10.1038/scientificamerican0606-14sp.

the garden; animals moseying along gracefully and peacefully; gorgeous flowers of purple, red, and orange covering the entire ground and tickling your bare feet as you walk wide-eyed and astounded through these grounds. Then, you catch a glimpse of the regal couple. No, not Megan and Harry, it's the beautiful and perfectly navel-free Adam and Eve. They frolic in the (almost) nude, since only recently they both fell from grace after consuming that forbidden fruit—more on that later.

They skulk into a hidden corner of the Garden. What are they planning to do there? Genesis 4:1 tells us, "And the man knew Eve his wife; and she conceived and bore Cain."

You may now take another full inhale and exhale, then slowly open your eyes.

Are you back? Good!

But wait! What is this euphemism for? Can't we simply say that the royal couple had sexual relations?

Kabbalah tells us that, in fact, no, we cannot. Stating this would deem this translation inaccurate. If Adam only engaged in intercourse with Eve then, yes, that would be applicable and accurate. But, since Adam's familiarity with Eve, on a soul level, is what enabled this holistic merging resulting in conception, they didn't only have sex, they engaged in the holistic act of *knowing* one another's core being, the very definition of intimacy! The choice of word, namely "knowing," was not incidental, but rather a particular choice of what an intimate soul connection entails.

OK, so we have the concept of intimacy in check. Now what? How do we acquire this sense of closeness with another, and more important, do all relational connections carry the potential of encompassing intimacy? I'm glad you asked, because this is where things may become a bit more complex.

# Your Soul and Soul Mate

You knew this was coming. In order to explore this very important topic, we first must ask, "What is a soul?" You may have a direct and concise response to it; something along the lines of "the emotional part of human nature," or "the principle of life, considered a separate entity from the physical form, i.e. the body."[2] These are spectacular and accurate (we haven't even begun to explore the question of soul and body relations, which we will soon). Nonetheless, if you entertain the primordial wisdom of Kabbalah for the definition of the soul, things start to expand and evolve to a point of no return. Here's a quick peek.

# Soul by Kabbalah

Kabbalah tells us that our soul is a Godly or divine essence compartmentalized in a physical form known as "the body." They are interconnected by the body's ability to manifest aspects of your soul via its very particular conditions, features, and construction. So, in other words, if I have a certain body and carry myself in a certain way, the alteration of these features (for instance, an intense weight loss, a diagnosis of a physical illness, and so forth) will eventually reveal different aspects of my soul—what we may relate to as *soul growth* or *personal development*. So far, so good; if you take a moment to carefully examine these definitions in your personal life experience, you will realize that radical changes in your condition do, in fact, create a myriad of new opportunities, experiences, and physical sensations that were entirely novel to you prior to the related transformation, as if you were a "new person." In fact, you are.

   Two imperative points come to mind in light of this interesting definition: First, the fact that your soul does not change, your body does. By the altered body, the soul is able to reveal itself in a variety of ways that were foreign to the "old body." Take a moment to repeat this notion

---

2   Dictionary.com. n.d. "Soul." In *Dictionary.com*.

in your mind; the prior and renewed manifestations of your external self were both encompassed in the soul, but its revelation, this way or another, is determined by your physical, earthly emitting. Second, in our common definitions, we tend to relate the "change of heart" of personal development to an "inner working of the soul," a change that came from within. But, according to the suggested Kabbalistic principle, the inner condition is static and was always existing. These different potentials were dormant and weren't revealed until the physical transformation, a platform that enabled the "changed position" of the soul, which was only "revealed" to you after many hours of spiritual work, meditation, and mindfulness practices. Is the revolutionary component of this definition apparent yet? The soul needs no growth, it is fully developed. What it does need is for the vessel she's held within (your delectable body) to allow the soul to shine in the most enlightening potential it can achieve. Don't take a breath just yet, I want to expand it just a tad bit further.

What does Kabbalah think of the mind?

The mind, by these teachings, is the expression of the soul merging through the great physical mechanism known as the brain. To simplify it, your brain is the machinery, while your soul is the energy going through it.

As if this isn't complicated enough, Kabbalistic teachings tell us the concept of *gilgul* (reincarnation) and how it relates to that precious soul we all carry.

It is usually thought that reincarnation takes place after a person passes from this world—after the death of the body—at which time or soon after the soul transmigrates into another body. Here, we are presented with a new definition called *Ibur* (gestation), a process that involves receiving a new (higher) soul, during one's lifetime here in this universe. Bear with me through this explanation: Ibur speaks of a new soul coming into a person's heart while he is still alive—thus the term Ibur—for one's soul to become impregnated with another soul while still alive. If you examine this phenomenon, you'll understand the deeper explanation behind the change manifested by extreme experiences we may encounter in our lives courses. We either undergo a change of mind about certain things, or change our lifestyles, and thereby ascend to the next spiritual level. This is also included under the general heading of gilgul-incarnation, because by receiving this "download," we are now hosting a new soul and acting as a vehicle for that soul's rectification. This is what occurs when a person is ready to advance in his soul evolution. This is why the soul enters five realms, each higher than the other, namely *nefesh*, *ruach*, *neshamah*, *chayah*, and *yechidah*. The Zohar tells us that the four levels of the soul usually enter a person during his lifetime. Alas, receiving access to the highest realm, yechida, isn't accessible to us humans during life here in this shallow level of existence called the world of action. The Zohar adds that Adam would have received it had he not sinned.

OK, that settles soul, for the time being. But how do we find or recognize our "soul mates," and what does that even mean?

Disregarding the pop definition of soul mates and temporarily with-holding the variety of tips regarding how to locate it, become it, merge with it, or separate from it, let's examine the Kabbalistic view of this concept.

Kabbalistic teachings state that the first person created (i.e., Adam or Adam Kadmon), by the specific Kabbalistic definition, encompassed a universal soul (in Hebrew its referred to as *neshamah klalit*) that included aspects of all creation; for this reason, even one "small" act on his part (like the consumption of the forbidden fruit) could have such powerful implications. After this particular choice, Adam's soul fragmented into innumerable sparks, which subsequently became clothed/incarnated in every human being that was ever born and will ever live. These particular fragments of the universal soul are placed in different bodies, thus when we relate to a "soul connection," one can potentially be attained with simply anyone because they are all a part of this universal soul—"relative souls" is the Kabbalistic term for that matter. However, when we encounter a specific soul that seems more "familiar" to us, this connection, or what we relate to as soul mate awareness, becomes more "tangible," if you will.

Kabbalistic teachings become even more intricate with the presenta-tion of the "principle souls" concept. Here, we are looking at a specific designation that each of these souls received upon the "big bang" of the primordial sin; each soul was designated to a specific part of Adam's body. Simply put, we have souls that are nestled in the head, ones in the feet, others in the hands, and so forth.

When two souls from the same "location" encounter one another, it is more likely that a certain bond will form, very much like the sensation two travelers from the same home town may experience upon running into one another while traveling in foreign, unfamiliar land.

So, if I am a "head soul" rather than a "foot soul," does it mean that I am a superior soul? Not in any shape or form. One must keep in mind that in the world of souls, no tangible criteria applies. The designated origin, by Kabbalistic views, is manifesting in the reflection of these location-based origins upon our personality traits. So, a head soul would be characterized in a more charismatic mannerism. That soul will be comfortable in a leadership position and will be less of a team player. It's imperative to make clear none of these traits or features are positive or negative in their essence, but rather have their implications in a more advantageous or less beneficial expression, by our interpretation of them in our daily lives. Feet souls will be more grounded, as an example, but being grounded could be a terrific trait when manifested as responsibility and accountability, and not so beneficial if creates anxiety over embarking into unknown terrains or being overly guarded.

## The Four Elements

Another component of our personality that can be utilized in our quest of a significant other, or a soul mate, could be the distribution of the four elements within us.

We encompass all four elements—fire, water, earth, and air—within us at all times, but one of the elements will be dominant, which will manifest in greater aspects of our character being influenced by it. The second influential element will be subdominant, the third supportive, and the fourth, sub-supportive.

What are the components of these elemental influences in our character?

A dominant fire principle will relate to the emotional state we are characterized by. The emotional flow is represented by fire. Here, too, we can notice a significant implication of beneficial versus less beneficial expressions of this dominant element. If I am high in fire, it may be expressed in overbearing, less tolerant, and intense components of my personality, which could be less inviting to be around. But, if I manage that high fire (very much like a stovetop burner) and utilize it toward passionate and all giving expression of my behavior, I can be experienced as a pleasant person who is "all heart," per se.

Air relates to communication. Personalities that are verbal, talkative, and express themselves well verbally are high in the air element.

Earth will manifest in a settled and calm nature, as we suggested in the more grounded "feet souls." Nonetheless, not all foot souls are dominant in earth; some may have a bigger water component to their personality, which will be explained below.

Water speaks of enjoyment. You must think, "Well, what does that mean and how could enjoyment be related to the grounded character?"

I'm glad you asked, because this particular element is a very interesting one, yet may be compared to a double-edged sword.

The idea of gratification and enjoyment will be determined as beneficial or less advantageous by its intrinsic nature; what I mean is that if a dominant water element is consumed by self-pleasure, indulgences, stimulation of the mind and body, experiences of constant titillation, and satisfaction, it will be expressed as an *external* water element, one that is mainly selfish and self-concerned.

Conversely, if that water element is experienced as an *internal* manifestation principle, the person will be more geared toward self-inspection, meditation, supporting others' spiritual paths, striving toward oneness, and so forth. They may be more comfortable being a part of a group rather than leading (in relation to a foot soul), and they'll dedicate most of their energy toward enlightenment and gratitude.

How does this all relate to soul mates? Does it mean that we must share the same "dominant component" in order to be complementary and compatible? The answer is in the question: dominant elements can be compatible *only* if they are complementary; in other words, the idea behind "opposites attract" isn't a superficial pop culture suggestion but rather based psychological law.[3]

Kabbalistic teachings, nonetheless, are aligned with the study referenced when stating that these gaps in dominant elemental features should be enough to intrigue us, but *not* overplay our essential requirements for a successful coupledom. In other words, a strong fire element can be drawn to, and get along famously with, a partner who is water elemented, but only if they both utilize their *internal* adaptation for the long run. For example, a water element partner being a spiritual and supportive character alongside a fire elemented partner who practices passionate and compassionate acts of giving. This adjustment can and should be enhanced once they are in the relationship. Love and desire could represent an aligned source or be completely opposing elements, as we will explore in the coming chapters.

## Quickstep Meditation

Most of us are very aware of our more intense disposition, but along our life experiences and as we grow older and wiser, this disposition may alter or adjust. Regardless of your certainty regarding your dominant element, try the meditation below to gain more certainty and grasp over this life principle.

Sit in a comfortable position, close your eyes, and take a deep breath through your mouth, all the way up to the top of your lungs. Now, purse your lips and let your breath out slowly as if you're whistling through them. Repeat this three times, and keep a comfortable posture while reverting to normal breathing.

Position one hand on the ground and the other on your chest over your heart.

---

3   Lindová, Jitka, Anthony C. Little, Jan Havlíček, S. Craig Roberts, Anna Rubešová, and Jaroslav Flegr. 2016. "Effect of Partnership Status on Preferences for Facial Self-Resemblance." *Frontiers in Psychology* 7 (June). https://doi.org/10.3389/fpsyg.2016.00869.

Go within and ask for guidance. Ask your intuitive knowing and this benevolent universe to direct you at your strongest nature.

Be attuned to the signals you receive; they may be very mild, or conversely, mighty and powerful, but stay in your intuitive mode and listen.

A random example of this explicit manifestation could be water elements sensing more of a vibe through their chest-positioned hand than the ground-positioned hand. A fire element may feel a rush in both; an earth element will be moved more by the ground hand, and finally, an air element may feel the need to lift both hands off their position. Stay in your breath and intuition, trust what is coming.

Once you feel secure in your gathered information, release your hands, and take another deep breath through your nose, exhale through your pursed lips slowly and gradually.

Open your eyes and remain seated.

Now, in this new enlightenment, take a look at the chart below, and without further contemplation, mark your position in the four elements.

Keep your chart and revisit it, both individually and with your future or current partner, for future reference.

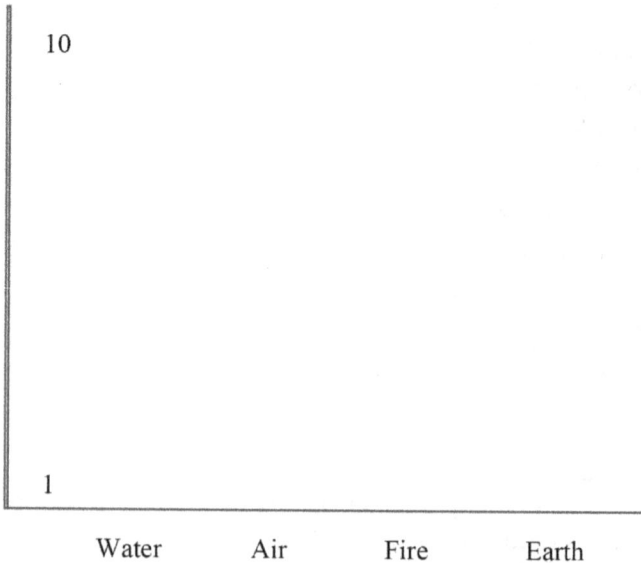

```
10




1
     Water      Air      Fire      Earth
```

# Unconditional Love

OK, so we are on our way to locate the perfect soul mate and align our dominant strengths with theirs in order to make it a successful dyad. But what does a successful relationship entail? Do we dedicate ourselves to one another entirely and limitlessly? Do we share all activities? Do we keep personal space? Are we allowed to have different emotions toward one another and still "define" this exchange as successful? Under the sweet and tangy taste of a romance novel, a Hollywood chick flick, or a "15 Tips for a Perfect Relationship" piece in a tabloid, we fail to notice the bitter and shackling aspect of these "norms" or social regulations we are all forced to subconsciously abide by.

Let's begin with the overly used and likely inaccurate term "unconditional love." To the general layman, it will sound like a positive thing, a supportive component in a relationship (any form, for that matter—not solely romantic) and a concept we should all strive for. But is it really? What is so flattering about my love being unconditional? If its unconditional, doesn't it cancel or eliminate the receiver of this love's particular traits, features, tendencies, characteristics, and so forth? If I love you unconditionally because you're my partner, doesn't it mean that anyone can step into your place and I will crown them with the same "unconditional" designation?

Kabbalistic views on this matter are intriguing.

The idea of "unconditional" is essentially frowned upon, and the concept of "love" in its juvenile, "candy cane" form, even more so.

Let's break it down to a more comprehensible picture.

Kabbalah suggests that if you or I matter in this dyad, it cannot be unconditional, because the you or I factor, is, in fact, a condition. I'm in this partnership with *you*, not just anyone, and thus, this is conditional.

Now, looking at love, these teachings have a few points to drive home.

Love, to start with, isn't the main component of a relationship. It isn't *the* relationship, no matter what the romantic hit list tells you; it is simply a feeling. It can be the spirit of the relationship, but it isn't the full definition of it. It would be correct to view it as a response to the relationship that is ideally present most of the time. Reverting back to the former point of "condition," I'm allowed (and by human definition must have) a myriad of emotions that should and will fluctuate in the relationship as it grows, progresses, and evolves. Therefore, I cannot "love you unconditionally," since at times I may be angry, unhappy, disappointed, hurt, and so forth; but, I can, and will (if I choose a fully committed relationship par excellence) be your committed partner, *unconditionally*. In other words, the unconditional factor is there, only attached to the commitment, not to love, which is, as mentioned, a feeling, and thus by its very nature, should fluctuate; to the situation we are in together, that is, the committed relationship, I'm unconditionally devoted.

By Kabbalistic views, a successful relationship (namely marriage in the more religious sense) is characterized by this selflessness of the commitment. As long as we are two separate entities "giving and receiving" love or any other emotional gestures, we are operating from the place of distance; the only way to merge and dissolve into this committed dyad is by removing the soul gap between us and allowing the true merging to take place.

As the Hebrew alphabet is viewed to be the "Holy Tongue" that the Creator used in order to form this universe, we use the analysis of the Hebrew terms for man and woman in order to relate to this sacred unity.

For the sake of this specific example I will mention that one of the most-used terms for the Creator is יה.

The word for man in Hebrew is איש, and the word for woman is אשה.

If we look at these two short words, we notice that they encompass two similar letters, *aleph* (א) and *shin* (ש); they differ in a single letter, *hey* (ה) for the woman and *yud* (י) for the man.

If we connect the yud and the hey, we find that they form the name of God יה, as mentioned above. So, under this mystical analysis, Godliness or a divine presence is always present in the unity of man and woman. But, if this unity is formatted in a complete dissolving and merging fashion, it will produce another factor; that factor is formed from the letters א and ש together, summing to the Hebrew word אש translated to English as "fire." In a holistic observation, this utter commitment and melting into one another, along with the divine presence, integrates the fire of passion and creation in this unity. This is the essence of infinite manifestation of the masculine and feminine factors in the particular relationship.

We can use the pleasant analogy of a jigsaw puzzle. A profound unity of a man and a woman in a committed relationship can be very similar to a complete and beautiful jigsaw puzzle, sans missing pieces. The puzzle pieces do not care much for their personal identification or placement; they all strive for one particular goal of making the puzzle whole and complete. They don't argue about where is a more dominant spot to be placed in the puzzle, they don't fuss about the actual details on their piece looking prettier or more sophisticated than another's; all they strive for is the formation of a holistic, complete goal. Now, does this mean a strong, committed relationship should strip us from our personal identity or remove any terms and boundaries from the dyad? Quite the opposite, actually, as we will discover in the coming chapters.

## The True Meaning of Oneness

We all strive to meet our kindred spirit, live a beautiful fairytale life in a supportive relationship, experience success, and have two-and-a-half children and a white picket fence—or at least a diluted version of it.

However, regardless of the chewed-up concept of living by example, or "being the change you want to see in the world," we are surrounded by erroneous manufactured concepts of love, devotion, and relationship, some of which were mentioned earlier.

As we already established, love is not the answer for all, "unconditional" is not necessarily a compliment, and the attainment of a true connection can only come from a full merging of the two participating parties. So now what?

The Kabbalistic concept of a marriage (or any form of a committed relationship for that matter) requires the establishment of a few basic foundations; three, to be exact.

# The Trifecta

The first foundation is **sanctity**; the idea of a committed relationship, albeit existing in a world of "no fault divorce" management, should be understood as a divine concept. The decision to enroll in a marriage is not an earthly, human concept, even though it appears as part of social structure, one that opposes our ancestral nature (more about that later). In fact, it is quite the opposite; if we choose to engage in such a commitment, we should take into account that submitting to a committed relationship is a divine concept, and therefore us humans are likely to struggle with different aspects of it. How can it be solved, thus, on a cognitive level? Keep reading.

Relating to our dyad as a sacred one holds the potential of eliminating the "quick on the trigger" notion that is being practiced in this regard.

The second foundation encompassed in this trifecta is **generosity**. We often fail to notice that as we progress in a committed relationship, we become pettier with our partner. If we take a conscious look at it, the means by which we relate to this unit would be considered obscene and insulting if applied to any source of communication outside of the marriage. We grow to avoid basic communication, give each other sarcastic remarks, disregard, unrelate, overlook, and insult our partner, while we wouldn't dream of acting in this fashion with a work colleague or other friendly associate in fear of eliminating them from our lives! Yet, we proceed with this pettiness, day in and day out, without ever giving it another thought.

Last but definitely not least is the third foundation of a committed relationship. That foundation is **dignity**. We can never have enough of it. Not only that the sanctity of this unit and the generosity required here are bound to be entangled with dignity, but in using this term, I mean a lot more than the basic idea of just being respectful toward one another. Having true dignity is sourced in the concept of not getting overly familiar with our partner.

What does that mean?

Well, there are many manners in which this can be incorporated, but protecting the atmosphere in our joint home is the onset of it all. Let me explain: if we share a home and both exhibit a lack of interest in our indoor appearance and our basic bodily functions, or our personal space is being breached, or the manner in which we speak to one another is undignified, we create an *overfamiliarity*. And you know what is the first and most essential ingredient in a passionate existence? Novelty.

In other words, we are very capable of creating a home status that will enable less familiarity without creating a distance.

A few examples could be found in the universal need to know and be aware of every single detail about our spouse. Do we really need to leave the bathroom door open while using it? If my partner has a physical feature she's less pleased with, do I really have to stare right at it and comment (or not) in hope that my words, or silence, will be aligned with her desired response from me?

Being physically intimate is another aspect that can be utilized here. This isn't a choice that will be acceptable by all, but if you dare go deeper into the core of human behavior, you may unveil its essentiality.

Creating personal space in our sleeping arrangements can be super beneficial to our intimate prosperity. In other words, if you're able and willing to attempt using separate beds or bedrooms, you may find they benefit your love life. The French are known for their lack of interest in cohabitating and their preference for separate habitats. You're not obligated to reach this great length, but if you take it from the "masters of love and passion," the distance may create the need for seduction, allurement, and, yes, initiative. If I'm laying right beside you in our joint bed and you prefer to watch a game of soccer over a physical exchange, I may find it insulting. But, if we are both enjoying our privacy and ability to make the actual nocturnal engagement special and sacred, we may find that we long for one another and go to extremes to find a new way to surprise one another in our coming rendezvous.

Another concept in Kabbalistic teachings sheds light on our roles in this divine dyad. As I mentioned earlier, we are human, and thus dealing with a divine program may be challenging. So, how do we really overcome our selfish needs and become selfless in this "dissolvement" into one another? The idea behind this is this is a transformation that each one of us must make. This transformation is called transitioning into a husband and wife, from a prior state of man and woman. You see, man and woman cannot and will not get along! We initiated that discord in the Garden of Eden, and we keep establishing it in the high and rising divorce rates. But, how many of us really considered the difference between a husband and wife versus man and woman? Being a husband or a wife isn't glamorous; it isn't exciting (in its mundane facet); and it entails many sacrifices. The mistake we make is attempting to remain who we were prior to the committed unity in order to "keep our identity" out of fear of losing ourselves. However, to attain and maintain a true committed dyad, we must melt into this pot rather than maintain our past identity.

It does not mean we become helpless and dependent, and it does not mean that we lose our voices; it does mean, nonetheless, that we become a *unit* rather than collaborating partners. In a marriage, we shouldn't be afraid to *need* our partner, we shouldn't be worried to be seen as weak, and we shouldn't be concerned more with the social view of our unit than what is taking place inside it; we change our status *and* our perspective, not only the former. Yes, it may be a difficult task, but who said being divine is an easy walk in the Garden?

# Chapter 2
## Facing Fear

Looking at this topic, you may ask yourself, "What kind of fear am I relating to?" Or maybe you tell yourself, "I am a fearless creator and my life is going smoothly," which is fantastic if it is (more about being that creator, soon).

Nonetheless, fear is a large component in the human existence, and yes, naturally it has its strong hold and impact on our love life and sustainability in a dyad.

Let's begin with a primordial idea. Do we face similar fears as men and women, unrelated to our relational status? For this very imperative contemplation, we are going to delve into a state of mind that may enable an accurate, personal reply.

## Quickstep Meditation

Since the "location of fear" isn't mapped, and one may feel or sense it in literally any part of the human body, you'll be encouraged to find the spot that *you* personally relate to the emergence of fear from past experience.

Sit in a comfortable position, close your eyes, and take a deep breath through your mouth, all the way up to the top of your lungs. Now, purse your lips and let your breath out slowly as if you're whistling through them. Repeat this three times and keep a comfortable posture while reverting to normal breathing.

Position one hand on your chest and the other around the area where you normally sense fear when it emerges. It can be your chest (if it is, place both hands on your chest), it can be your throat, your feet, your head, or your neck. Feel free to roam and explore.

Go within and ask for guidance. Ask your intuitive knowing and this benevolent universe to direct you to your source of fear. Where does it appear and what is its nature? Does it have a color, a smell, a specific sound, or a ringing? Try to give it as much detail as possible in order to later narrow it down.

Once you feel you have acquired your desired information, remain in this position, and breathe into the location of fear. Spend a count of three breathing in and out of the hand positioned around the fear factor, and then another three seconds of breathing into the chest. So, if your fear locator is based in your neck, you'll inhale into it to the count of three, then exhale there to the count of three. Then, proceed to the chest inhaling to three and exhaling to three. Rotate between the two locations and repeat for five cycles. If the fear is located in your chest, you may want to still double the count.

Once you feel secure and peaceful, slowly regain normal rhythmic breath, and open your eyes.

Write down a few notes for future reference so you can have a base to return to, should you need to revisit your fear.

Now that you've accomplished the important task of fear location, we can probe into the more philosophical nature of fear in your life, because that is the source of all your challenges.

We mentioned that there's a primordial factor to be observed here regarding fear.

If, even on a subconscious level, we base our knowingness on our "story of origin"—that is, our story of creation—we are told that man was created from dust and woman was created from man (for the sake of this discussion we will disregard what part of the human that relates to).

If our subconscious contemplates these mere facts, we may be astounded by the true source of all miscommunication in a committed relationship.

The idea that man is sourced in dust—that is, nothing—and that woman is sourced in man—that is, something—can shed an immediate light on what troubles us in a dyad, and why is it so different. Allow me to simplify it.

When a man is engaged in a relationship, his biggest fear is to be reverted back to his nothingness.

Relatedly, a woman partner, being unaware of this sensitivity, may walk right into the abyss of relationships. Let's use a real-life example to make this idea clear.

If your partner aims to replace a lightbulb, and you, his female partner, mention the simplicity of it or claim that you are very capable of handling it yourself, it isn't your partner's ego that is being compromised here, it is his mere existence—the core value of your male partner—that is being jeopardized, albeit unintentionally. Note that we are not relating to an actual physical extinction or a real threat to his existence on a conscious level, but the incompatible reaction that a scenario of this sort may produce, which is sourced in that very basic fear. This is also the reason men tend to "provide solutions" when all you needed was for him to listen to you and hold your hand. This does not come from a need to overpower, but from an actual fear of not being needed or relevant and, thus, reverting to nothing.

Bear with me through this idea.

So, if this is a genuine concern, what is the gender difference, and what source of fear are women challenged by? Great question; it is one that has a precise answer.

Since a woman was created from something—that is, man—a woman's biggest vulnerability or source of subconscious weakness is not reverting into nothingness, but the fear of losing her identity to a man and experiencing gender-based injustice. This female sensitivity to the latter is likely the source of the emergence of the feminist movement. Unfortunately, this sensitivity to injustice can also produce a justification-based tolerance, which can explain the female leniency toward abuse. An abused wife who stays by her abusive husband's side and keeps sharing their home isn't necessarily a woman who lacks self-worth or is oblivious to the risks she's facing, but rather she's a woman who finds "justification" for her condition, as absurd as this may sound to an outsider. "Oh, he slapped me? It's probably because I forgot the food in the oven and it burned. If I do a better job, this won't happen." The woman excuses and justifies her spouse's behavior by providing a "logical" explanation for the abuse.

These gaps between the female weakness and male fear may also lead to aggression, which is obviously gender related and more common in males; the need to prove a "worth" can generate acts of bravado or machismo that can wreak havoc on the relationship or a general relational conduct. The fact that men thrive in challenging situations or combat is similarly related, due to its ground to provide "solutions," proving the male necessity. A woman is free to be a nurturer in nature because she's not in a constant "threat to her existence" like her male partner, thus she can be completely content with caring for things as they emerge, rather than running around in search of "fixing." These are basic gender-based differences that are not conscious or practiced on a daily level, mindfully.

They lay under the surface yet lead our lives in the direction we, at times, wish they did not. When we jokingly relate to men and women as alien species, we are not so far from the truth.

## Soulful Consciousness

Now that we've discussed the ins and outs of gender-related fears, we can more deeply comprehend how the cliché that "men are from

Mars and women are from Venus" materializes in our physical lives, conducts, and stressors, and how it may jeopardize or flat-out eliminate our chances of attaining—and maintaining—a strong bond with our better half.

Since fear is the ultimate soul-depriving mechanism, it is imperative to understand how it is so, and what can we do to eliminate it.

How can this task be achieved? Simply put, we can achieve this reality by living consciously. On a larger, more intricate scale, it may require establishing of a whole new way of thinking, feeling, and, finally, conceptualizing our mere existence.

# The Tree of Life

If you have ever been exposed to any Kabbalistic teachings, you may be familiar with the Tree of Life.

According to this school of wisdom, the Tree of Life—which is a well-established symbol of creation and existence in Judaism as well as in other monotheistic and esoteric doctrines—is depicted as the ten interconnected nodes, or *sephirot*, as they are called in Kabbalistic teachings. Some interpretations of this term compare these sephirot being luminaries to sapphires—thus the name—while others relate to them being simply levels of interactions in a counting mode, from the Hebrew word to count (*sephira*). According to these teachings, the ten sephirot are the foundation of the divine realm. Each sephirah represents a certain aspect of creation and human existence, while being manifested in the human form by its location, by its color, sound, and personification, as the unification of the ten sephirot should amount in restoring harmony to creation.

According to Kabbalist scholars, the Tree of Life holds various capacities and values. Among these are:

The Tree represents a series of divine emanations from God's creation out of nothing, what is known as *Briah*, an act that is solely divine and can never be replicated in lower realms or by humans. These emanations represent the nature of revealed divinity, the human soul, and the spiritual path of human ascension.

The symbolic configuration is made of ten spiritual principles (the ten sephirot, more on this shortly), but under certain conditions, they amount to eleven since the top configuration, called "crown," and the fourth semi-configuration, called "knowledge," are interchangeable.

Kabbalists credit the Tree of Life to be a diagrammatic representation of the very process by which the universe manifested in its tangible form as the world of action, here on earth.

Each higher realm of existence "hovers" over the top configuration of "crown." The highest realm of existence is related to as "emanation," where the infinite light of the Creator—*Or Ein Sof* in Hebrew—resides.

The Ten Configurations or sephirot are (sans interchangeable factor mentioned prior): the top triangle, also referred to as "supernal," is composed of crown, wisdom, and understanding; the second triangle is composed of loving-kindness, strength, and beauty; the third triangle is composed of victory, splendor, and foundation; and the last configuration is called sovereignty.

For the sake of this particular section and the following meditation, we will simply look at the layout of the Tree of Life and follow the rhythm and sequence of the sephirot.

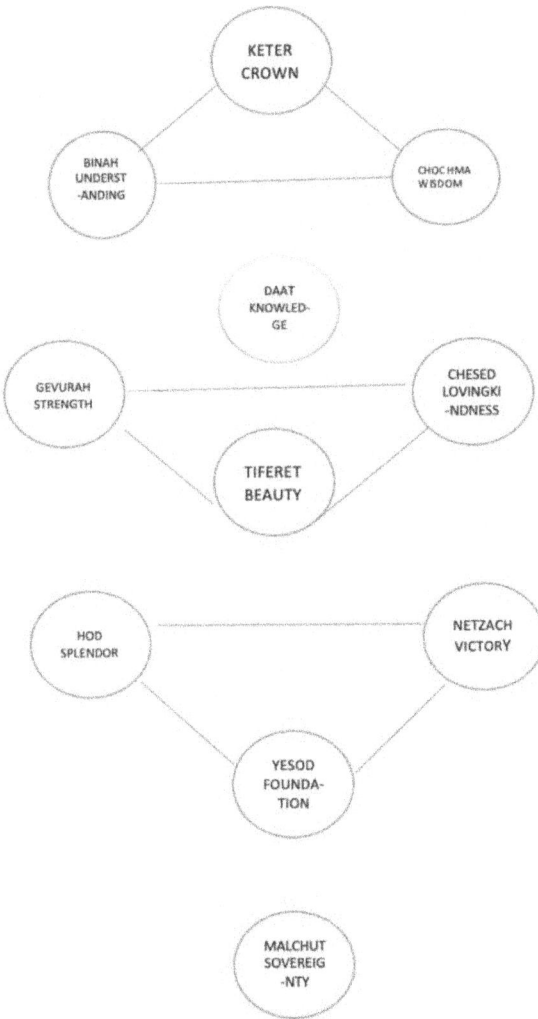

```
                    KETER
                    CROWN


  BINAH
  UNDERST                        CHOCHMA
  -ANDING                        WISDOM


                    DAAT
                    KNOWLED-
                    GE

  GEVURAH                        CHESED
  STRENGTH                       LOVINGKI
                                 -NDNESS

                    TIFERET
                    BEAUTY



  HOD                            NETZACH
  SPLENDOR                       VICTORY


                    YESOD
                    FOUNDA-
                    TION



                    MALCHUT
                    SOVEREIG
                    -NTY
```

Within the middle pole of the Tree of Life, we see the second-from-the-top sephirah called *Daat*. Daat—or in its translated definition, "knowledge"—is not considered an actual sephirah among the ten accounted for. If you look at the image, you'll notice that this particular sephirah is floating around the upper part of the Tree, disconnected from the other pillars, yet very present.

The reason for this unique position is that Daat is the core of our fearless existence, our true soul consciousness. To drive this point home, we can use the example of an ultrareligious individual who follows every rule and law in the book, yet he may exhibit a complete lack of the awareness and knowledge required to love consciously and be soulful. This may manifest in careless acts, dismissal of others, self-gratifying tendencies, and so forth, while all in the realm of religious adherence. Knowledge of self, therefore, is the exact point we need to lean on in order to acquire that soulful existence that we are striving for.

By following the route toward this knowledge, we can quiet our attention-demanding ego and allow our higher self to shine through.

How does all of this relate to fear and relationships? Directly.

We all live under a certain threat of a few principle and relational dynamics, which will be aligned here shortly.

The acquisition of your inner knowledge enables a life in which these challenges may still lurk in the back of your mind, yet they are not allowed to run a puppet show out of your life.

The potential habitual fears in relationships are:
Fear of rejection
Fear of failure
Fear of the unknown
Fear of the loss of control
Fear of pain and suffering

It is not uncommon to be entangled with a full range of all five, or to bounce between one or two more dominant fears while the others hibernate only to be awoken and fully activated again.

So, what is the process of attaining freedom from this chaos, or fear gang, that sneaks up on us uninvited?

There's no quick fix, yet the utilization of breath work with meditation on the Tree of Life—and in particular the Daat sephirah—can produce quite miraculous results and improvement in our well-being.

# Quickstep Meditation

Observe the Tree of Life for a few minutes before going inside. It will likely not be coherent and apparent to your meditative mind just yet, but you may look again in the midst of it, or simply take it in slowly and derive the unique qualities you'll give this particular experience while enhancing future ones with a more elaborate vision of it.

Sit in a comfortable position, close your eyes, and take a deep breath through your mouth, all the way up to the top of your lungs. Now, purse your lips and let your breath out slowly as if you're whistling through them. Repeat this three times, and keep a comfortable posture while reverting to normal breathing.

Start moving from the top sephirah (Keter/crown) through the right sephirah (Chochma/wisdom) to the left sephirah (Bina/understanding) and down to the middle semi-sephirah (Daat/knowledge).

Move with this line, and allow your mind to follow methodically until it flows effortlessly between the four circles. Remind yourself that the Daat sephirah is clear and unbound.

Once this becomes easy, you'll add a layer of color to this meditative state.

Picture the top Keter as a clear halo, and as you shift, let it dissolve into the right-hand Chochma, with a full ranged rainbow of color, an array of all colors you can imagine.

Keep moving to the left sephirah of Bina, and while dissolving the full ranged rainbow of the Chochma, picture Bina in bright green. Remain there for a few seconds.

Then, take a full, deep breath and push your breath out in an exhale into the Daat circle. The Daat circle is crystal clear, and appears like an angel's transparent wing. It floats in midair.

Allow all the prior colors and feelings to fill the Daat circle with a full-blown energy and sensation.

Remain there for a minute while breathing freely.

Once you feel satisfied, return to the top and start the circle of shift and colors once again. Repeat up to five times, or until you feel you've mastered this section. Remain seated, regain your normal breath, and slowly open your eyes.

# Chapter 3
## Getting Acquainted with Your Serpent

A lot has been discussed and suggested when it comes to the story of creation.

Kabbalistic teachings go even further in this pursuit and suggest a few "out of the box" and even unsettling versions of this dual story (yes, there were two different references of the human creation), but we will attempt to remain focused on the relational aspect of these stories—man unto himself—as well as man unto his committed other.

Let's briefly go over both references of the story. We can view in Genesis 1:27 the passage, "And God created man in His own image, in the image of God created He him; male and female created He them." And then, shortly after in Genesis 2:22, we read, "And the rib, which the LORD God had taken from the man, made He a woman, and brought her unto the man."

OK, we know that the biblical scripts are not scattered, and if something as significant as the very creation of human life is mentioned twice, we should examine it further.

What is behind these two contradicting references? First, we are told that the divine created man, and that there were male and female present at this significant occasion. Then, a short chapter later, we are told that man was alone, and God decided to create a "help meet" for him via his kind organ donation of a rib. For the record, the Hebrew script—which is deemed to be the original—translates the word *tzela*, or "rib," as "side," so the actual organ from which Eve was formed wasn't necessarily the all-time favorite rib.

Which is true? Why are they contradicting? An array of commentaries suggest anything from an initial androgynous creature that was only untangled in the second story, by the removal of the rib that was a connective tissue, all the way to the story of Lilith as the initial rebellious and feminist wife who demanded to be equal to man and thus was removed from this sacred environment, as we are later told all sinners are destined to.

More on Lilith and her upheaval later, but for now, let's revert to the final product, woman out of man's body: Eve. What was the purpose of her creation?

In Genesis 2:18, we read, "And the LORD God said: 'It is not good that the man should be alone; I will make him a help meet for him,'" yet another certification of the elimination of whichever female counterpart who was present before. Looking at this more holistically, Kabbalistic views tell us that woman is a form of spiritual compass for man. She's there to direct his path in the dark, and giving her ability to nurture, and freedom from extinction anxiety (as discussed earlier) she exists in order to make the important decisions, very much like what to consume, how to behave, and so forth.

Given this, we are not surprised when we realize that Eve was in fact the one who made the decision to consume that forbidden fruit (Any idea what fruit it was?) and generously feed her beloved partner with it, as we are told in Genesis 3:6: "She took of the fruit thereof, and did eat; and she gave also unto her husband with her, and he did eat."

What strikes you as the most perplexing factor here? If Eve was created to be a beacon rather than a destroyer, why send the serpent to her and convince her to stray from the divine path? Was this a test?

Kabbalah tells us that Eve is not only a compass, but also the primordial concealed ego that already exists in Adam. So, when the time comes to execute the human to the divine connection, the serpent appears before Eve: "And he said unto the woman: 'Indeed, God has said, "You shall not eat of any tree of the garden."'"

Because Eve is the egotistic part of Adam and lacks that fear of extinction, she initially resists the serpent (Genesis 3:2) because she wishes to keep Adam untainted. She only follows the serpent's suggestion due to her curiosity and serves as the "regal food taster" to validate the serpent's claims. If we look at this in this manner, Eve did not actually tempt Adam, but rather intended to nurture him with the knowledge bestowed from the consumption of this fruit, but only after she examined it first, in order to protect her husband. We can relate that dynamic to a modern dyad by acknowledging a wife's role in a committed relationship as the guardian of her partner's well-being and, in fact, downright existence.

Now, let's tend to this promiscuous fella known as the serpent.

What was the nature of this "intruder" or solicitor that was placed in the garden by the Creator himself, in order to carry out a certain task? If we jump ahead to current conditions and revert back, we can derive many consequences. In a study released in 2016, researchers report that limb reduction and loss are the hallmarks of snake evolution. Although advanced snakes are completely limbless, basal and intermediate snakes retain pelvic girdles and small rudiments of the femur. Moreover, legs may have reemerged in extinct snake lineages, suggesting that the mechanisms of limb development were not completely lost in snakes.[4]

So, when we think of this scene, we are likely looking at a good-looking, well-spoken, conniving, two-legged creature, who attempts to persuade Eve into the very condition the Creator aimed for; the loss of

4    Leal, Francisca, and Martin J. Cohn. 2016. "Loss and Re-Emergence of Legs in Snakes by Modular Evolution of Sonic Hedgehog and HOXD Enhancers." *Current Biology* 26 (21): 2966–73. https://doi.org/10.1016/j. cub.2016.09.020.

divine mode and the progression into humanness, in order to allow for soul development, which we spend a lifetime pursuing, only to reunite with our divine nature.

A few nuggets regarding Mr. Serpent: In Hebrew (and in the biblical verse), the word for serpent is נחש. This term has another definition in the holy tongue of Hebrew: "to assume."

Kabbalistic teachings tell us that the role of the serpent—in the Garden and thereafter—in a proverbial sense, enables us to examine our souls and soul connections. In other words, as soon as we allow an "assumption" of a more benefitting option—better partner, better life, better anything, more, grander, and so forth—we are bound to pay the price of being "thrown out of our heaven."

Looking at this interpretation from a more realistic, modern standpoint, we are propelled to examine our egotistic nature at all times. When we lose sight of that aspect in us, we face the risk of disillusionment and bewilderment. Our sacred dyad, thus, functions as an anchor or, then again, a compass toward an enlightened path that should be treasured.

Yes, this information is immensely profound, and may sound esoteric, but remain open-minded and holistic before delving into the upcoming meditation.

# Male and Female Aligned

We have discussed the principle of Daat within the Tree of Life. In the prior meditation, we practiced focusing on that principle, color, and feeling aligned, in order to achieve a level of soul growth.

Before we proceed to our next quickstep meditation, I'd like to introduce the principles that enable a soulful merging within a committed relationship.

Take another look at the Tree of Life structure.

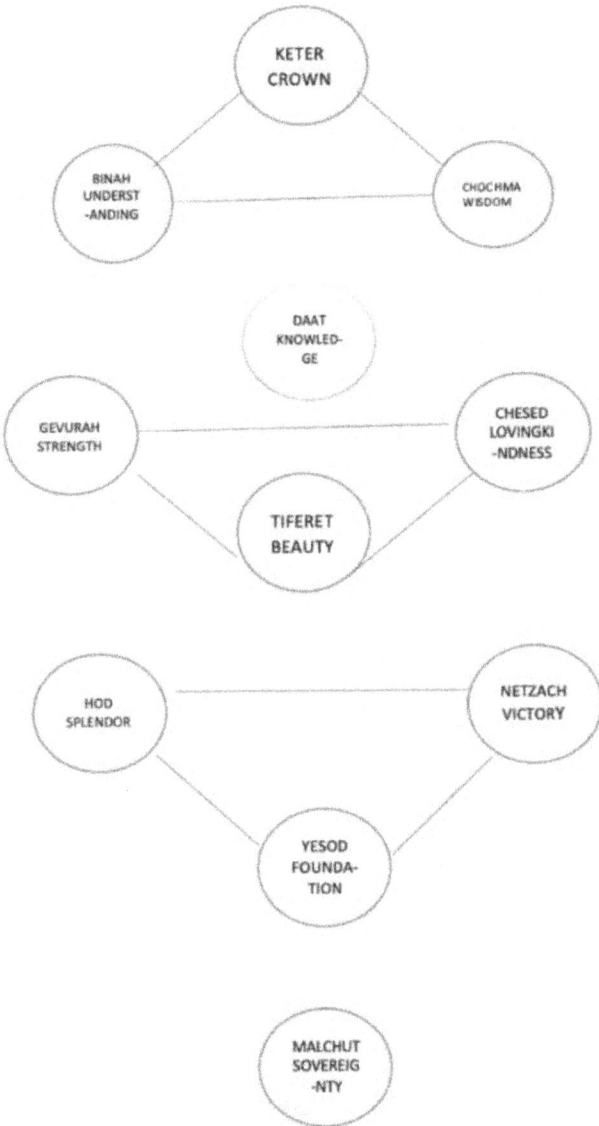

We are focusing on the fourth (Chesed/loving-kindness) and fifth (Gevurah/strength) principles of the Tree, on the right and left poles.

These two principles are highly essential, and actually a must, in a long-term relationship. The right, male principle of Chesed is a component that will instill a kind and soft layer into the relationship. It will allow a smooth transition into different stages of the dyad and will enable a benevolent relational conduct and exchange between you and your partner.

The female counterpart of Gevurah on the left, conversely, will keep a strict element in the sacred relationship that will prevent a loss of identity into one another; a component that, as mentioned previously, is one of the leading if not the top vulnerability factor for females.

By integrating the two well and allowing a smooth flow of energy between them, the relationship can only grow and prosper, rather than disintegrate or deteriorate on the account of miscommunication, a lack of fragility, or an overload of rigidity.

## Quickstep Meditation

Observe the Tree of Life for a few minutes before going inside. It will likely not be coherent and apparent to your meditative mind just yet, but you may reobserve, or simply take it in slowly and derive the unique qualities you'll give this particular experience while enhancing future ones with a deeper vision of it.

Sit in a comfortable position, close your eyes, and take a deep breath through your mouth, all the way up to the top of your lungs. Now, purse your lips and let your breath out slowly as if you're whistling through them. Repeat this three times and keep a comfortable posture while reverting to normal breathing.

Start picturing your energy flowing through the top, supernal triad, from the top sephirah of Keter, through the right polar Chochma, to the left sephirah of Bina, through the semi-sephirah of Daat.

Here, take a deep breath and generate the full energy you've acquired into the next sephirah of Chesed on the right and in a straight line into Gevurah on the left. Keep shifting your energy between Chesed and Gevurah in your mind. Envision a white light moving between the two poles, generating heat and brightness, while intensifying gradually as you focus on the energy floating between these two components.

Once you feel strong enough in your visualization, return to the top and begin adding colors.

Remember, the top sephirah of Keter is clear, then shifts into a full range of rainbow colors when the energy arrives at the right-hand Chochma, then turns green when it arrives at the next base of Bina, then dissolves into a diaphanous ray of light moving downward to Daat.

Here, pause again, and shift the full energy, color, and sensation into Chesed; add a light blue color to the sephirah and remain there focused on it for a minute or two. Gather your energy, shift it to the left-hand Gevurah, and add a layer of bright red here. Start pitching the stream of energy from the right blue Chesed to the left red Gevurah. Keep shifting the energy back and forth until it becomes strong and intense. Once you feel satisfied, release the energy, relax, and revert to your normal breathing. Take a few deep breaths and open your eyes.

## Polarity and Strength

As the theory claims, and as we solidify oftentimes in our daily practice, two opponent forces existing in the same sphere is a recipe for success.

When observing this very common perspective, we must ask ourselves how it relates to the state of love in a relationship. Can love be sustained? Does it disappear? If so, where does it go, and what is left in its absence?

Since we exist in a universe that created a sense of mystery and elusiveness around the concept of love, we are in a dire perplexity over what is it, how to attain it, how to maintain it, and how to be worthy of it.

It is thus imperative to make clear: love is abundant. It is always here, surrounding us and enveloping our lives. The definition we give it nonetheless is a different story.

So, taking it back to the facility of a committed relationship, we find "someone to love" and then a number of years later, we sense that we "fell out of love." We don't know how or why, or perhaps we justify this notion via a variety of claims and rationales as we move on to the next "true love" relationship, only to find out that we are facing this very predicament again.

What are we doing wrong? Let's start with the understanding that love doesn't disappear, or leave, or wane. Love may change its face and evolve or arise as a different structure, but it's always present. An adjacent force that accompanies romantic love in its budding phase is desire, or lust, and *that* is a component that loses its stance in our relationship *if* it isn't maintained.

Consider this claim; throughout our lives, we have our ups and downs with our offspring; they annoy us, disrupt us, show disrespect to us, or even completely alienate us, yet, we don't fall out of love for our children. So, the partner *we* chose, out of the entire universe, to share a full life with, with that partner we are so quick to fall out of love? If you break it down, it doesn't make much sense.

But, since the component of desire is so intense in a romantic relationship, we tend to get perplexed and confused when combining the two. What we might have encountered is the "dismissal of choice." Kabbalistic teachings tell us that we have the freedom of choice 100 percent of the time; we once chose our partner as that beloved one, so the very act of non-choosing at this point in life, is, in fact, our choice— and as such, it can be altered.

First, let's make clear that desire represents separation while love represents closeness, oneness. We only desire what we do not have, and once we have it, it no longer applies to the definition of desire.

Thus, these are two different entities; nonetheless, does that mean we should strive to live a life deprived of that immaculate sense of craving and yearning known as desire? Not at all.

How can we revive it? As mentioned previously, the feeling of familiarity isn't your best ally when it comes to attraction and pull. We need a level of segregation in order to "keep the flame burning." For some, the idea of different beds/bedrooms/homes may suffice, but for some, we will need a recollection of the very day we joined forces in full-blown desire—our day of nuptial.

If you are in a marriage, a reenactment of that day, even simply for the two of you, can create wonders. You can roleplay, wear the same or similar outfits, enjoy the same activities on that day, and engage in the lustful sensual act you shared that day.

It may sound farfetched, but certain memories entrapped in our hippocampus may arouse the very sensations and feelings we once shared, if they need to be reintroduced.

If you're not married, you may use a similar technique of "re-kindling" by reintroducing your alluring selves to one another, following the same path suggested above.

These tools are often dismissed as silly or embarrassing, but we fail to realize how simple it really is to stimulate our brains into a desired sensation, pun well intended.

## That Thing Called Love

What is love? It is likely the world's most notorious, ancient, and baffling question ever asked. Throughout millennia, generations, backgrounds, cultures, and climates, the question of love—what it is and how it fits in our lives—has always been a pressing one. We are addicted to love, seek love, crave it, will betray our closest people to attain it, and go to great lengths to prove its existence. But what is it, under all these heartwarming slogans and valentine-worthy cards?

And, more important, before we attempt to suggest some form of title to this elusive, peculiar "thing" we so crave, let us ask, "Could that love be applicable to anyone, is it one size fits all?" Does that make sense?

## Kabbalah on Love

By Kabbalistic views, the concept of love is by far greater and more complex than we can even begin to imagine. Does the Creator love us? And do we love him? And if we do, why are we "breaking his laws" on a daily basis?

And if he adores and loves us, why are we being tested constantly? Why do "bad things happen to good people," and what is the purpose of all this "love"?

The more holistic, esoteric perspective of love suggests that it cannot be restricted to one narrow definition. For example, we cannot really define love by any standard known to man. Nonetheless, what we can in fact derive out of this confusion is that our frustration and miscommunication in our relational dyads emerges from the fact that we attempt to create a staple definition of "what is love," and if the existing circumstances do not follow that staple, we reject it by claiming that we "do not want to be loved *this* way but rather *that* way."

What about the position of love in our lives? Do we look at it as "the pursuit of closeness?" And if so, do we always want to be close to the people we love? If we do not, does it mean we do not truly love them? Let's take it to the next level of entanglement by stating that we all want love in our lives, but "under our terms," in the particular right amount, and to not have this "love" trespass to where we want to maintain boundaries.

If we assume, on a very hypothetical level, that all these preposterous details and requirements are being kept, will that certify the maintenance of this love? Or will we still fall "out of it" after a while?

The truth is, as stated before, we have the tendency to confuse love with desire, so when this alleged love (desire in disguise), settles down and relaxes in our relational exchange, it goes to the back burner to rest and be forgotten because, as mentioned prior, once it's attained, we are no longer in pursuit of it; it is officially in high supply and low demand.

So, how do we try to ignite it? Well, we all know the answer to this question, yet fail to identify it as simply that.

We attempt to reignite that supposed "love" by creating a distance (remember, love is viewed as the pursuit of closeness), by fighting, arguing, infidelity, disagreement, betrayal of trust, and so forth. And we do this, even if subconsciously, in order to create room for that closeness again. In layman's terms, we call it "make up sex" and it feels oh so good…

The imperative question here is this: Do we really have to go to these lengths in order to ignite something that can always be present and simply requires a different form of maintenance? In short, we do not.

If we look at this concept of love as a multifaceted, omnipresent force that can be maintained by recruiting the "less familiarity" factor discussed before, then the need to struggle for, in quest of, and in the name of love, can be put to rest.

Another angle of this concept that is important to keep in mind is the instability or transitory nature of love.

Love is anything but static, and if it is a flat line you're looking for, it isn't attainable in the world of the living.

What is there to do? Creating a "situation" that is loveable—that is, a kind and confident dyad, a family, a formed and committed life together—can act as an anchor for this unstable ship called love. Then, when the sea is stormy and rocky, we have the structure of the well-maintained ship of our relationship to get us through love's unstable tides.

Are there any factors to consider in this establishment?
Of course.

Our compatibility, our joint goals, our appreciation for this dyad and one another, as well as our understanding of the sacredness of this exchange. Wait, this sounds way too complex, doesn't it? It may very well be, but if we are connected with our partner on soul level, everything falls into place. The latter means that this connection, this committed exchange, is gratifying us with soul growth so that we feel we can actually expand to a new apex in light of this dyad.

Not that we can "tolerate" this living situation, but rather it enables our growth and ability to thrive, new ideas and paths, and spiritual elevation. Does this mean it is always easy and good? Quite the contrary; a good soul compatibility may be challenging at times, but can and will lead us to a better version of ourselves.

One last component mentioned before, as sacredness should be emphasized here; if we remind ourselves that a committed relationship or marriage is a divine concept, and thus isn't "mine to own" but a path directed by a far greater force, we will be able to ease and relax into it with a full conviction and trust that it is taking us in the right direction. Trying to micromanage every single aspect of it may deprive it of the oxygen necessary for its prosperity and growth. We need to adopt the full belief that this relationship was deliberately and specifically created for our partners and us on a profound custom template.

"Sure," you say, "easier said than done." And you'll be exactly right. Yet, it is well worth the time invested.

# Chapter 4
## A Sinful Mind in a Divine Body

In the '80s chick flick *Working Girl*, alluring Melanie Griffith tells overwhelmed costar Harrison Ford, "I've got a mind for business and a body for sin."

If we observe the Kabbalistic views of a committed relationship in the service of your soul quest, the ideal combo would be a divine, tastefully presented appearance, incubating a very elaborate sinful mind. Why is that?

Your mind can be provocative and profound enough to source the fuel for your wildest fantasies; yet, in order to maintain a long-term relationship that promotes monogamy and soulful connection, we need to maintain a level of respect and tamed conduct so our partners can feel at ease and, most important, gain confidence derived from their exclusive exposure to our "goods."

Kabbalah teachings tell us that in order to have a successful, luscious, and evergreen relationship that is long-term and faithful, we need to integrate a few steps.

First and imperatively so, we need to define what that committed relationship is in our eyes, and we need to align it with our prospective partners' views. So, if my idea of a marriage or committed relationship involves sharing a home and never traveling solo, while my partner's idea is a lifetime of mono attractions and an occasional night together within an overall separate home situation, we are not compatible in our vision of this important quest. And so, this exchange is bound to fail.

The Tree of Life teaches us that a true committed dyad means striving for oneness. Like the Tree of Life that holds the masculine faculties on the right and the feminine faculties on the left, our unity should provide a platform for oneness, which can be attained only via full commitment to this dyad and transitioning from man and woman to husband and wife, along with all its less appealing aspects.

The next component here would be the challenge of embracing your partner's weakest traits.

This category may include the tolerance of a messy partner by Ms. Hospital Corners, the tardy wife by a punctual control freak, or the profound introvert by a mass extrovert.

All of these assignments may be immensely challenging to deal with, but since we are discussing soul growth, there are two points to keep in mind here;

First, a successful dyad is never free of struggle—the opposite of happiness is comfort; thus, we should never strive to be overly comfortable. Second, a soul mate is not someone who enables a fluffy, diaphanous existence, but rather one who may push us to our spiritual apex and allow us to achieve the soul growth we are intended for.

If we made it this far, we are moving in a very good direction; nonetheless, our job isn't finished.

If we are in this successful relationship, in order to maintain it, we must acknowledge that our egotistic tendencies must be replaced by a more malleable choice. We must embrace the things that are important to our partners, as if they're important to us.

It's not so out of the blue that tomorrow you would wake up with a keen affection toward college baseball, but it does mean that if your partner is so anxious to catch the next game and his dream is for you to watch it with him, your soul growth involves biting it and "taking one for the team"—sans sarcastic remarks of course, otherwise no growth would be achieved.

Going back to the lust and desire factors, we're often so consumed with not "letting ourselves go" or keeping appearances. Yet, you see plenty of husbands and wives walking around the palace of their shared relationship in tainted rags and with unkempt and dreary appearances, unaware of the fact that the most important individual to impress is hanging around them every moment of the day or night.

When did the outside world become more important? We don't have to be uncomfortable in order to be presentable, but we are obligated to keep ourselves attractive in the presence of our beloveds.

These basic terms of conduct may seem harsh, uncomfortable, or perhaps even unbearable to some.

Nonetheless, the truth is, if you dig a bit deeper inside, all these suggestions were once a given to you, not anything you ever dreamed of overlooking.

The principle behind a long-term dyad is the idea of maintenance and pursuing every day together as if each day was your very first date where your first impression could turn your life around.


# As above So Below

As we progress through the inspirational points of how to attain, and especially maintain, a committed, soul-sourced relationship, we keep bouncing back to the very core of our existence; our oneness.

Now, let's go back to the Tree of Life and focus on the Kabbalistic interpretation of all this verbal expression.

Kabbalah views the Tree of Life as a joint source of masculine and feminine energies coming together to form a holistic creature, in a sense, a manifestation of God's image, as stated in Genesis 1:27: "And God created man in His own image, in the image of God created He him; male and female created He them."

But what is God's image? Haven't we established that God does not have a physical image, that he's omnipresent, and that his "form" is in every single thing on the planet? Indeed, we have.

To override this trivial interpretation of "God's image," we accept the Kabbalistic explanation of being created in the image of God; not as the tangible physical manifestation of it, but rather as his vibrational essence—the fact that we, too, are *creators*.

This point carries plenty of responsibility in our general everyday conduct because it eliminates our "fixed product" state of mind and reminds us that we always have a choice, and that the creation of our lives, our sustenance, and our relationships, is in our *creative* hands.

Let us go back to the ten sephirot in the Tree of Life.

Take another glance at the tree to be reminded.

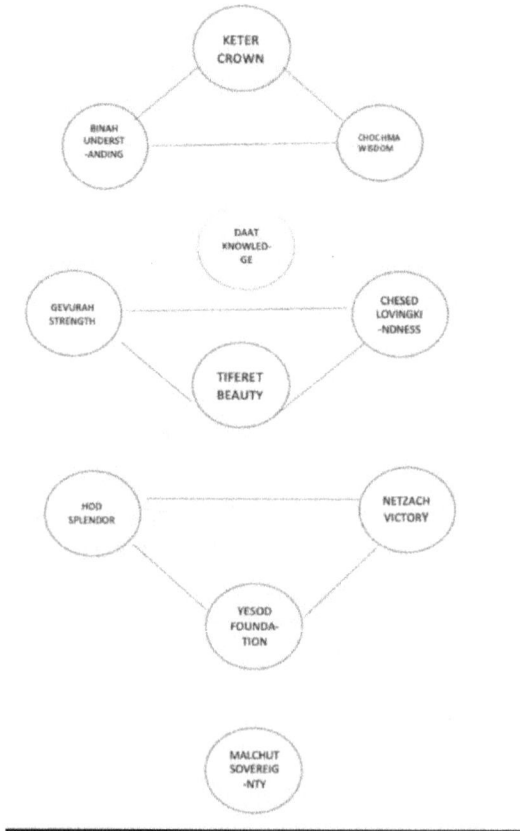

The top sephirah of Keter (crown) and the bottom sephirah of Malchut (sovereignty) are our main focus here.

By Kabbalistic teachings, the top sephirah of Keter represents the masculine energy.[5] In a sense, this top energy, closest to the metaphysical sphere, is all of life in its intricate manner, in potential. In other words, in this top vibration, we hold the entire possibilities of our lives.

Then, we look at Malchut, the bottom sephirah. This sephirah represents the feminine energy, all of life in actualization, of life's potential.

The principle behind a spiritual and fulfilling life in all its aspects, a committed relationship being the main focus, is the ascension and mutual interconnectedness of the bottom sephirah with the top.

If you observe the translation of these two sefirot, you'll notice that the top Keter is a crown, and the bottom Malchut is sovereignty.

In practice, any sovereign requires to be crowned as part of one's core function, while a crown can only be placed on a regal devotee once they're declared worthy of this holy title.

This, essentially, requires a complete and holistic exchange between the masculine and feminine forces in order to form the perfect human, thus enabling the soul quest to proceed on its way to locate its equally perfect soul mate.

How is it done? Through many practices, one of which will be applied next in our quickstep meditation.

--------

5   It is imperative to make this statement in relation to the divine nature of this practice, due to common inquiries. The top sephirah of Keter being defined as masculine while the bottom sephirah of Malchut being defined as feminine is anything but a gender-related statement. There's absolutely no relation to dominance or subordinance in this structure; Kabbalistic teachings tell us that humanity as a whole is considered the feminine component of creation, while the creator or God is the only masculine, overseeing it all. The fact that a masculine needs a feminine source in order to create, can be manifested in gestation, in a committee marriage or the simple unification of feminine and masculine energies in a quest of upgraded spirituality and meditative practice. Thus, the creator needs humanity in order to create, or "gestate," any form of new creation, and so humanity acts as a feminine component to the creator's masculinity.

# Quickstep Meditation

Observe the Tree of Life for a few minutes before going inside. It will likely not be coherent and apparent to your meditative mind just yet, but you may reobserve while at it, or simply take it in slowly and derive the unique qualities you'll give this particular experience, while enhancing future ones with a more elaborate vision of it.

Sit in a comfortable position, close your eyes, and take a deep breath through your mouth, all the way up to the top of your lungs. Now, purse your lips and let your breath out slowly as if you're whistling through them. Repeat this three times, and keep a comfortable posture while reverting to normal breathing.

Imagine the Tree of Life in your mind.

See the top Keter vividly and then spiral down to the bottom Malchut to see it vivid and clear in your mind's eye.

Repeat this sequence for few times until you're feeling comfortable and satisfied in the practice.

Allow the entire structure of the Tree and all its ten sephirot to fade into the background while keeping a focus on the top and bottom sephirot.

Now, stretch a bright ray of light between the top and the bottom sephirah, and start transmitting your energy through it. As you intensify your focus, the pillar of light should become more vibrant and tangible. It can appear electric, like a Jedi's sword.

Keep focusing on the white light shifting between the two, and then slowly add the diaphanous shade to the top sephirah of Keter.

Keep pushing the energy downward toward the bottom Malchut, then add a dark blue shade to the bottom sephirah. Keep intensifying the flow of energy between the two, allowing the pillar to become more vivid and vibrant.

After a few moments, when you feel the energy is strong and can be left undisturbed, focus on Keter again, and within the diaphanous shade it holds, write the letter א (aleph) inside it. Move downward to Malchut, and within its bright blue shade, insert the letter מ (mem) in the bottom sephirah. Keep focusing on the energy shifting via the light polar between the two, putting more emphasis on the letters within the top and bottom sephirot.

Once you feel satisfied in your energetic work, allow the entire Tree of Life to reemerge from its background, and fade the top and bottom sephirot in the wholeness of the Tree.

Take a few deep breaths and open your eyes gradually.

"Remember. The way you make love is the way God will be with you."

—Rumi

# What Sex Has to Do with It

As we move along the spiritual connection between male and female energies, we are bound to touch the most sacred aspect right in the eye of the hurricane, the thing called sex, or a sexual exchange.

In our modern climate, sex has become a trivial tool of communication. We all engage in it, or want to; it shrieks at us from every piece of advertisement or media content, we are all aiming to be crowned "good at it," and we use it as a general commodity, in all its versatile faces.

Nonetheless, the Kabbalistic views of the sexual union are a far cry from the pop culture perspective.

First, we need to acknowledge that the Kabbalistic relation to sex is never as a prohibition. Sex is advocated as a commandment and as a source of bliss that isn't only suggested, but absolutely required, for the sanctity and prosperity of the committed relationship.

In fact, the Jewish stance on sex is that its vibrant existence is one of the three basic rights of women, and thus obligations of men, upon a nuptial unity.

The married woman is entitled to the right of food, clothing, and pleasure, or as the biblical verse states, "שְׁאֵרָהּ כְּסוּתָהּ וְעֹנָתָהּ לֹא יִגְרָע," or, "If he take him a wife her food, her raiment, and her conjugal rights, shall he not diminish." (Exodus 21:10)

Thus, we are presented with a man's legal obligation to fulfill his wife's needs; should he not be willing or able, the wife may exercise a divorce.

The Talmud (the Jewish body of civil and ceremonial law) has set complex rules governing sex. These laws of *onah*, or "conjugal rights," require a man to provide his wife with sufficient pleasure during the sexual act, as well as regulate the frequency of "performing the conjugal duty."[6]

If quoting Maimonides, "A husband is forbidden from holding his wife's matrimonial rights for sexual relations."

The frequency of sexual relations is based on the man's profession in order to accommodate his ability to fulfill his spousal obligation and still perform his professional duties. For example, a sailor who is absent from the "home base" is only obligated to perform conjugal duties once every six months, but the local commuter will be obligated to a much more frequent timetable. By these related laws, it is accepted for a man to withhold these pleasurable rights from a woman during the time of *niddah*, or menstruation.

So what can we derive from all this? Essentially that the sacred value of a sexual exchange is of very high importance and significance. Kabbalistic views see sex as the ultimate act of unification between souls. God's masculinity can only be manifested in its divine nature by the unification with human femininity. Thus, in the "micro" act of unification, we are practicing the whole concept of creation, par excellence.

Kabbalah tells us that everything we encounter in this life is a metaphor for a spiritual concept, including sex.

In this relation, Kabbalah expands on the idea of casual sex. Before we proceed, we must remind ourselves that the discussion isn't leaning on cultural, relational, or civil spheres, but on a soul elevation matrix.

Here we are told that casual sex doesn't only stray from our soul quest, but that it can deter us from this quest altogether if we don't

---

6   Biale, Rachel. *Women and Jewish Law, An Exploration of Women's Issues in Halakhic Sources*. New York: Schocken Books, 1984

give the sexual union its important role in our lives as a merging of two halves in the quest for oneness.

This may be emphasized by the concept "intercoursal nuptial," or in Hebrew, ביאה קידושין. This practice is obsolete and isn't pursued by any denomination in Judaism, yet in ancient times, the idea of a man and a woman merging in the act of sexual intercourse could suffice as a legitimate status of marriage between the two, if the male announced to his female counterpart "you're hereby pronounced as my wife." Yes, it had to take place in the presence of two witnesses and the actual declaration needed to be verbalized, but consider today's climate, where online streaming could be debated as a sufficient source of that component.

How else can we benefit from these ancient divine teachings if they are not applied to our modern views of sexual unity? Kabbalah tells us that the sex position we call "missionary" is the most sublime position in which we can maximize our spiritual growth. Not only for the biological factor, as this position maximizes the chances of gestation and procreation, but for the soul connection infused in it due to the face-to-face, body-to-body factor.

# Chapter 5
## Your Guardian Angels

The most intriguing and surprising aspect of the holy ark in the biblical temple (*Mishkan*) are the cherubs positioned on the ark's cover. What are cherubs? The Torah describes them in detail in Exodus 25:20: "The cherubim shall have their wings spread out above, shielding the cover with their wings. They shall confront each other; the faces of the cherubim being turned toward the cover."

Tradition has a rich history of interpreting the mythical cherubs in numerous fashions. Nevertheless, the extensive findings from the ancient Near East make it clear that the cherubs historically represented either frightening beasts used as guards, or the equivalent of flying horses harnessed to chariots; these images fit a number of biblical passages.

In the Mishkan, however, they served as buffers surrounding the deity.

Kabbalah mentions that when the people of Israel were ununified inside the temple, the cherubs would turn and face away from one another, while on occasions when the people adhered to God's laws and conduct, the cherubs would face one another. Similarly, the spiritual act of unification via the sexual union, and particularly while utilizing the face-to-face "missionary" position, stands as a replication of this very divine act. The cherubs facing one another invited the **Shekinah,**[7] the "feminine" face of God (as depicted in the Malchut sephirah in the Tree of Life), to participate in the act of creation and soul elevation.

In accordance with these views, the divine source is the male, and thus a giver, and humanity is the female, thus the recipient.

Life, and the act of sexual union, is an ongoing courtship between the Creator and us, humanity.

Even deeper than that is depicted in in Proverbs 12:4: "A virtuous woman is a crown to her husband." The Tree of Life top sephirah of Keter (crown) is the ultimate point in which the human soul merges and unifies with the Creator's divine light while in this life on earth. We are told by Kabbalistic teachings that humanity is the engine igniting that unification and soul elevation. The Creator, being infinite, needs our finite tangibility in order to create and procreate the human race. So, in fact, humanity courts the Creator, not the other way around. The dance is mutual, yet the wooing is orchestrated by us humans in a shape of soul seeking and acts of kindness, of committed unity, and of striving to make this a better universe for us all.

# Soul Mates

We are fascinated with the concept of soul mates, always have been, and likely always will be. Why? For various reasons of course, but prominently because the idea of a cosmic connection that was custom made just for us and matches every aspect of our, let's admit, somewhat narcissistic existence, is charming and fanciful.

The Kabbalistic views of soul mates isn't as glamorous or Hollywood-like, but it is quite fascinating, nonetheless.

Why are we even assigned soul mates? From a Kabbalistic point of view, aside from the divine soul growth plan, the Creator assigns these

---

7    Note that the words Shekinah and Mishkahn are sourced in the same Hebrew root שכן , which means to reside; i.e. the dwelling place of the Shekinah took magnified presence within the sacred temple.

matches because that is the core "mechanic" of creation. Every creation encompasses a feminine and a masculine energy, and thus, very similarly to the duality of our limbs, the "core soul" holds both gendered entities before it is "split" in half pre-gestation and begins the tangible quest of both parts of a whole in order to achieve the Creator's source plan. We are taught that every single person on this planet has a soul mate. That soul mate is assigned its specific dual counterpart forty days before conception and is the perfect match for our soul. Now, here lies the first disparity between the Hollywood version of soul mate and the Kabbalistic teachings.

According to the latter, a soul mate isn't a perfect match on a physical "earthly" level. In other words, it's not like the typical female fantasy of a tall, dark, and handsome Latin lover bound to manifest in the shape of Valentino in the flesh, who is created and provided on a silver platter along with his magnificent Italian ride of choice (I mean he must drive a Ferrari, it is a given.) while flashing a sardonic smile.

Kaballah actually explains that our soul mate is a component for soul growth—emphasis on the soul, not our earthly quests. Moreover, if the match is erroneously assumed to be based on a physical or tangible contribution, (physical attraction, financial status, professional achievement), it is likely not a soul match and is bound to be short-lived. Not that your soul mate should be unattractive or appalling, but in the world of souls, physical attraction isn't a component.

A soul mate serves to elevate the spiritual state so that it can benefit from this duality in the "coming realms."

And, regardless of the fact that we are assigned a soul mate, we are not guaranteed to ever find them; we may cross paths with a soul mate, but the earthly conditions may not allow for this match to materialize. How so? Our souls may benefit from another experience under particular conditions.

So, you might ask, "Who could I end up with?" Hang in there, we are getting to it, but not before I mention that a soul mate could potentially appear as a person you don't even particularly like, yet their existence serves your soul elevation, thus pursuing its divine purpose.

We may, by Kabbalistic views, end up with a "good enough match," referred to as a "deed assister," or alternatively, "soul *match.*" This alternative match suits our needs in this life in order to facilitate spiritual growth, and we can attain a very happy life alongside it.

How does this assignment work? The soul mate comes to this world as a result of your gestation. Wait, what? Does it mean that if they arrive in this world later, they cannot be a soul mate, or that only a partner of similar age could be a soul mate? They can't be younger, older, or any other combination?

Not quite; your soul mate could be older, younger, or of similar age because their creation isn't on a physical level, but rather soul level.

Here, Kabbalah introduces us to another concept called *Ibur.* Translated, it means "conception." What Ibur means is that as you carry your spiritual work on this earth, you may be a match to your soul mate, but if conditions on the ground didn't allow it (different social status, remote locations, and so on), your current partner (who, of course, already possesses a soul that is a qualified match to yours) will be granted a second soul that will inhabit the same body. No, it's not an "exorcism" kind of situation, but a divine intervention designed to allow you to attain your spiritual goals with your soul mate under the current circumstances.

How and why does a situation like this arise? The way we conduct ourselves on a spiritual level enables our matches according to what our souls need in order to be elevated to a higher level. And so, if we invest time in our spiritual growth, we may, at one point in our tangible existences, be elevated to a frequency or a level of spirit that allows a more advanced match, or perhaps the very match that was originally assigned to us, yet didn't make it to the "meeting point" at the time ,due to various conditions on the ground.

Another very prominent disparity from the Hollywood version of a soul mate is the concept of happiness. Kabbalistic teachings tell us that we are not entitled to or "have the right" to pursue happiness for the egotistic self! Yet, we are not only entitled, but rather obligated, to create the terms to make the Creator happy by our soul growth, as stated in Deuteronomy 28:47: "Serve the LORD thy God with joyfulness, and with gladness of heart, by reason of the abundance of all things." We are propelled to meet our soul mates and do our spiritual work in order to be elevated to the position of gratifying the Creator.

Are there different souls from different levels and different locations? Indeed, this is a relevant and important point. Our soul *group* is human; we do not come from the vegetative or inanimate soul group (although through the process of reincarnation, one may end up there), but rather the human soul group; nonetheless, there is a diverse group within the human soul group. We can find seventy soul subgroups based on race, religion, and so forth.

It is important to add that your soul mate serves your soul quest, not only your relationship. So, its purpose could manifest in a myriad of ways, not only in your inter-relational experiences.

# First and Second Soul Mates

Kabbalistic teachings introduce us to the concept of first versus second soul mates. What are they? There are a few different interpretations and commentaries that relate to this concept, but we will focus on a focal explanation and then finalize with a viable example.

The first commentary that relates to this concept claims that the initial match is the actual one who was chosen for you; thus, the second match is a later choice. Here, the definition is that a second match is a "deeds match." In other words, due to a person's conduct (for better or worse), a different match is assigned in order to match the person's circumstances and elevate them from that particular point on. As an example, if a person strayed and immersed in illegal activities, or unfortunately encountered a life of addiction, his second match would be someone who can help his soul recover and elevate it to its rightful position. Similarly, if one repented and became an immensely giving individual, engaging in acts of kindness and devoting his life to the betterment of the world, his soul may be elevated to a place where a new match is due in order to help him ascend to an even greater sphere.

In a biblical story of spiritual elevation, we are told the fascinating engagement of Jacob, Leah, and Rachel in Genesis 29:16-18:

> Now Laban had two daughters; the name of the elder was Leah, and the name of the younger was Rachel.
>
> Leah's eyes were tender, but Rachel had beautiful features and a beautiful complexion.
>
> And Jacob loved Rachel, and he said, "I will work for you seven years for Rachel, your younger daughter."

The plot thickens when Jacob finishes the course of serving Rachel's father for her hand in marriage only to find out the morning after his celebrated nuptials that he bargained for the wrong sister, and now laying in his marital bed was Leah.

Jacob insists on the beautiful Rachel, goes around to serve her father for another seven years, and finally marries her.

By Kabbalistic views, there was a course of reason and action to this long and intricate soul journey that Jacob needed to complete.

First, we are introduced to Jacob's soul elevation by this "bait and switch." We recall that in Genesis 27:20–23, a similar act was carried on by Jacob himself, along with the kind assistance and encouragement of his mother, Rebecca.

> And Jacob said unto his father: "I am Esau thy first-born; I have done according as thou badest me. Arise, I pray thee, sit and eat of my venison, that thy soul may bless me." And Isaac said unto his son: "How is it that thou hast found it so quickly, my son?" And he said: "Because the LORD thy God sent me good speed." And Isaac said unto Jacob: "Come near, I pray thee, that I may feel thee, my son, whether thou be my very son Esau or not." And Jacob went near unto Isaac his father; and he felt him, and said: "The voice is the voice of Jacob, but the hands

are the hands of Esau." And he discerned him not, because his hands were hairy, as his brother Esau's hands; so he blessed him.

If Jacob paid for this action by being promised Rachel and receiving Leah, why was any additional godly demand required?

We are told that Leah's soul was an elevated one—she was introspective, a master meditator, and an internal conversationalist—while Rachel's soul was gentle; she was charismatic and appealing to others. She was a natural influencer.

Both Rachel and Leah mothered the Jewish nation. Rachel contributed the influential and Jacob's favorite, Joseph, while Leah provided the foundation required for the purpose of gratifying the Creator.

Jacob's soul was bound with both, and although Rachel did in fact hold tremendous qualities that were essential for the future of the Jewish people, Jacob was particularly drawn to her beauty. The earthly component was beneficial and necessary for a good dyad, yet Jacob's soul required a steeper climb, which could only be enabled by the contribution of Leah's side of this triangle. On a soul level, it was the dyad with Leah that even enabled the final creation of Rachel's children, who ended up playing a crucial role in leading the children of Israel to their holy land and prosperity.

If we compare the concept of first and second matches here, we are bound to see that Rachel was Jacob's first match, but due to Jacob's elevated and enlightened path, Rachel was removed (by her early passing) and his soul was then elevated to the second match embodied in Leah, a match that will bring him to a soul apex.

# Love and Marriage

We have examined the idea of soul mates from a number of aspects and exemplified it with a theological reference. Yet, we may still be left a bit baffled and uncertain about the existence and validity of it all, not to mention the innumerable questions that may arise as we contemplate on this subject further.

We said that our soul mate is designated for us, meaning there's no direct correlation with any physical, emotional, or professional attributes that we may fancy. And we are told that we may not even like our soul mate. Here, I'd like to add another layer.

Once more, the principle of a soul mate is designed to elevate us, and essentially to provide a mirror or ground for us to recognize the areas in us that require work. If simplified, the most punctual person may be assigned a soul mate who is a "complete flake," thus making the soul quest a work toward a rational and patient reaction to this unagreeable conduct. It is important to add that none of these interpretations are judgmental or questionable, as we are not dealing with social, cultural, or historical norms, but rather soul-sourced requirements that are tailor made for a particular soul.

Striving to locate our soul mate often sets us off the path of removing our ego and actually unveiling our pitfalls and the aspects of ourselves that keep us stuck. The focal point of all this confusion is to allow for universal consciousness in every aspect of life and to see others as an opportunity to enhance the spiritual connection to our souls—ours as well as theirs.

What is the stance of marriage and divorce in this relation, if so?

Kabbalistic teachings tell us that we are unlikely, yet potentially able, to divorce a soul mate. This situation may arise for a number of reasons, but to remain focused, let's emphasize two.

## Where Is My Soul Mate?

We may begin our quest of soul exploration on ground level alongside our partner, yet potentially grow to different levels of spirituality in which our assigned soul mate concludes their work and we are ready to grow to a different soul connection, or soul compatibility, like the Jacob story.

Divine intervention is a real and legitimate concept. Think for a moment about the endless occasions in which you felt the hand of the Creator "rescuing you at the very last minute" from a car accident, from boarding a plane that went down, from signing a deal that turned out to be a scam, and so forth. So, if I'm being directed and saved from personal decisions, how does my free will play a role in this life? Am I merely a pawn?

Kabbalistic teachings refer to a man's will as a source of consideration for the Creator. In other words, if you're pining for a certain relationship that may not serve you, or even harm you, yet will not bring you to an early demise, the Creator will allow it; so, we can enjoy our free will and take a detour as long as the assigned time here and desired goal is kept, because we are immersed in co-creation, the dynamic between us and the divine source is constantly engageable.

## Thou Shall Not Covet Thy Neighbor's (Sexy) Wife

Is it possible for us to meet our soul mate while married to another? Kabbalah teaches us that this isn't a plausible situation. We are not meant to meet our soul mate while married to another because we cannot be presented with a viable option when the circumstances are debilitating and so not allow us to pursue it.

# Chapter 6
## Sexual Healing

Anywhere one turns, the luring cling of hedonism flashes us with its luster. What is the Kabbalistic involvement with pleasure? Is it a sacred concept? Is it frowned upon? Are we supposed to pursue our desires in their sexual form, or inhibit them and follow the holistic practices of our soulful existence? How can all of this be determined, and how is it functionally pursued?

The principle of higher consciousness and becoming one with your core is often misinterpreted as an act of seclusion, which requires celibacy or disinterest in the art of love as a prerequisite. Judaism as a whole, and Kabbalah in particular, do not share this view. From a Kabbalistic perspective, sex is a spiritual instrument that connects us to the Light of the Creator. However, since light cannot be visible in the absence of darkness (which may be referred to here as the shadow self), we need to take into account that desire, sexual desire included, is composed of two poles: one representing the light, also known as selfless desire, and the other, its opponent that represents the shadow self, which can be referred to as selfish desire. While the latter is actualized by the need for self-fulfillment, self-gratification, full indulgence in the resources, and immediate delight, the former lies on the needs of our partner, being immersed in satisfying the other's needs, not as a means to an end (my pleasure, reciprocity, and so forth), but rather for full indulgence in the other's joy. In the (unrelated) polyamorous community, the term *compersion* is similarly used to exhibit an empathetic state of happiness and bliss that is derived from a partner's sexual indulgence or profound emotional gratification provided by other partners within the adjacent relational connections.

So, that is it? Just feel empathetic and altruistic toward my partner's physical and sensual joy? Easier said than done, as our egotistic nature propels us to seek indulgence—and more of it as soon as it's winding down—which essentially reflects the nature of addiction. We are bound to fall back into habitual tendencies, even if we aim to remove ourselves from them. The idea behind succeeding in the path of sacred or spiritual sex is to be entirely mindful of that tendency, to not be discouraged should it rear its less attractive head, and to continue to shift back into the desired practice of selfless intimate exchange.

Why is it even necessary? Can't the union between two bodies, as we are in fact created in the "divine image," be sacred enough? Sure, it can, but since sheer joy and indulgence is short-lived, we aim to enhance, extend, and elaborate the potential of this particular sexual union.

First, we need to change our view of lovemaking as a whole. If we look at it in a broader view, there should not be an actual "fore-play" in lovemaking, only play, as a whole. All interactions between lovers—from gazing, to kissing, to touching, to climax—should be a part of the "play."

This view eliminates the entire "means to an end" stance because there is no end, but rather a long, creative, blissful dance of two souls manifesting their potentialities via earthly bodies.

The Zohar speaks about fundamental yet trivial acts that enable this connection. In one verse, it's translated (the Zohar is written in Aramaic[8]) to, "A kiss of love is spreading to the four directions, while these four directions are reconnected by it, as one."

---

8   "Zohar 2:147a." n.d. Www.Sefaria.Org. Accessed September 8, 2020. https://www.sefaria.org/Zohar.2.147a?lang=bi.

In the eyes of the Zohar, all human souls encompass masculine and feminine energies within them. This verse is a beautiful analogy to the scenario where in the sexual union (or even a mere kiss), the two spirits (two within each lover) gather through the kiss, and birth four souls, summing them to the four directions.

Real intimacy, by these means, shifts us from the world of separation—which is infinitely represented by the triviality of desire (we only desire what we lack)—into the world of oneness, enabled through this unity, where our soul (on its dual components) finally feels liberated.

In order to achieve this wonderful sensual union, we are requested to eliminate our separate egos and merge as one.

## Dropping Preconceived Notions

The Western views of masculinity versus femininity will jump to the conclusion that the speedy and goal-oriented quest of climax is the "masculine energy," while taking the time in the details, kissing, gazing, and caressing, are sourced in the "feminine energy." But these are unrefined assumptions based on a cultural climate that truly have no relation to soul connection or spirituality. These two forces are not opponent, but rather complementary, and exist in both males and females alike. Yes, women are more geared toward the aspect of "being," in contrast to the male nature of "doing," but these qualities are stronger and weaker in different individuals and could even manifest differently in the very same individual upon soul growth.

The Kabbalistic teachings of the Baal Shem Tov (the seventeenth century rabbi, mystic, healer, and founder of the Hassidic movement) were profoundly accurate even before modern neuroscience connected the limbic system, or the *fight or flight response*, to our ability (or lack of it) to relax and enjoy pleasure. Taking our time in sensual exploration enables that relaxation, and thus infuses the act of sacred sexuality with its necessary component for growth and enhancement. The French refer to a sexual climax as *la petite mort*, an expression that likens the postorgasmic sensation to death. In a sense, we need to look at this view as a source of contemplation. If we are adventuring together in this scenic, less-traveled terrain of sexual union, and immerse entirely in the merging of our feminine and masculine energies, we can arrive at the point of the "death" of the two separate halves, and the rebirth of the *new* entity as a whole creation.

Keeping these subtleties in mind in the act of lovemaking is essential. Can we still enjoy a brief spark of sexual quest, or an afternoon delight? Of course we can. We should, nonetheless, keep in mind that the brief encounter is a part of the prolonged play, and it shouldn't be regarded as a single act that requires a summation. In other words, Eastern and Kabbalistic perspectives are aligned in their view of postponing climax in the quest of a more profound buildup and/or soul connection. Whether this act is referred to as awakening your kundalini, or a practice of sacred sexuality in Kabbalistic terms, we are aiming for the same treat: a more profound and holistic experience, rather than the instant gratification numbness, the very one that creates remoteness immediately after climax. Allowing the slow path to stead for that immediate rapture has the potential of inviting a plethora of advantages, both in and out of the bedroom.

# Quickstep Meditation

We are now focusing on the ninth sephirah of Yesod (foundation). The sephirah of Yesod is vital since it represents the core of our sexual union, which is synonymous with the sacral chakra in Eastern teachings.

Observe the Tree of Life for a few minutes before going inside.

Sit in a comfortable position, close your eyes, and take a deep breath through your mouth, all the way up to the top of your lungs. Now, purse your lips and let your breath out slowly as if you're whistling through them. Repeat this three times, and keep a comfortable posture while reverting to normal breathing.

Move from the top of the Tree slowly descending through the sephirot of Keter on top, to Chochma on the right, and through Bina on the left.

Continue through Daat floating in the middle, and proceed to Chesed on the right; gear left to Gevurah, and down to Tiferet. Continue breathing naturally, and maintain your vision on each sephirah as you move along the Tree. Proceed to Netzach on the right, and move to Hod on the left. When you arrive at Hod, pause and take a deep breath. Merge all of the sources and sephirot in your mind and clench your abdominal muscles before breathing your accumulated energy out in a strong, releasing exhale into the sephirah of Yesod. Remain there for a few moments. Observe how you feel, sitting in this unique energetic place. Place your hands on your abdomen and feel your inhalation and exhalation through this diaphragmic breath. Remain here and gradually dissolve all the prior sephirot into an unfocused background. Stay in Yesod, focusing on your sensations, and then gradually shine a strong light on it. Remain in the light, then add a diaphanous shade of orange to this sephirah. Focus on it and allow it to enhance, gradually covering your entire energetic field like a bright orange sun. Immerse in it and feel the warmth cradling your entire body.

Remain here for a few moments, then take deep breath; inhale and exhale. When you feel satisfied and relaxed, slowly open your eyes.

# I Want You for Your …

The simplicity and triviality of exchanging vows and untying them has become a casual phenomenon. The rates of divorce and separation rise with every breath we take. The concept of no-fault divorce enables a couple to pursue permanent parting without ever communicating in person again.

Sure, modern life requires adjustments, and we all need to step up and elevate our conduct to these advances, yet Kabbalah views parting from a spouse very critically. Kabbalah teaches us that the importance of one's spouse is akin to a limb or any other vital organ; thus, the parting from that partner is analogous to an amputation. The teachings go even further, stating that no one—not a parent, nor children, let alone anyone else who is considered close in the couple's life—is more imperative and crucial than one's spouse. It is thus frowned upon to compare this sacred dyad to a "love connection" because love is simply a commodity.

In fact, the approach is that love—like money, like appearances—is expandable and perishable if not maintained correctly. Thus, a view of the common nuptial rationale, namely, "I would like to be in a committed relationship with someone who is _____ (fill in the blank: wealthy, beautiful, career savvy, and so forth)" is completely irrelevant within the unity of souls.

Not only because it eliminates the sanctity of this unit (as we stated that marriage is a divine concept, not a legal, human one), but it also alludes to the fact that these factors are *the* focal point of the union, when these are all materialistic manifestations that have nothing to do with the quest of our soul or soul mate.

So why is it less offensive to state that you're marrying for love, or for someone's attractive features, than it is to state that you're after your partner for their finances? Because of your ego. Simply.

Love, becoming this noble idea, or beauty being something that is (erroneously) unique to the prospective partner, are romantic and sexy to consider. But wealth is something accumulated and could also be attained from other similar partners, which makes it all less "personal" and socially incorrect.

So, what is the component most imperative to a long-term nuptial?

First, as an homage to the Hollywood romantic views of love conceptualized, we must learn to appreciate the sense of belonging, or exclusivity, as a much more appealing source of closeness or oneness. The idea behind exclusivity is the sense of belonging, the idea of "home," as a place of solace and refuge, if need be. Sure, we can indulge in multiple romantic exchanges, but will it jeopardize that sense of security? Experience can shed light, and we are the only ones who can decipher whether we are willing to venture on this path to begin with.

Kabbalistic teachings tell us that a sacred dyad is similar to the universe's constant evolvement, or infinite creation.

If the "creator" was interested in a status quo, nothing would die or come to life, no discomforts would distract our peace of mind, and all would be very similar to the Garden of Eden before the consumption of that forbidden fruit.

Yet, in order to maintain that sacred unity, we need to evolve beyond our inept sense of *existence* and graduate into our united sense of *living*.

Let us break it down a bit. When we are in existence mode, we take care of "number one"—or if we compare it to our relationships, we first think of our own comforts, constantly dread "losing ourselves" in this dyad, and we are defensive, protective, and uneasy.

In the mode of "existence," we occupy a space that may or may not entangle with our partner's space, and that creates a collision and a potential inability to coexist. Because "space" is a commodity in the existence mode, if you take more space, it leaves less of it for the other (this can be applied to any aspect of social exchange). But, if your mindset is in "living mode," after graduating mutually into this sphere, you're now manifesting your space by your contribution *to* the dyad, not *from* it.

Simply put, when you *exist*, you're "in need" of this, that, or the other, but when you *live*, you are the source of support to someone else's "needs." This creates a dynamic that enables not only a sustainable life, but one full of beauty, passion, and appreciation for every moment.

To clarify it further, look to the element of fire. Fire is an important element when considered as an existing source versus a living source. When fire is in its existence mode, it takes up space by spreading out, which can be hazardous and detrimental if handled incorrectly. But, when fire is in its living mode, its contribution is heat and warmth.

Another example that closely relates to this sacred dyad is the concept of gestation. Very similarly to a marriage, if we are in existence mode, we feel overwhelmed. "My house is not my own any more" is a common complaint of the prospective mom—that constant discomfort. The gestating woman "loses her body" to the fetus; she is not herself, her features change, someone is taking up space that was hers, and she cannot even choose her favorite foods to consume, as her "needs" are no longer her own. Yet, if she keeps in mind that life is being formed in this process, her whole view of this experience can alter.

If we remain in existence mode in our relational dyad, we can extinguish it after a while, because we can't afford to "lose our space." But if we progress to living mode, we can thrive.

# Chapter 7
## Sexy Kabbalah

The sexual imagery of Kabbalah is profound. These teachings note that "the very origins of the universe is a never-ceasing process of arousal, coupling, gestation, and birth, within the life of a God, who is both male and female, and proclaim this complex inner flow of divinity, described in the most graphic of sexual terms, to be the highest of mysteries."[9]

Yes, these statements allude to the leading commandment of procreation, but it also relates to sex as a profound source of pleasure given to the human race to be enjoyed and celebrated.

The interesting underline in this Kabbalistic view is the third factor (along with procreation and pleasure): the principle of "holiness," or in Hebrew, *Kedusha*, as primary purpose of sexuality.

It is in the moment of sexual union that we come closest to wholeness. Instead of alienation and disparity, we become one flesh. How does that transform from our primal urges into the holiness of soul connection and the light of the Creator? Harmoniously.

---

9   Strassfeld, Sharon, Michael Strassfeld, Mark Nulman, Nessa Rapoport, Levi Kelman, Stuart Copans, and Adrianne Onderdonk Dudden. 1999. *The Second Jewish Catalog: Sources & Resources*. Philadelphia, PA: Jewish Publication Society of America.

To love the Creator and appreciate his sublime work, one must first love another human being; even prior to that, one must first love oneself.

In the Kabbalistic realm, the adage "love thy neighbor as thyself" isn't an allegory for narcissism—or, alternatively, a complete altruistic stance—but rather a first and important concept of getting closer to that oneness of light. When you do in fact nourish your soul and "thyself," you engage in a number of actions. You affirm the Creator's perfect creation; in this rationale, questioning this creation doesn't apply as humility, but quite the opposite. The reason for it being a divine-negating act is that one may view his assumptions as more accurate than the Creator's.

When you love yourself, you also allow yourself to gradually seep from *existence* into *living*, thus removing a layer of "dirt" from your soul, which is essential in the quest of spiritual growth.

When you love yourself, you become more and more established in sharing this love with another, and since you can only give what you have, the first step is to acquire that love internally.

How do you unblemish your soul? Through mindfulness, spiritual practices, kindness, and breathwork; through simply living, rather than existing.

Why would you ever want to sacrifice you own comfort for the sake of another? Because that's your soul quest! Your soul needs to be heard before it can join another on the path to soul unity, also known as the soul mate relationship. Your soul is very quiet, and listening to your soul requires you to balance the loud volume of the cacophony of everyday life.

Once you go through the elaborate steps of enabling this genuine growth, together with the other loved ones we can restore the world to peace, wholeness, and harmony.

Kabbalistic teachings do not set boundaries on the powerful sexual urge. Rather, they see sexuality and its highest form—love—as critical gifts of holiness given to us by creation to live by, in this world and beyond.

Kabbalah tells us that even more profoundly than other pleasurable acts or needs, like food consumption, the act of sexual union involves another person, and for that mere reason, should be treated very delicately and cautiously.

The principle of treating another person with respect is called *kavod ha-beriot* in Hebrew. The potential of damaging another person's very core is particularly high during sex, because the act, no matter how "casual," involves vulnerability. You are naked physically and emotionally before another without the protective "walls" you carry around on a daily basis. Thus, while acknowledging our common vulnerability, we need to be especially protective of the other person in their nakedness.

Poet James Baldwin puts it beautifully when he writes, "Love takes off the masks that we fear we cannot live without and know we cannot live within. I use the word "love" here not merely in the personal sense but as a state of being, or a state of grace—not in the infantile American sense of being made happy, but in the tough and universal sense of quest and daring and growth."

## Quickstep Meditation

We are now focusing on the sixth sephirah of Tiferet (beauty).

The sephirah of Tiferet is vital because it represents the love we genuinely carry in our souls, yet consciously or subconsciously spend our entire lives aiming to conceal. It is located around the heart, and is synonymous with the heart chakra in Eastern teachings. This sephirah represents a certain harmonious relationship between love and order or discipline, and between the flowing unbound love and restriction. It's the uniting component between two partners.

Observe the Tree of Life for a few minutes before going inside.

Sit in a comfortable position, close your eyes, and take a deep breath through your mouth, all the way up to the top of your lungs. Now, purse your lips and let your breath out slowly as if you're whistling through them. Repeat this three times, and keep a comfortable posture while reverting to normal breathing.

Move from the top of the Tree, slowly descending through the sephirot of Keter, to Chochma on the right, through Bina on the left. Continue through Daat floating in the middle, proceed to Chesed on the right, and gear left to Gevurah. When you arrive here, remain silent. Place your hands on your chest and spread your fingers. Gather your breath, and then in one flow, "shoot" your energy forward and down to Tiferet. Enhance this sephirah in an immense energy, and focus on it, potent and strong, aiming to break the barriers of the cage your heart settles in.

Remain there for a few moments, and then slowly invite the beautiful lavender shade to immerse Tiferet, as if you are the Creator and just now blew the breath of life into it through a very small aperture.

Fill Tiferet with the purple light, slowly fade the background of the rest of the Tree, and remain focused on this location. Take a few deep breaths and proceed shining through it, in and out, left and right, up and down, all around.

Once you feel strong and settled in it, revert to your normal breathing. Keep your hands on your chest, and then slowly lower your hands to your knees or the ground. Open your eyes gradually, and breath normally.

## The Trifecta of a Committed Relationship

Kabbalistic teachings speak elaborately about the sanctity and importance of a committed relationship. Among other advantages, we are introduced to the interesting "relationship guarding trio" of *wall*, *blessing*, and *peace*.

The concept of *wall*, provided by a dyadic unity, is referring to the "wall against misfortune and misdeeds."

In other words, the fact that we are in a committed nuptial means that the strength of the dyad provides us enough space for mistakes and vulnerability within so that we are less prone to exhibiting these vices externally to the dyad. It shields us from venturing out into the open space of the universe because our partner can buffer most of our misbehaviors or mishaps.

Then, we have the principle of *blessing*; here we are taught that a blessing of happiness, calmness, serenity, prosperity, and so forth is in direct relation to our dyad.

Here's how: say for instance that you have a highly rewarding career and a terrific paycheck, while your partner is a "stay at home" mom.

Kabbalah tells us that the very source of your terrific financial gain is in your wife's buffering, or operation in the "back office." In other words, yes, you may have skills and/or education, but were it not for your supportive soul match, these gains would not have been possible to the degree they are manifested today.

The last but not least component of *peace* is interesting; it represents peace of mind. Both Western and Eastern views tell us that for a person to have a clear mind and healthy body, one must have peace of mind. Kabbalah comes in merely to affirm that very logical notion, and to add that peace of mind is a representative of your soul growth. As long as your soul struggles and aches, this state will "bleed" into your mind and body's functionalities. If you experience peace of mind, therefore, it is due to the "blanket" or "shield" provided by the sanctity of your dyad.

## You Get What You Need

It has long been established that us humans are a very successful creation, yet exceptionally limited. Our perception of reality is infinitely distorted by the confinement of our five senses. If that isn't enough, one may add to it a sense of unworthiness, guilt, shame, and remorse, and there you have it, the perfect imperfection.

Yet, the Creator's larger plan is for us to use all avenues of our lives in order to enhance the time we spend here on earth, even within the limitations of our physical bodies.

How can it be achieved? Through our soul, and more specifically, our soul connection.

Let's use an easily comprehensible analogy. If we are faced with a wildfire, what is the source that can extinguish it and regain equilibrium? It isn't a trick question, and you know the answer. Of course, its water. You are correct.

Nonetheless, water alone, as powerful as we know it is, cannot extinguish the fire all by itself. The water needs to be channeled through a hose, directed by a human hand, or, more safely, a certified firefighter. What do we derive from this analogy? Simple. The universe and creator are constantly providing us with strengths that are embedded and can be easily and readily utilized into forming a sublime life for ourselves as well as others around us. Yet, the Creator cannot direct these strengths all by itself, or rather *chooses* not to, as this is the core establishment of a relationship. It needs us (the firefighters) to take this enormous power, light, strength, or whichever title you fancy, and channel it toward the source of need; be it ours or others. That's essentially our goal and purpose in life in general, and in our relational exchanges in particular.

In order to safely drive this point home, I'd even progress and mention that not only are we obligated to act as vessels and channels to our strengths to enhance our lives and the lives of others, but even the act of enabling a person who refuses to take initiative and thereby "forces" us to provide all of his needs can be viewed as a violation of our purpose. We must progress with conviction and kindly, yet firmly, remove obstacles or other factors that aim to entangle that vessel we carry in the direction of the light and enlightenment. Here, one needs to act with caution nonetheless, and tread lightly. That means that we can lose view of the general agenda, and instead turn it into a personal one. The divine agenda is selfless and benevolent; it's infinite and knows no boundaries; it has no shelf life or limited stock. Conversely, our selfish or self-centered agendas are very limited, narrow, and can dim or extinguish in a heartbeat.

Let us use another analogy to make this clear. The idea of pleasure, which is supremely relevant to relationships: After the pleasure is attained, where does it go? After all, it felt so powerful when it was present, didn't it? At times, you could even say that it may have felt all-consuming and greater than your own existence, so what happens to it after it is experienced? It is gone, evaporated into a black hole.

Why?

Because its source is finite and human; that is, selfish, not divine.

If we adopt the divine agenda in our conduct, relationships, pleasures, choices, and the like, we will come to the understanding that it is never-ending and sublime.

How can I, nonetheless, as human in this body, on this earth, enjoy my life here now?

The answer is simple. We were directed here in order to do just that: maximize the divine agenda, here, while we are alive, as humans, and by doing so, maximize that experience for others like us, anywhere around the globe.

If we take it to a more personal level, we are in our relationships in order to ascend the spiritual conditions of ourselves *and* our partners through different actions and choices. Going back to the story of creation, this is precisely why the "primordial sin" took place. This wasn't a manipulation of the divine, or a bad inclination by the serpent (if you read carefully, he was sent by the Creator himself to carry out this task), but rather an agenda for us to remove ourselves from the divine, undisturbed life there in the pleasant Garden onto the more challenging manifestation here on earth, because, once more, we are that vessel needed to carry out this valuable task.

What about our wants, our needs?

These are different from one another, and maybe even miles apart. Simply put, our wants are based on our distorted 1 percent perspective of life here, manifested by the five senses. There's plenty we cannot see, hear, smell, touch, or taste, yet we assume that what we want is the ultimate, based on this distorted view.

Conversely, our needs are the Creator's agenda. They are based on what we cannot foresee in the infinite realm. Our challenges emerge when we fail to trust these assigned needs and cling to our wants like a toddler to his blanket.

We cannot let go, we don't care to look further, we *want* this now!!! Yes, it doesn't matter who we are or where we come from, this is applicable at one point or another in our lives. In particular, this is prevalent when the divine "agenda" fails to align with our own, and what follows are our misaligned wants versus needs. The principle of mindfulness aims to target this very challenge: trusting that the agenda we cannot yet see is the precise and unquestionable path suitable for us. It is not an easy task, and the road there is paved with disappointments, heavy hearts, and discombobulation, yet, when we arrive at this understanding and gain trust, we remove the strings of attachment to the selfish and connect to the infinite charger of the selfless.

Now, this does not mean checking into a Buddhist monastery and wearing white or orange togas all day, nor does it mean a hermetic lifestyle. It does mean, however, that we need to practice a higher consciousness toward the broader sense of wellness, rather than our own small pond of it.

Let's use one last analogy for this section to make this much more coherent. If life was a jigsaw puzzle and we were given that puzzle folded neatly like a blanket, complete and whole as soon as it is rolled out of the box, what kind of interest or intrigue would that have evoked in us? We would have dismissed it altogether, or even protest as to its misleading nature. Similarly, our lives, in all their intricate factors, are jigsaw puzzles waiting to be aligned correctly. But only if we take the time to align the pieces where they belong will we arrive to witness the beauty of their wholeness.

Trust, anyone?

# Chapter 8
## Soul Mate Compatibility

Evolution has taught us that males and females are designed to sense an attraction to one another in order to procreate and keep the human race alive.

That is correct and has been affirmed throughout eons.

Nonetheless, the Kabbalistic view of this primal need is more profound. Kabbalistic teachings speak of the soul recognition of its counterpart in another's presence. Not only on an evolutionary level, but also in the core, romantic, sensual sense.

Essentially, it whispers, "You have what I'm missing." That is an oversimplification of a soul connection. Naturally, one needs to be aware of his own soul and what it's lacking in order to find that missing piece.

A key element in relationships is compatibility. From early on in the acquaintance phase, and all the way up to the more solidified dyad stages, discord can make or break relationships. How do we define compatibility? How many types of compatibility are there? Is it a "one size fits all" kind of sphere? Or is there a certain type of compatibility that can sustain a relationship?

In order to find your soul mate, match, or connection to the divine light, you'll need to fist analyze your own soul and its attainment, since lack of awareness of your own core cannot yield a successful match.

Let us review the different levels of soul connection. Kabbalistic teachings tell us that the soul has fiver levels of existence. [image]

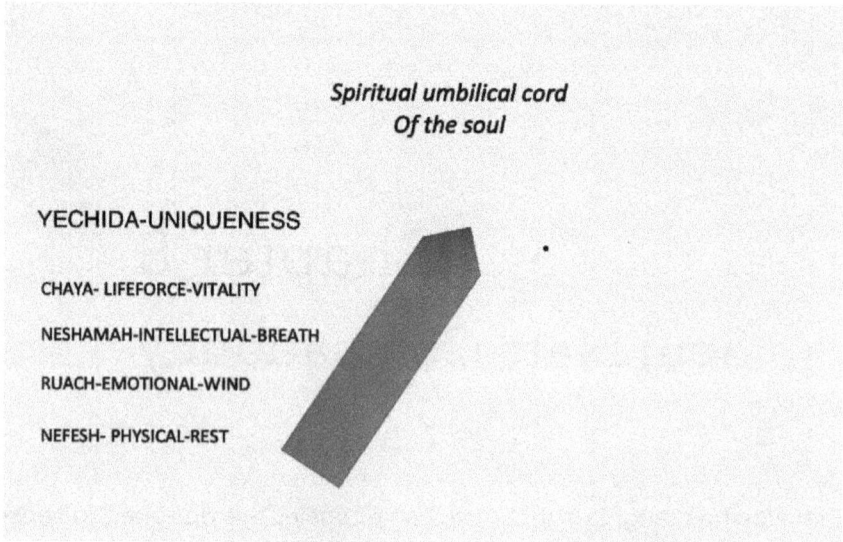

**Spiritual umbilical cord**
**Of the soul**

YECHIDA-UNIQUENESS

CHAYA- LIFEFORCE-VITALITY

NESHAMAH-INTELLECTUAL-BREATH

RUACH-EMOTIONAL-WIND

NEFESH- PHYSICAL-REST

Starting from the lowest realm called Nefesh, this realm represents the physical sphere, and is assumed to be an actual energy field hovering right above the head—or "crown"—where the spiritual world connects to the tangible body. Then there are the emotional, intellectual, and lifeforce realms in between, and finally, the highest sphere, Yechida represents a complete and sublime oneness with the universe or the divine, it is a state of uniqueness, reserved for the divine.

# The Different Realms of Soul Connection

## Physical Compatibility

Physical attraction to one another on the material level is essentially the nature of the Nefesh sphere. Here, we establish the initial connection, as it is vital for partners to be physically drawn to one another, and physical compatibility is clearly based on a subjective set of preferences. Nevertheless, it is an important component in a relationship.

It is imperative to comprehend that this sphere is rewarding and lovely, yet highly limited. If one remains in this realm, the relationship may be compromised or potentially have a short shelf life, as a physical component is ever changing and isn't static; thus, what is appealing now may become less enthralling in time.

This sphere is also representative of the existence mode; here, we are not yet elevated to a higher realm of spirituality, or even physical evolution, but rather dealing with maintaining the basics.

## Emotional Compatibility

The next element of Ruach, or emotion, is a higher soul level connection. This sphere enables arousal and stimulation on a more profound level than the flesh. You can be attracted to someone physically, but if there is no emotional connection, the relationship cannot endure. How does this manifest differently from the prior sphere? Think of a familiar scenario: a potential partner may look beautiful on paper or in real life, but when you meet and talk to them, you don't feel a thing—there is no "click." Every healthy relationship needs a feeling of trust and commonality, as well as emotional nurturing.

## Intellectual Compatibility

Now we arrive at the third realm of Neshama, or mind connection, which is an imperative phase, since this is the last one of the five that is transitory.

Once you cross this threshold, things take an interesting turn.

Intellectual compatibility between two people who respect each other's intelligence and are profoundly aroused on a cerebral level can be miraculous and absolutely igniting.

The term sapiosexuality refers to this sphere.

The couple can share, and are stimulated by, each other's ideas and/or shared intellectual interests.

They value each other's opinions and thoughts.
They find each other's knowledge compelling.

## Eternal Compatibility: Transcendence

The element of Chaya refers to the subconscious or vitality and can take the shape of just about anything in your life; from love, to nurturing, to sexuality, and so forth. This connection elevates you to a higher state where you share a common goal or purpose with your partner that is by far greater than either of you, or greater than its parts. The fourth element of compatibility, which infuses and lifts a relationship to another dimension, holds the potential of what fairytales may call "eternal love." Since all is transitory when it manifests on an earthly, materialistic level, what connection can ensue the infinite? This fourth soul connection sphere holds a higher prospect, and this very potential.

It is called spiritual compatibility: two people who share a vision and a mission—a vision that transcends their needs and their every-day life interests. The partners constantly inquire: "What transcendent vision do we share, and how can we contribute to the greater good of all? What mark do we want to leave on the world?" It even relates to one's close environment when you ask as a unit, "What kind of feeling do we want to project to our close environment? What legacy are we leaving?"

In contrast to the first three soul connections, which are all subject to change (due to age, life circumstances, emotional evolvement or lack of it, etc.), this fourth dimension may last a lifetime and more.

This is a divine dimension where you suspend your selfish quests in order to ascend to a higher realm beyond yourself. You immerse in the mutual cause to the degree that it becomes much more profound and potent than your personal experience.

No matter what changes or challenges one may go through, a vision does not change. Your vision and mission can take on different shapes and forms, yet your core personality, your essence and life mission do not change. When two people find a partnership on that level, their relationship is able to evolve throughout life.

"How is this realm even reachable?" you may ask. Naturally, it requires a solid and unquestionable commitment.

Say you decide to volunteer at a soup kitchen once a week. You stick to it as a shared experience and you don't "give yourself breaks" based on selfish whims. You are fully committed to the mission. This in turn creates a layer of true intimacy because you were able to mutually rise above your egotistic nature. This must be firmly infused into your very nature in order to be sustainable.

## Final and Sublime: Oneness

This final and completed level of soul connection, called Yechida, or uniqeness, is the concept and principal of oneness.

In this realm, you are at peace with yourself to a degree that you cannot say, "I'm at peace with a certain experience but less at peace with another," because there is no experience; your mere presence is an ongoing continuance of blissful *being*, not *doing*, and of inner satisfaction, and so is your unit. Here, you experience serenity and a sensation of fundamental love that is always present at a core level. This isn't influenced by experience, mood, and so forth, but rather embedded firmly into your being. It's akin to a feeling of being "in the zone," perhaps such as when you mediate or act on other forms of mindfulness. You come to a place where you're no longer a body or even a vessel, but simply an essence, and that essence is infinite. We are not discussing a sensation because that would imply the material physical involvement in it, which is the source of disparity from prior realms. You melt into one another, in complete harmony, at your core level.

Here, there's no action, simply a state of being.

## Quickstep Meditation

In this quickstep meditation, we will pursue a slightly different route. Here, we will aim to reveal where on these soul connection levels we are positioned, and where we would want to go.

Sit in a comfortable position, close your eyes, and take a deep breath through your mouth, all the way up to the top of your lungs. Now, purse your lips and let your breath out slowly as if you're whistling through them. Repeat this three times, and keep a comfortable posture while reverting to normal breathing.

Imagine the five simple steps for soul connection we just discussed, and place yourself on an energetic level (preferably) at the bottom of the scale.

Position one hand on top of your head where the crown or halo would be, and the other one on your abdomen.

As we are aware that our highest consciousnesses is greatly influenced by our intuitive notions, we are aiming to involve a dynamic between the two by the hand placement.

Feel yourself within the realm of Nefesh, or body. Are you comfortable here? Do you feel at ease in this location? What does your "gut" tell you? Rate yourself imaginatively on a scale from one to ten, one being uncomfortable and aiming for higher, and ten being your natural habitat.

Remain there for a few moments and climb the stair onto the second level of Ruach, or emotion. Scan your mind and body and ask yourself this same question. It's quite common to feel unsure or indecisive. Don't pressure yourself, you can go back here later.

Repeat this process on all levels until you arrive at the highest level of Yechida.

Remain there for a few minutes, and retain normal breathing and comfort.

When you feel satisfied, remove your hand from your head, and place both hands on the ground. Remain in Yechida, and ask yourself, "Does this feel attainable and desirable to me?" Rate your sensation from one to ten, one being, "Not at all, get me out," and ten being, "What a feeling, finally."

Repeat this process as you descend down the stairs of soul connection until you reach and complete the Nefesh, or physical realm.

Retain a normal breath and keep your eyes closed for a few minutes before returning back to your comfortable and leisurely position. Open your eyes and relax.

# Healthy Relationship: What Is it?

Bringing up this inquiry seems basic and elementary, yet Kabbalistic teachings once again tell us that it is far from it.

If the trivial views of a functional relationship can mean that the partners get along, perhaps share a common interest, enjoy similar activities or are wise/strong/yielding enough to stay out of one another's hair when needed, Kabbalah lists very different elements that comprise this "well baked cake."

I'm using this analogy not to belittle the concept of a unity—of course a cake is much more easily attained—but a well baked cake isn't the opinion of some versus others, but rather a fact, unlike the *taste* of the cake.

Similarly, a healthy relationship is not questionable. The *flavor* of it may be favorable to some and less so to others, yet the actual "readiness" of it should be a factor that is likely agreeable by all.

So how do we measure this healthy relationship? As we started and exemplified with the cake analogy, we can look at the results of this dyad. If this relationship is healthy, it will yield two healthy and pleased human beings, and it will likely permeate to the close surrounding; for example, children, neighbors, friends, family, and so forth.

You may ask, "That's all very nice and palatable, but what are the actual components that are a necessity in this recipe in order to make it considered heathy?"

# The Trinity of a Healthy Relationship

First, we need to include a symbiotic exchange.

A good dyad means that both partners are active in the foundation and the ongoing functionality of the relationship. We don't see one partner being *dragged* into a lifestyle or course of conduct that is only entertained due to fear of losing the relationship, we don't see a partner who simply acts apathetically and obeys or tries to walk on eggshells to retain the status quo. We see two partners who are mutually responsible for the creation of a successful, healthy unit.

There's a very beautiful verse in Proverbs 27:19 by King Solomon that reads: "As in water face answereth to face, so the heart of man to man."

Simply put, that means that your partner should be connected to you, or the way your heart and soul relate to your partner should resemble your reflection in the water. Unlike the similar narcissistic notion of the mythological Narcissus who fell in love with his own reflection, here you are bound to love, appreciate and nurture your partner *as* yourself, as if they're literally your own reflection—because they are, on a soul level.

Another important factor of a healthy relationship is the solid foundation of personal self-esteem. Self-esteem is crucial to the successful health of the relationship, because a person who is not appreciative of their values cannot require that appreciation from another. In fact, that person isn't even readily available to create a successful relationship, because the energy that is emitted from one's conduct and overall being will immediately draw a similar frequency from another. And thus, a coupledom comprised of two very unstable and troubled individuals who view themselves as unworthy has a very low probability of being the epitome of health.

The last but not least important factor that cannot be overlooked in a healthy dyad is the principle of accountability. If we are not accountable for our mistakes or misjudgments, we can never correct them. Place these factors in a work environment, and you will witness a complete collapse in light of unaccountable conduct. If things are rocky in a business, or if I made an investment mistake, or any related decision, yet I fail to take responsibility for it, dismiss it, fault others, or belittle its effects, the business will soon liquidate.

## Quickstep Meditation

We are now focusing on the tenth sephirah of Malchut, or sovereignty.

The sephirah of Malchut is vital, since it represents the self-esteem that is required for the ongoing success of a committed relationship. Malchut can represent the "feminine" ground that complements the "masculine" top sephirah of Keter, among other functions, and is considered the female component of the divine via another name assigned to it often, namely the Shekinah. Yet, for the purpose of this practice, we will focus on the component of self-esteem.

Observe the Tree of Life for a few minutes before going inside.

Sit in a comfortable position, close your eyes, and take a deep breath through your mouth, all the way up to the top of your lungs. Now, purse your lips and let your breath out slowly as if you're whistling through them. Repeat this three times, and keep a comfortable posture while reverting to normal breathing.

Move from the top of the Tree, slowly descending through the sephirot of Keter, to Chochma on the right, through Bina on the left. Continue through Daat floating in the middle, and proceed to Chesed on the right. Gear left to Gevurah and then immediately descend to Tiferet. Remain here for a few moments and practice deeper breathing; inhale and exhale to the count of four.

We stop here since it is midway to our goal sephirah of Malchut, and we are gathering our energy in that direction.

Proceed to Netzach on the right and straight to Hod on the left. Descend to Yesod and pause again.

When you arrive here, remain silent. Place your hands on your abdomen and spread them open fingered one above the other, toward your chest. Gather your breath, and in one flow, "shoot" your energy forward and down to Malchut. Enhance this sephirah in an immense energy and focus on it, stay in your gut with all your might. Now, lower the "volume" of this energy and allow it to settle in. We would like to allow the sanctity of this sephirah to slowly seep in, in its indigo shade. Slowly begin to fade the entire Tree in the background while emanating the dark blue shade, and then circle your energy around it, over and over, clockwise.

Remain in your comfortable seated position and allow the energy of the Shekinah to overtake every barrier you may have established in the past, anything that may emanate from feelings of unworthiness, or lack of completion. This energy is now being eliminated and "reverted back to factory settings" where you are a perfect and complete creature of light.

Remain in this place until you're satisfied, retain normal breath, and open your eyes.

# Chapter 9
## Outsourcing

We explored the various paths and requirements for a prosperous relationship, but does following this "recipe" religiously guarantee a long and reliable relationship?

Let us examine infidelity. Modern societies have been progressing to view the frequency, prevalence, and legitimacy of this notion far more leniently than any prior generation. In our "modern fare"—albeit somewhat frowned upon in some more traditional circles—the idea of playing the field is not only legitimate, but it is advertised, and at times even celebrated[10] by establishments that promote the idea of an affair as a token of posh and open-minded lifestyle. But enough about what we all know about the industry and its abilities to propel audiences toward a particular action. The Kabbalistic views of infidelity are different. Here, we are looking at the sacredness of a committed dyad, not on a religious level, not on a social level, not even on a relational level, but actually on the spiritual, metaphysical level.

The prospect of exiting the sacred unit is a breach within the energetic balance that is established within such a unit. So, in other words,

---

10 Ashley Madison. n.d. "Affairs & Discreet Married Dating: AshleyMadison. Com®." www.Ashleymadison.com. http://www.ashleymadison.com.

the lack of presence, or the diminishing, justifying words we run through our heads that may satisfy our cerebral dissonance, does not provide any Band-Aid for the soul. The energetic sphere between a couple is compromised by an affair, and it may erode on a very profound level after the action.

To make this clear, it doesn't matter one bit if your partner knows of the act, if your partner suspects, or if they'll never find out; on a soul level, there's been a disruption, a breach, that must be equalized in order for the universe to gain balance. How will it be remedied? It can take different forms and cannot be managed on a tangible level. Perhaps it will manifest in a liquidation of this dyad, in a misfortune or hardship of some sort, or in a similar act on your partner's end, in future relationship—it doesn't matter, but the equilibrium must be achieved.

We tend to justify the difficulty of maintaining this sacred union on its mono level by comparing it to our ancestral relation to other primates that founded their social lives on sharing their shelters, food, and sexuality. Yet, not only would we never consider sharing our home with some stranger off the street, we established laws against invaders and do anything in our power to protect what's "ours." More important, we are not our "ancestral" primates, we are an evolved creation that has acquired tools and abilities to deal with challenges of any form, including the staleness of a "familiar dyad." I'm not referring to the "right or wrong" concept of conduct, as these are materialistic, social, even emotional stances. What is discussed and suggested here is the spiritual end of it. "So how," you ask, "can novelty be attained? I mean, if it's not a new partner, what will it be?"

Forget the *Cosmopolitan* advice columns (with all due respect), the only way to maintain novelty is by the constant revitalization of the dyad through the less familiarity stance.

The curbing of 100 percent sharing of every single moment or thought can leave some room for surprises. The choice to use separate beds or bedrooms; to be seductive, alluring, and mysterious rather than bored, forceful, or degrading; the reintroduction of kindness and compassion into your sexual exchanges while engaging the entire soul when the sexual union does happen can greatly revitalize the relationship.

Another factor that plays a role in infidelity is the notion of "feeling relevant and vibrant." We all suffer from a "life crisis" at any age. We fear losing ourselves in the relationship, in the other's domination, in society. We want to stand our ground. Yet, it's imperative to understand that a merging of two souls, when it is a true connection, is anything *but* diminishing and deteriorating.

In fact, the whole becomes greater than its parts.

Kabbalistic teachings refer to the story of creation in Genesis 1:27 as the creation of the initial Adam (human, in Hebrew), who was dual gendered and was established initially in an attached mode—one gender facing the front and the other facing the back: "And God created man in His own image, in the image of God created He him; male and female created He them."

Thus, by Kabbalistic views, a soul unity strives to do just that: to merge into one creation together. Only now, since the dyad is a sacred and nurturing one, the result will be upgraded in comparison to the initial "product," because now we are bound face to face, thus the valued "missionary position."

A factor that is worth mentioning here is the component of gender when it comes to relevance. As previously discussed, man, having been created from "nothing," has a more burning need for validation, and may be more prone to seek that validation elsewhere, statistically.

We are told in Genesis 2:18, "And the LORD God said: 'It is not good that the man should be alone; I will make him a help meet for him.'" And then, further in Genesis 2:24, we read, "Therefore shall a man leave his father and his mother, and shall cleave unto his wife, and they shall be one flesh."

The message behind these verses is gender sourced because it relates to that male need and does not state the equivalence to it in the female. Sure, a woman needs the support and validation of her partner, but since this is stated and experienced on a less tangible level, we need to keep in mind that the masculine challenge is well founded and should not be taken lightly.

We will further our discussion into energetic balance and sacred sexuality in the next section, but first, it is time to go inside.

# Quickstep Meditation

We are now focusing on the fourth sephirah of Chesed, or loving kindness.

The sephirah of Chesed is vital because it represents self-love, as well as love for another. This love reference is not secluded to close circles, but it is a complete love for anything and anyone, as an expansion of self-love, that is required for the ongoing success of a committed relationship.

Observe the Tree of Life for a few minutes before going inside.

Sit in a comfortable position, close your eyes, and take a deep breath through your mouth, all the way up to the top of your lungs. Now, purse your lips and let your breath out slowly as if you're whistling through them. Repeat this three times, and keep a comfortable posture while reverting to normal breathing.

Place one hand on the floor for strength and grounding, and the other on your right shoulder. Keep your hands in this position throughout the entire meditation.

Move from the top of the Tree slowly descending through the sephirot of Keter, to Chochma on the right, through Binah on the left. Continue through Daat floating in the middle, and gaze at its diaphanous nature.

Before shifting down to Chesed on the right, take a deep breath to the count of three, and exhale to the same count. Repeat these three times, or more if needed.

Once you're ready, gather your entirety and push your energy into Chesed on the right. Breath into it, as the Creator breathed the initial breath of life into Adam in the Garden of Eden. Remain there and practice intense breaths in order to waken the self-love that resides there.

When you feel strong enough in the image and sensation, fade the rest of the Tree into the background, and add a shade of light blue into Chesed (Tchelet, in Hebrew).

Circle the light blue around and inside it, like a clear sky on a mid-summer day.

Circle it and breathe into it repeatedly. When you feel satisfied, gradually allow Chesed to fade, slowly remove your hands from their positions, and move them back to your knees or thighs. Slowly open your eyes.

## Energetic Balance and Sexual Connection

We began discussing the component of energy within the sexual union, but we may also approach it from the angle of the sexual component within a spiritual connection.

We have established that sex, in Kabbalists views, is sacred and divine; a commencement of the very primal creation on a micro level, and if carried on wisely, holds the potential for complete transcendence, or as some would say, a religious experience.

Jokes aside regarding the "Oh, God" factor within the sexual practice, this unity truly deserves an emphasis and scope in order for its legitimacy and necessity to the spiritual path to be comprehended. Since we live in a world where sex is used as an outlet in any way shape or form—too long of a list of ways to even begin to utter—we are the ones responsible for making it qualify as the gate to a spiritual transcendence *and* ascendance.

In Kabbalistic teachings, we acknowledge that casual sex, the kind that strips the experience off of any spiritual and emotional connection, is not beneficial and is downright harmful. Not to the body (although it can be), not to the mind (although thoughts are energy, so ...), and not even to one's social status or how they are perceived or perceive themselves; it is neglectful to the cosmic energy in a sense that it is being "contaminated" with an empty vessel of a physical form that lacks any spirituality. Let's use a simple analogy: we know that artificial sweeteners are harmful to your body. The list of disadvantages is long, but what I'm aiming at is the basic idea that your body is being "tricked" into believing it is being fed something sweet. For example, it prepares itself for the process of breaking down insulin, but then it is left with this charade of a supply that it doesn't know what to do with—*pumping gas in neutral*, in a sense.

Now, apply this simple analogy to your sexual union. Your soul is triggered that here you are in the very presence of the act of creation, yet all it ends up with is a little "shake down" at best, perhaps some genital arousal, and that's it, done.

What the soul is left with is a big gaping void that is not sourced in a neediness or oversensitivity, but rather a "promise" of fine sugar which turned out to be Splenda.

Yes, the physical body craves stimulation. We are divine beings, yet we are placed in this carrier called body that has needs and wants, but we must keep in mind that in all our actions, we awaken the soul component of our being, and we must take responsibility for it.

Gender unrelated, the energy flowing between the souls is "politically correct," and so any exchange, whether between heterosexual partners or homosexual lovers, applies as an exchange of divine and spiritual energy.

The caveat relating to multiple relationships, as mentioned prior, is also applicable here on the energetic level. Since the complete unit encompasses two souls, by expanding that exchange into a number of dyads, we may create an imbalance.

Wait, does that mean that we need to act prudishly, avoid provocative clothes, act sheepishly in the bedroom, and so forth? God, no (pun well intended).

Regarding the exhibitionism factor, we can choose our wardrobe and act as we choose, but we must take that similar responsibility in the understanding of the energy that is being emitted. That same energy returns to us. So, if I choose provocative outfits, they simply must create a sphere of similar energy driven toward me; these are not religious or social rules, these are the laws of the universe.

Regarding a kinky, experimental zest in the bedroom, Kabbalah puts no restrictions on these acts, in any way. One may experiment and enjoy every wild idea that comes to mind while being engulfed in a soul-connecting exchange.

## In the Garden

What really took place in the Garden of Eden that we are constantly being thrown back to? Well, we investigated it a bit earlier in the book with discussions of the serpent and his role, and with the Creator's choice to approach Eve rather than Adam with this matter, but for the sake of discussion, let us go back to some details again.

The consumption of the forbidden fruit is obviously what launched this slippery slope down the rabbit hole of humanity. It is interesting that although we are often presented with the apple as *that* fruit, in modern iconology, no source provides firm evidence of its validity. Kabbalistic teachings tell us that the answer is in the story, right there in front of our eager eyes. In Genesis 3:7, we are told, "And the eyes of them both were opened, and they knew that they were naked; and they sewed fig-leaves together, and made themselves girdles."

Have you ever taken a luscious bite into a fresh fig? It's almost obscene looking, and yes, the assumption is that the tree was, in fact, a fig tree, but we are not tending to this for the sake of its identity. What is interesting here is the fact that later in this chapter in verse 21, we are told, "And the LORD God made for Adam and for his wife garments of skins, and clothed them."

In all imagery relating to the story of creation, we are presented with the erroneous assumption of the known human form being covered in fig leaves, garments, or other options.

Yet, what we fail to comprehend is that these fig leaves were not intended to be placed on a human body—the first humans didn't have bodies. Adam and Eve were divine creatures. The debate regarding the actual form they possessed prior to being given the "garments of skin" is vast, but what we need to acknowledge is that only on this very important occasion were they given the shape and form we are familiar with—the *skin garments* we call a body. And so, the soul is lying right beneath it, and every single sensation we allow in our physical form relates directly to our soul like a delicate, perishable item.

# Self-Deprecation

We all know and are aware that humility and selfless conduct is a desirable trait, especially spiritually. Yet, it is important to discuss what true humility really is, that it can serve, elevate, and transcend a relationship, conversely to arrogance in disguise.

Since all our relational choices are sourced in the manner in which we perceive ourselves, these views of the self are important and can be detrimental to the sacred dyad if mishandled.

Let's begin with the innate, yet sometime elusive, notion that humans hold a divine place or spark in this world, thus making our role *here* indispensable. It is not a matter of interpretation or an opinion; by Kabbalistic teachings, it simply is. Now, conduct or behavior that is supportive of this notion will exhibit acts of kindness, caring for others, and humility.

But, is a person who states, "I'm nothing important. My place here on earth is insignificant" a humble or an arrogant person? By Kabbalah, this kind of self "deprecation" is considered one of the most advanced acts of arrogance for two reasons: Firstly, the "tangible you" walking around this earth is simply a loan from the Creator. As such, you are not the manufacturer of this creation and thus have no say or control over its relevance. You're simply occupying it for the time being.

Secondly, since this this body isn't yours to keep (only for this lifetime), who are you to override a divine decision as to its importance or relevance? This isn't your place to question, nor are you allowed to deprecate the very holy vessel you were given for safekeeping.

This notion is staggering if you contemplate it, because we all walk this earth as the actual masters of this, or any, creation. Now, that does not negate the fact that you are a cocreator; you're, in fact, collaborating with a higher divinity and source in order to keep creating, given that this universe is ever evolving.

But you're not the "manufacturer" as stated, you're the carrier, and as such should act respectfully toward yourself and others.

How can you create a more sacred ground acknowledging this very notion?

Morning and nocturnal affirmations of your soul and divine existence can be beneficial in the service of this acknowledgment.

The morning chant מוֹדָה לְפָנֶיךָ מֶלֶךְ חַי וְקַיָם שֶׁהֶחֱזַרְתָ בִּי נִשְׁמָתִי בְּחֶמְלָה, רַבָּה אֱמוּנָתֶךָ:

"I am thankful before You, living and enduring King, for you have mercifully restored my soul within me. Great is Your faithfulness." (Courtesy of Sefaria)

And the nocturnal chant of בְּיָדְךָ, אַפְקִיד רוּחִי: פָּדִיתָ אוֹתִי יְהוָה--אֵל אֱמֶת.

"Into Thy hand I commit my spirit; Thou hast redeemed me, O LORD, Thou God of truth."[11]

These are simple yet creative and efficient ways to affirm your role in this divine matrix. They can give your soul a boost, when needed.

Another channel to generate this profound godly force in you is to activate your "love muscle." In a very similar manner to which feeding your body the correct nutrients yields physical fitness and healthier muscle tone, acts of kindness like volunteering or rewarding others with no expectation of anything in return exercise the *giving dimension* within you and will yield an elevation of your state of mind and the volume of your soul.

We are familiar with the idiom "I'll believe it when I see it," but Kabbalah teaches us that only the ones who foresee these miracles will witness them, not the other way around.

---

11  Ps. 31:6 KJV

# Chapter 10
## How Do You Love

Progressing in your spiritual path is unquestionably beneficial to your dyad.

How do you know what the level of soul connection with your partner is and whether it can grow further? Kabbalistic teachings tell us that there are three levels of bestowing your beloved.

The *first i*s simply obliging your partner's requests and attempting to fulfill their needs and wants to the best of your genuine ability.

The *second* level of this exchange is elevated from the former naturally and is sourced in noticing certain cues in your partner and listening carefully for suggestions or "hints" they may spread along the dyadic path. In this level of communication, you're in such higher sync with your beloved that most commonly you "pick up" on their cues and provide you're the particular quest.

Now, the *third* level of a good and sacred exchange requires no words or insinuation, since speech, directions, or even implied attempts are a human trait manifesting within a human body. But a true divine soul connection between partners will allow one to simply know and acknowledge what will bring the partner pleasure, and for one to then *simply* provide it.

In other words, your soul connection becomes so highly sensitive and elevated that you're fully aware of your partner's needs, perhaps even before the thought itself emerges in your partner's consciousness.

This level of exchange is unique, yet attainable with the practice of humility and mindfulness. You might think, "Wait, what does that mean? That I'm only here to serve my partner?"

Not at all.

You're here to be a conduit to a divine power that you hold inside, and to use it in a symbiotic fashion that allows a greater soul elevation for both you and your partner.

Needless to say that there are no *scores* being kept and no quid pro quo kind of exchange; a loving soul connection entails an effortless state of bestowing.

Let us revert back for a moment. What is love? Is love a need like nourishment and shelter? Love, in a holistic view, is not a need, but a transcendence, and if applied to the sacred dyad, love is not a need, but *being needed*. It's not a self-fulfilling act, but a self-giving act; it isn't a means to an end, but the main goal.

# Quickstep Meditation

We are now focusing on going through the Tree of Life in a different fashion than practiced previously—in a flowing motion.

Observe the Tree of Life for a few minutes before going inside.

Sit in a comfortable position, close your eyes, and take a deep breath through your mouth, all the way up to the top of your lungs. Now, purse your lips and let your breath out slowly as if you're whistling through them. Repeat this three times, and keep a comfortable posture while reverting to normal breathing.

Place one hand on the ground (this hand will remain on the ground for the entire session, while the other can shift to different locations throughout), and place the other on top of or over your head as a halo.

Start from the top Keter and imagine nothing but a flow of light bouncing from the top, descending down. Shift your moving hand to the right Chochma and place it over your right eye. Remain there for a moment, and shift to the left Bina, moving your hand to your left eye.

Continue at this pace, descending your moving hand to Daat, and place it on your mouth.

Continue to the right to Chesed and shift your hand to your right shoulder. Continue breathing and move to the left Gevurah, shifting your hand to your left shoulder.

Keep descending to Tiferet, and place your hand on your chest over your heart.

Take a breath and keep moving to the right Netzach. Place your hand on your right thigh. Breathe and shift the energy to the left Hod, and place your hand on your left thigh. Take a single breath and descend to Yesod, placing your hand on your lower abdomen, before shifting downward to Malchut and placing your hand on your feet or anywhere extended from your bottom limbs.

Concentrate and imagine a circle of energy surrounding your body as the Tree of Life, and shift all of it back up to Keter. Switch hands and repeat.

We are aiming to make this transition as flowing and as smooth as water sliding down a slope. Simple and effortless. When you are satisfied with your progress, revert to normal breathing and open your eyes.

# Miracle Workers

Kabbalistic teachings tell us that we are cocreators of the universe we live in, that we possess an insurmountable influence on our existence as well as that of others, and that we should thus tread very lightly when it comes to our choice of actions, thoughts, and overall conduct.

Right as the book of Genesis opens with the story of universal creation (Genesis 1:2–10), we are presented with the four elements that are the building blocks of any formation: *earth*, *wind*, *fire*, and *water*. All of these, we are told, were created as a foundation of *everything, out of nothing*. In direct relation to this fact, we are advised that all of us carry these four components within us, but only our own perspective or determination of which aspect to use in which direction can make or break our influence in this world as cocreators. The relevant question often emerges as to the Creator's initial plan. Why does a powerful force that established every single life-form or inanimate object on the planet need our inept intervention? I mean, we are only human, aren't we?

This is where Kabbalah thinks and teaches otherwise. In this perspective, we are not *only* human—far from it. We are divine sparks, covered in tangible "human" bodies, yet the soul comprising the four elements is able to create and demolish every single thing.

This ability can manifest in our physical bodies. In terms of health, or lack of it, it can manifest in our work situations, in terms of prosperity or poverty; it can be infused in our relationships, in the experience of love; and it can be prominent in our environment in a sense of chaos and disarray, or conversely, as peace, harmony, and protection.

So why do things break down or deteriorate, including, most profoundly, our bodies, our health, our relationships, and so forth?

Because this is the only way the divine can ensure our involvement in the process.

Let's say we knew our expiration date in advance, and also that up until then, nothing can harm us in any way. What kind of motivation, in your view, would that knowledge infuse us with? Would it encourage us to push to our spiritual apex in search of answers and enlightenment?

Kabbalistic teachings are aligned with other sources of spirituality in relation to thoughts being an actual creative force, but this is where things branch out. Kabbalah doesn't direct us to visualization solely, but rather pushes us to visualization and *then* physical action, because regardless of the subatomic particles that are very capable of being realigned by state of mind, the soul is not. The soul demands action, and thus placed us in a tangible body in order to carry out the deeds that will allow and enable its elevation.

## Naturally Unnatural

We are often introduced to the notion of "natural" occurrences in the universe; the likes of *natural* disasters, *natural* physical deterioration, *natural* relational decline, and so forth.

Yet, Kabbalistic teachings advise otherwise. By the latter, the meaning with which we infuse a certain area of our lives receives the necessary nourishment, and thus can evolve differently and not allow a predetermination of a certain outcome or condition.

If put simply, Kabbalists suggest that chaos, war, earthquakes, and floods are *unnatural*! The natural state of universal equilibrium is, in fact, accord, harmony, energetic flow, and peace. This similar equation may be directly applied to our personal and interpersonal lives. We are not forced to witness the wilting of our relationships and surrender to the two-year-desire shelf life prescription; we are not doomed to age, get sick, and perish in a way that doesn't dignify our sacred souls; we are not victims of a declining planet.

Let us use a simple analogy to exemplify this point. You are well aware of who you are, your strengths and weaknesses, and your overall nature. Yet, if evaluated anonymously by a group of people, they'll all have a very different view of you—not based on who you are, but based on who *they* are!

And even that can potentially alter, because who you are today isn't who you were ten years ago, and thus our perspective of events, situations, and people has changed.

In a similar fashion, we are the "creators" of our realities, by a perspective point. So, if we decide our input and involvement in the betterment of our physical, relational, and emotional condition is immense and valuable, it will simply be just that. Kabbalah cites the story of the ten plagues of Egypt not as a story of nations, people, religion, or even miracles, but as a story of believers versus nonbelievers. In a nutshell, what enabled Moses to turn blood back into water was not exclusively sourced in him being a messenger of the divine, but that he believed he could make things happen, contrary to Pharaoh. Essentially, what this story tells us is that the honest and definite fear we have of "catching an illness" if someone around us isn't well can be similarly applied to health and bliss. These two can be contagious, and since we, as are the bacteria or virus, are made out of atomic energy, we can spread this health and blissful existence in the same fashion the COVID-19 disaster presented a total disablement of the entire universe.

The impact the "one red nuclear button" has on the world as a whole could be similarly applied to one person's determination to send love and health energy throughout; in the close circle (physical health, good relationship), or in the global sphere (peace, calmness, harmony, and growth). The most important idea to embrace here is that we truly do not need to strive for perfection, but rather aim for the existential intent, and the rest will follow naturally.

# The Seventy-Two Names of God

The ancient Kabbalist Rabbi Shimon bar Yochai wrote in the Zohar that the parting of the Red Sea was not only a miraculous action exhibited by Moses under a divine infusion, but it was also the power of certainty, alongside the utilization of the sacred divine names, that granted Moses, the messenger, his divine ability to alter the subatomic realm of nature.

These divine names are the Seventy-Two Names of God. The seventy-two sequences were composed of Hebrew letters (derived from Exodus 14:19–21) that hold an extraordinary power to overcome the laws of nature in all forms, including human nature.

The seventy-two names are each composed of three-letter sequences that act like an index to specific spiritual frequencies. Since they were derived from the very letters that comprise the biblical verses, aligning the parting of the sea, by either gazing at the letters or visualizing them with closed eyes, chanting them, or scanning them digitally, one can connect with these frequencies.

We can liken this practice to nucleobases, which are nitrogen-containing biological compounds that form nucleosides, composed of all of the monomers that constitute the basic building blocks of nucleic acids. The ability of nucleobases to form base pairs, and to stack one upon another, leads directly to long-chain helical structures, such as ribonucleic acid (RNA) and deoxyribonucleic acid (DNA).

Five nucleobases—adenine (A), cytosine (C), guanine (G), thymine (T), and uracil (U)—are called primary or canonical. They function as the fundamental units of the genetic code, with the bases A, G, C, and T being found in DNA, while A, G, C, and U are found in RNA.

Each of the base pairs in a typical double-helix DNA form a unit; either an A paired with a T, or a C paired with a G.

In a similar fashion, Kabbalistic teachings tell us that practicing the energy of these three-letter sequences is exceptionally powerful for a mind *and* body transformation because they hold a divine energy.

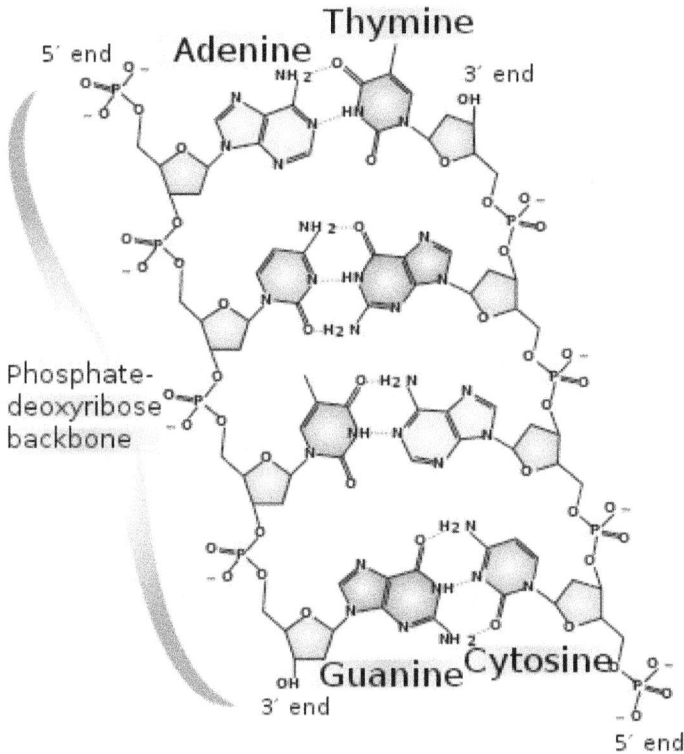

These names of God, when uttered, scanned, touched, or visualized, project an actual act of formation, on a micro level. In other words, their power allows one to truly use the divine spark within oneself in order to miraculously enliven or completely form changed conditions.

# Chapter 11

שְׁלֹשָׁה הֵמָּה **נִפְלְאוּ** מִמֶּנִּי (יח)
וארבע [אַרְבָּעָה] לֹא יְדַעְתִּים:

דֶּרֶךְ הַנֶּשֶׁר ׀ בַּשָּׁמַיִם דֶּרֶךְ נָחָשׁ עֲלֵי צוּר דֶּרֶךְ־אֳנִיָּה בְלֶב־יָם וְדֶרֶךְ גֶּבֶר בְּעַלְמָה: (יט)
Proverbs 30:18-19

In this beautiful verse from the book of Proverbs, thought to be written by King Solomon himself, it says: "There are three things which are too *wonderful* for me, Yea, four which I know not: The way of an eagle in the sky; The way of a serpent upon a rock; The way of a ship in the midst of the sea; And the way of a man with a young woman."

This subtle reference to the most miraculous mergers in the universe is magnificent and enchanting, because it emphasizes how natural yet phenomenal these mergers are, including, of course, the exchange between a man and a woman.

## Withholding Pleasure

The *Shulchan Aruch*[12] (in Hebrew, שֻׁלְחָן עָרוּךְ) is the Code of Jewish Law and the most widely consulted of the various legal codes in Judaism.

---

12 "Shulchan Arukh, Even HaEzer 76:11." 2020. Sefaria.Org. 2020. https://www.sefaria.org/Shulchan_Arukh%2C_Even_HaEzer.76.11?lang=bi.

In this very detailed and well-established manual, we learn the importance and validity of a sensual and sexual union. In fact, the *Shulchan Aruch* suggests that it is altogether prohibited to deny a woman her pleasure.

It says:[13]

יא) (אָסוּר לְאָדָם לִמְנֹעַ מֵאִשְׁתּוֹ עוֹנָתָה; וְאִם מָנְעָה כְּדֵי לְצַעֲרָהּ, עוֹבֵר בְּלֹא תַעֲשֶׂה דְּ''עֹנָתָהּ
לֹא יִגְרָע'' שְׁמוֹת כא, י ; (וְאִם חָלָה אוֹ תָשַׁשׁ כֹּחוֹ וְאֵינוֹ יָכוֹל לִבְעֹל, יַמְתִּין שִׁשָּׁה חֳדָשִׁים עַד
שֶׁיַּבְרִיא, שֶׁאֵין לְךָ עוֹנָה גְּדוֹלָה מִזּוֹ; וְאַחַר כָּךְ, אוֹ יִטֹּל מִמֶּנָּה רְשׁוּת אוֹ יוֹצִיא וְיִתֵּן כְּתֻבָּה:

(11) It is forbidden for a man to withhold conjugal duties from his wife. If he did so with the intent of causing her pain, he has transgressed the prohibition of "Do not reduce her conjugal obligation" (Ex. 21:10). If he is ill or weakened and he is unable to have intercourse, hes allowed to wait six months until he becomes healthy, for this is longest period of conjugal duties [the denial of, that is]. After that period, he must divorce her and pay the Ketubah [the Jewish legal-financial contract being granted upon nuptials].

What we witness here is an unquestionable obligation of a husband to his wife. Not only does the law require the regular practice of this important exchange, but the laws elaborate even further on the regulations, choices, practices, and frequency of the "act of creation," as it is often referred to.

We are told that intercourse is a holy and pure thing, when it is done at an appropriate time and with appropriate intentions. The fact that this act is referred to as "knowing" *translates* as an act that can never be considered blameworthy or perverse.[14]

---

13 Haezer 76:11

14 "Noam Elimelech." n.d. www.Sefaria.org. Accessed September 11, 2020. https://www.sefaria.org/Noam_Elimelech%2C_Additions%2C_ Iggeret_HaKodesh.1?lang=bi.

To explain further, the same resource states that neither sexual organs—genitals and more—nor sexual intercourse (in all its shades, colors, or practices) are obscene, for this act is a divine obligation. If a divine force created man and woman and all their organs and functions, there can be no obscenity in any of their practices. Sexual intercourse is not only regarded as an important and healthy physical exchange, but one that benefits the soul altogether. The sages go to a great length by stating that the sexual unity is so highly valuable that no act of flesh and blood compares to it.[15]

Commentators explain that "God considers good intention as if it were a deed" (it's sufficient that you hold a good intent in high rank and deliverance to make it as strong as an actual deed) to mean that intention can actually create deeds. In continuance to this notion emerges the Kabbalistic view of mindfulness and meditation, where meditation is not simply contemplative, but can also design and activate reality; in that manner, it can be even utilized as a tool on its own *and* as a means to an end. The holiness of sexual union is therefore the full merging of the spiritual and physical realms.

In Tibetan practices, these acts of sexual union are utilized to allow the soul to dissolve into a complete emptiness; this level of soul connection that enables emptiness and a plain "being" rather than acting is aligned with the Kabbalistic notion of Yechida (also referred to as *unique*), the previously mentioned level of soul connection or compatibility that is ranked the most holy and is a direct connection to the divine and the original creation.

## Quickstep Mediation

In this new quickstep meditation, we will aim to chant, scan, or visualize one of each of the three-letter combinations of the Seventy-Two Names of God.

---

15 "Avot DeRabbi Natan, Trans. by David Kasher, 2019." n.d. Sefaria. sefaria.org. https://www.sefaria.org/Avot_D'Rabbi_Natan.37.5?ven= Avot_DeRabbi_Natan,_trans._by_David_Kasher,_2019&lang=bi&with= About&lang2=en.

By choosing one of these sequences, we are changing the frequency of the desired outcome in our mind and enabling the emergence of a solution, or an overall *betterment* of our close and extended surroundings.

Observe the chart of the Seventy-Two Names of God below before we begin. Don't worry, you will not be requested to memorize all these sequences; you can slowly and gradually get accustomed to them. For our purpose, this time we will choose the combination of ירת, which signifies a frequency of connecting to spirituality and enabling a silent "partner," or a stronger sexual energy to be emitted from one to another.

| | | | | | | | |
|---|---|---|---|---|---|---|---|
| כהת [8] Tav Hey Kaf Defusing Negative Energy | אכא [7] Aleph Kaf Aleph DNA of The Soul | ללה [6] Hey Lamed Lamed Dream State | מהש [5] Shin Hey Mem Healing | עלם [4] Mem Lamed Ayin Eliminating Negative Thoughts | סיט [3] Tet Yud Samech Miracle Making | ילי [2] Yud Lamed Yud Recapturing the Sparks | והו [1] Vav Hey Vav Time Travel |
| הקם [16] Mem Kuf Hey Dumping Depression | הרי [15] Yud Resh Hey Long Range Vision | מבה [14] Hey Bet Mem Farewell to Arms | יזל [13] Lamed Zayin Yud Heaven on Earth | ההע [12] Ayin Hey Hey Unconditional Love | לאו [11] Vav Aleph Lamed Banishing the Remnants of Evil | אלד [10] Daled Lamed Aleph Protection from Evil Eye | הזי [9] Yud Zayin Hey Angelic Influences |
| חהו [24] Vav Hey Chet Jealousy | מלה [23] Hey Lamed Mem Sharing the Flame | ייי [22] Yud Yud Yud Stop Fatal Attraction | נלך [21] Kaf Lamed Nun Eradicate Plague | פהל [20] Lamed Hey Pey Victory over Addictions | לוו [19] Vav Vav Lamed Dialing God | כלי [18] Yud Lamed Kaf Fertility | לאו [17] Vav Aleph Lamed Great Escape |
| ושר [32] Resh Shin Vav Memories | לכב [31] Bet Kaf Lamed Finish What You Start | אום [30] Mem Vav Aleph Building Bridges | ריי [29] Yud Yud Resh Removing Hatred | שאה [28] Hey Aleph Shin Soulmate | ירת [27] Tav Resh Yud Silent Partner | האא [26] Aleph Aleph Hey Order From Chaos | נתה [25] Hey Tav Nun Speak Your Mind |
| ייי [40] Zayin Yud Yud Speaking the Right Words | רהע [39] Ayin Hey Resh Diamond in the Rough | חעם [38] Mem Ayin Chet Circuitry | אני [37] Yud Nun Aleph The Big Picture | מנד [36] Daled Nun Mem Fear(Less) | כוק [35] Kuf Vav Kaf Sexual Energy | להח [34] Chet Hey Lamed Forget Thyself | יחו [33] Vav Chet Yud Revealing the Dark Side |
| מיה [48] Hey Yud Mem Unity | עשל [47] Lamed Shin Ayin Global Transformation | ערי [46] Yud Resh Ayin Absolute Certainty | סאל [45] Lamed Aleph Samech Power of Prosperity | ילה [44] Hey Lamed Yud Sweetening Judgment | וול [43] Lamed Vav Vav Defying Gravity | מיכ [42] Kaf Yud Mem Revealing the Concealed | ההה [41] Hey Hey Hey Self Esteem |
| פוי [56] Yud Vav Pey Dispelling Anger | מבה [55] Hey Bet Mem Thought Into Action | נית [54] Tav Yud Nun Death of Death | ננא [53] Aleph Nun Nun No Agenda | עמם [52] Mem Mem Ayin Passion | הוע [51] Shin Chet Hey No Guilt | רני [50] Yud Nun Daled Enough is Never Enough | והו [49] Vav Hey Vav Happiness |
| מחי [64] Yud Chet Mem Casting Yourself in a Favorable Light | ענו [63] Vav Nun Ayin Appreciation | יהה [62] Hey Hey Yud Parent-Teacher, Not Preacher | ומב [61] Bet Mem Vav Water | מצר [60] Resh Zadik Mem Freedom | הרח [59] Chet Resh Hay Umbilical Cord | ייל [58] Lamed Yud Yud Letting Go | נמם [57] Mem Mem Nun Listening to Your Soul |
| מום [72] Mem Vav Mem Spiritual Cleansing | היי [71] Yud Yud Hey Prophecy & Parallel Universes | יבמ [70] Mem Bet Yut Design Beneath Disorder | ראה [69] Hey Aleph Resh Lost & Found | חבו [68] Vav Bet Chet Contacting Departed Souls | איע [67] Ayin Yud Aleph Great Expectations | מנק [66] Kuf Nun Mem Accountability | דמב [65] Bet Mem Daled Fear of God |

You may digitally scan the letters or gaze at them, you may view them in your mind with your eyes closed, or chant them to the sound of YARAT ; if you choose one of the two former options out of the 4, you may want to copy this sequence on a small piece of paper that you keep in a safe and respected spot in order to utilize this power. You may also incorporate all four utilization options and switch from one to another as you progress.

Gaze at this sequence for a few minutes before going inside.

Sit in a comfortable position, close your eyes, and take a deep breath through your mouth, all the way up to the top of your lungs. Now, purse your lips and let your breath out slowly as if you're whistling through them. Repeat this three times, and keep a comfortable posture while reverting to normal breathing.

Slowly allow the three-letter sequence of ירת to appear before you and float in your mind's eye.

I like to see these sequences as if they are floating on water as tiny ripples moving toward me and back as I gaze with my eyes closed. Allow the letters to form and heighten in your memory, and breathe "the breath of life" into them. Merge the goal that you have for this sequence, and then combine it with the energy you form.

It can be a soulful and beautiful connection with a potential soul match (narrow goal), or you can go further and enter a peaceful existence to all societies in their relational and sexual exchange (advanced goal). You may also alternate or gradually arrive at a higher-level goal as you advance and progress in the practice.

When you feel safe and strong in this frequency and the light it emits, gradually allow both your hands to touch the ground and revert to normal breathing. Gradually and slowly open your eyes. You may want to remain in this position for a few moments before getting back on your feet. Drink a glass of water to quench the energy you've emitted.

# Solomon Says

In the famous and invigorating piece of alluring poetry called the Song of Songs, we are presented with a fascinating display of two lovers who lure one another into a scene that appears as if it was taken out of a Harlequin novel.

There's a unique dynamic between the two forces or lovers in this biblical creation; read at face value, it can be misinterpreted or misunderstood. Many commentaries were suggested for it, and they all offer a (slightly or vastly) different view of it.

In Kabbalistic teachings, the commentary analyzes the Shekinah—the feminine divine presence—as the sephira of Malchut, the vessel of kingship, who is embodied in the song as a beautiful young woman and is representative of the Jewish people.

The young *fawn*'s beloved is identified with the male sephira of Tiferet and is the central principle of divine emotion, which represents God. In the body, Tiferet stands for the male torso, uniting through the lower sephira of Yesod as a sign of the male genitals, thus the sensual aspect of this poetic hymn.

The application of the circumcised organ of procreation (the male penis) as a symbol to the act of creation, enables this poetry to stand for the actual foundation of the world, referred to in Hebrew as בראשית מעשה, which often relates to the sexual union.

Within this sacred union, we witness many allegories of a passionate exchange, but for the sake of this discussion, we will rest on the verse, "I am my beloved's, and my beloved is mine."[16]

This unique and not necessarily comprehensible verse holds the core foundation of the relational dyad.

By Kabbalistic views, the structure of a sacred unit is based on dividing the verse into pieces, where "I am" is separated from "my beloved" and stands apart from "my beloved is mine" as well.

Looking at these three components, Kabbalah tells us that the "I am" part of the sacred exchange is the focal point of the ego. Therein lies our challenge in entering a sacred relationship and "giving up" or "letting go" of our selfish nature, our ego, or our "need" for individuality.

The target is for us to avoid viewing the unit as a threat to our independence, and instead see it as an enhancement of it, one that can only be attained by uniting forces with our lover.

---

16 The Song of Songs 6:3 KJV

Looking at the second part of the verse—"my beloved's"—it is suggested that we adopt a stance of vulnerability and become truly acquainted with our beloveds and their needs. Here we are told that even good deeds or positive intentions can be met with a negative response if they are not tailored and monitored specifically to the beloved's needs. We can use the analogy of water. It gives life and is absolutely essential for survival, yet if one fails to control water, they may flood and cause a disastrous outcome. Similarly, our acts of "love and giving" in a relationship cannot be egocentric, but rather externally directed at the quests of our partner. The third part of this verse—"my beloved is mine"—is reflected in our acceptance and integration of our partner's relation to *us*. In other words, here lies the most important and final resolution that can make or break a sacred dyad based on our ability to adjust and be malleable.

In a simple analogy, a functional system like our physical body would fail, crash, and disintegrate if one organ negated the importance or functionality of another. The only way that a body can maintain vitality and resilience is by allowing a harmonious collaboration of all parts by lowering the volume of one area while another needs to be intensified, by creating equilibrium for the sake of the whole, by holistically existing. Similarly, our interpretation of our partner's response needs to be specifically harmonious and accepting in order to allow success. It does not relate to self-sacrifice or self-cancellation; in fact, quite the opposite. It means that we hold an understanding that the ultimate result can only be achieved by a mutual collaboration, rather than by domination or submission.

## Quickstep Meditation

Observe the Seventy-Two Names of God chart before we begin. For our purpose today, we will choose the combination of לאו, a sequence that represents removal of ego and a true dedication to a harmonious collaboration and equanimity.

Remember that you can digitally scan the letters or gaze at them, visualize them with your eyes closed, or chant them to the sound of LAO. If you choose the two former options out of the four, you may want to copy this sequence on a small piece of paper that you keep in a safe and respected spot in order to utilize this power. You may also incorporate all four options and switch from one to another as you progress.

Gaze at this sequence for a few minutes before going inside.

Sit in a comfortable position, close your eyes, and take a deep breath through your mouth, all the way up to the top of your lungs. Now, purse your lips and let your breath out slowly as if you're whistling through them. Repeat this three times and keep a comfortable posture while reverting to normal breathing.

Slowly allow the three-letter sequence of לאו to appear before you and float in your mind's eye.

I like to see these sequences as if they are floating on water in tiny ripples toward me and back, while gazing with my eyes closed. Allow the letters to form and heighten in your memory and breathe "the breath of life" into them. Merge the goal that you have in relation to this sequence and combine it with the energy you create.

It can be a soulful and beautiful connection with a potential soul match, or you can go further and expand into a peaceful existence to all. If you are aiming to unite with your current or hopeful partner in a respectful and harmonious manner, that will definitely and unequivocally serve the greater goal of a harmonious, sacred, and everlasting relationship. You may also alternate or gradually arrive at a higher-level goal as you advance and progress.

When you feel safe and strong in this frequency and the light it emits, gradually allow both your hands to touch the ground, and revert to normal breathing. Gradually and slowly open your eyes. You may want to remain seated in this position for a few moments before getting back on your feet. Drink a glass of water to quench the energy you've emitted.

# Chapter 12
## Surrender, Anyone?

There is no doubt that this is the era of new age teachings, spirituality doctrines, the reemergence of enlightenment, and the quest for meaning. As part of it, we are greatly accustomed to the concept of surrender. Just let it go and surrender to the cosmos, the universe, the Creator, your pain, your challenges, your anger, your bliss, and so forth. Albeit positive encouragement, this approach may leave one baffled and indecisive about to whom, to what, or when to apply these great teachings.

Kabbalah tells us that surrendering is more than the act of letting go, and it is more than the act of trusting and allowing things to unfold or manifest. In fact, contrary to other spiritual teachings that promote the idea of taking a back seat and simply visualizing and allowing the particles to come together interfered by action, Kabbalah tells us that we have a role in this matrix that isn't demoted in significance from the Creator himself, as we are cocreators. In a sense, the fact that we were placed here is "proof" of our significance, and the reason we are kept here is to serve the ongoing, never-ceasing dynamic that is required between the Creator and us. This means that we cannot sit back and solely trust, we must take action. Is that equivalent to micromanaging? Not in the least. Yes, the component of trust is imperative, but if we don't exemplify the path into enlightenment, soul elevation, and spiritual growth by our own actions, not only will things not appear, but they may also disappear.

Let us try and present a scenario for this principle to become more comprehensible.

In the Book of Formation (ספר יצירה), we are told that there are four levels of soul, and that our universe, or the world of the living, is the world of action (עשייה), which is the least challenging form of soul existence.

This is not stated in a belittling sense, but on soul level.

In order to be elevated to the next level of formation (יצירה), we must engage in different forms of mindfulness, meditation, and enlightening actions.

It is imperative for us to understand that as humans, we can only arrive at this level of existence, or formation, since the human can only form but *not* create. This is where we witness the necessity of our collaboration with the Creator on the coming level of *creation*(בריאה) , as well as on the top level of אצילות, or emanation.

1. In אֲצִילוּת, or Emanation, the Creator's light (Or Ein Sof) radiates and is still united with its source. This supernal revelation therefore precludes the souls and divine emanations from sensing their own existence, or their shadow (from the word צל). In Atzilut, the ten sephirot emerge in revelation, with Chochma (wisdom) dominating, and the lowest sephirah of Malchut (sovereignty) connecting and sustaining the lower worlds.

2. In בְּרִיאָה, or creation, we refer to creation, but sans shape or form. Beriah is the realm of the "Divine Throne" where emanation (from the higher level) descends like a king onto a throne. The sephirah Bina (understanding) predominates this level of world.

3. In יְצִירָה, or formation, the created being assumes shape and form. The emotional sephirot, starting with Chesed and ending with Yesod, predominate. This ascent *and* descent channel the divine vitality down through the worlds, furthering the divine purpose. This world is also called the "Lower Garden of Eden."

4. In עֲשִׂיָּה, or action, the creation is finally completed and differentiated due to the concealment and diminution of the divine vitality. However, it is still on a spiritual level; the lowest sephirah of Malchut (sovereignty) predominates this world.

So, what does all this have to do with our relationships? Kabbalah tells us that by taking an active part in our spiritual growth, we can elevate our existence on all levels, including our relationships, in the service of enlightenment. In practicality, this may mean avoiding impulsive needs or actions that may later disserve us; being highly attentive to our partners; avoiding a dismissal of another's sensitivities; and appreciating the dyad through the "spiritual eyes of our souls" rather than the "physical eyes of our bodies."

These choices and actions may completely alter our world in general and elevate our soul levels in particular. How many times have you acted on a whim when feeling a bit low on attention, worthiness, or a sense of divinity, and then the very moment you acted upon that whim, you immediately knew on a gut level that your choice is at least disserving, and may even turn chaotic at its worst.

The responsibility we take over our choices may not always be conscious; often, it is practiced on a subconscious level and enhanced every time it is utilized. Yet, the decision to follow a changed path needs to be conscious and firm, otherwise, one cannot be a creator, but rather simply a by-product of circumstances.

## Quickstep Meditation

Observe the Seventy-Two Names of God chart before we begin. For our purpose this time we will choose the combination of מיה , a sequence that represents unity through sensitivity and tolerance.

Remember that you can digitally scan the letters or gaze at them, visualize them with your eyes closed, or chant them to the sound of MIA. If you choose the two former options out of the four, you may want to copy this sequence on a small piece of paper that you keep in a safe and respected spot in order to utilize this power. You may also incorporate all four utilization options and switch from one to another as you progress.

Gaze at this sequence for a few minutes before going inside.

Sit in a comfortable position, close your eyes, and take a deep breath through your mouth, all the way up to the top of your lungs. Now, purse your lips and let your breath out slowly as if you're whistling through them. Repeat this three times, and keep a comfortable posture while reverting to normal breathing.

Slowly allow the three-letter sequence of מיה to appear before you and float in your mind's eye.

I like to see these sequences as if they are floating on water in tiny ripples toward me and back, while gazing with my eyes closed. Allow the letters to form and heighten in your memory and breathe "the breath of life" into them. Merge the goal that you have in relation to this sequence and combine it with the energy you create.

It can be a soulful and beautiful connection with a potential soul match, or you can go further and expand into a peaceful existence to all. If you are aiming to unite with your current or hopeful partner in a respectful and harmonious manner, that will definitely and unequivocally serve the greater goal of a harmonious and sacred, everlasting relationship. You may also alternate or gradually arrive at a higher-level goal as you advance and progress.

When you feel safe and strong in this frequency and the light it emits, gradually allow both your hands to touch the ground, and revert to normal breathing. Gradually and slowly open your eyes. You may want to remain seated in this position for a few moments before getting back on your feet. Drink a glass of water to quench the energy you've emitted.

## Consummation and Intimacy

Kabbalistic teachings elaborate greatly on the very core of intimacy and what it means to become one with your partner. Achieving this sense of oneness isn't a given, and although a relationship should not be viewed as a chore or something one needs to "work on," our natural state as ego-based creators who strive for immediate and instant gratification demands constant tending and adjustment.

Ancients scriptures suggest, for example, that if a man commits to a marriage with a woman (paid the sum of dowry, in antiquated form) and hasn't yet reached her presence physically in order to pursue that marriage (due to battle or different obstacles sourced in physical conditions), he is not only advised but rather required to avoid anything prior to marrying his wife-to-be, lest he lose his chance of doing so to another suitor.[17]

Not only do we see this imperative requirement as urgent, but if we apply this suggestion to modern life, we can offer a real-time upgrade to common courtship.

The evaluation is that most attempts in entering a committed relationship are plagued with common misunderstanding, failure to follow up, *pride galore*, and additional factors that may interfere with the actual consummation of the relationship. Of course, the source of this lack might be in the limited form of communication, such as soulless text messages and icons used regularly instead of a real expression of feelings.

The obstacle of a "battle" that is being referred to in the ancient scripts is alive and kicking today, only it is now dressed as endless variety, the selfish quest of frequent novelty, and spiced with a touch of pride.

This ancient advice elaborates further and suggests that even the "soldier" assigned for a mission should be released in the first year of his committed relationship in order to keep his wife content, better known as "happy wife, happy life."[18]

These suggestions are extremely relevant in the consummation of intimacy. We live in a world that demands constant division of attention, 24/7 multitasking, and an unacceptable view of self-care. Although we created a much more *selfish* self, the relevant self-care that relates to personal growth and soul elevation has been axed out of the winning formula.

17  Deuteronomy 20:7 KJV

18  Deuteronomy 24:5 KJV

# Your Better Half

This discussion holds a preliminary notion regarding the relevance of a committed relationship. To begin with, in the current climate, the idea of traditional choices may be frowned upon (i.e., marriage and children) even by a traditionalist. If he or she already established the parental role, they might choose to pursue this path, solo. Kabbalistic teachings tell us that the state of aloneness—note that it isn't the same as loneliness—is ill-advised and inhibits soul elevation and spiritual growth.

Since these acts of ascension are based on the spiritual and emotional exchange of two components in the quest of establishing one whole unit, the individual who chooses a life of singlehood removes himself from that potential.[19]

## Quickstep Mediation

Observe the chart of the Seventy-Two Names of God before we begin. For the purpose of seeking what our soul needs rather than what the ego wants, we will choose the combination of והו , a sequence that represents that very intricate and complex choice between the ego (selfish) and the soul (selfless). When applying this sequence, look deep inside and compare these choices to a broader spectrum of relation; not only the strength it requires to be a giver versus a receiver, but what tremendous change this applied attitude could have on a cosmic, universal level if we distinguish our actual needs from our wants.

Remember that you can digitally scan the letters or gaze at them, visualize them with your eyes closed, or chant them to the sound of VAHU. If you choose the two former options out of the four, you may want to copy this sequence on a small piece of paper that you keep in a safe and respected spot in order to utilize this power. You may also

---

19 Genesis 2:18 KJV

incorporate all four utilization options and switch from one to another as you progress.

Gaze at this sequence for a few minutes before going inside.

Sit in a comfortable position, close your eyes, and take a deep breath through your mouth, all the way up to the top of your lungs. Now, purse your lips and let your breath out slowly as if you're whistling through them. Repeat this three times and keep a comfortable posture while reverting to normal breathing.

Slowly allow the three-letter sequence of והו to appear before you and float in your mind's eye.

I like to see these sequences as if they are floating on water in tiny ripples toward me and back, while gazing with my eyes closed. Allow the letters to form and heighten in your memory, and breathe "the breath of life" into them. Merge the goal that you have in relation to this sequence, and combine it with the energy you create.

It can be a soulful and beautiful connection with a potential soul match, or you can go further and expand into a peaceful existence to all. If you are aiming to unite with your current or hopeful partner in a respectful and harmonious manner, that will definitely and unequivocally serve the greater goal of a harmonious, sacred, and everlasting relationship. You may also alternate or gradually arrive at a higher-level goal as you advance and progress.

When you feel safe and strong in this frequency and the light it emits, gradually allow both your hands to touch the ground, and revert to normal breathing. Gradually and slowly open your eyes. You may want to remain seated in this position for a few moments before getting back on your feet. Drink a glass of water to quench the energy you've emitted.

# Chapter 13

Kabbalistic teachings tell us that the Ein Sof is the world of the divine located right above the initial sephirah of crown. The merging of these two is said to be the source of the nine lower sephirot. The final sephirah of sovereignty is considered the *feminine* component of the divine, and is directly opposite of the *masculine* crown—although, as mentioned previously, in the Kabbalistic views, humanity as a whole is the feminine to the Creator's masculine.

The relationship between the two is represented in a very sensual and sexual union. In detail, we are introduced to two esoteric "dyads." The top is of a divine nature (the two upper sephirot of Chochma and Binah) who has "two arms" in different directions versus the physical dyad depicted in the Song of Songs, portrayed by the sephirot Tiferet and Malchut, which are parallel one to the other.

Kabbalistic teachings tell us that when the earthly dyad engages in sexual ecstasy, the divine world of Ein Sof is filled with bliss, which is transferred through the sephirah of sovereignty to humanity as a whole.

The Zohar tells us that the initial condition of Malchut was a blissful existence because it was connected to the divine. Its masculine counterpart engaged in a constant sensual exchange with it. Alas, the Garden serpent interfered and created chaos that can only be remedied by the "patching" of the path back into a divine merging. This merging can be enhanced and utilized by our own contributions here on earth.

Our role is to reunite the shekinah—the feminine force—with the masculine force with our meditative practice, the principal of "tikkun," fixing ourselves and the world around us, and in the practice of a sacred exchange with our soul mate.

When portrayed in this manner, we understand why and how a meaningful sensual exchange is crucial for this purpose in particular, and our general human healing in general.

## Quickstep Mediation

We will now focus on flowing through the Tree of Life in a different fashion than practiced previously.

Observe the Tree of Life for a few minutes before going inside.

Sit in a comfortable position, close your eyes, and take a deep breath through your mouth, all the way up to the top of your lungs. Now, purse your lips and let your breath out slowly as if you're whistling through them. Repeat this three times, and keep a comfortable posture while reverting to normal breathing.

Place both hands on your knees or on your sides before we begin. Later in the meditation, you will be asked to shift your hands to different locations.

Start from the top Keter and focus solely on a flow of light bouncing from the top, descending down. Shift your hand to the right Chochma, and place it over your right eye. Remain there for a moment, and with your other hand, shift the left to Bina, and place your hand on your left eye.

Here, remain and meditate on this exchange between the divine dyad on top. Imagine an intense white light shifting between Chochma and Bina, back and forth. Imagine them merging together in an erotic harmony; it can alternatively take a psychedelic form, like Pink Floyd's *The Wall*.

When you feel satisfied with this intense sensual sensation, gather all of this energy, place one hand back on your knee or the ground, and shift the other swiftly below to Daat, around your neck.

Continue to the right to Chesed, and move to the left Gevurah. Keep moving downward to Tiferet, and place your hand on your chest over your heart.

Take a breath, and place both hands on your torso/chest. Remain there and start building an intense energy again while breathing more deeply. When you feel satisfied, move your energy to the right thigh, Netzach, and swiftly to the left thigh, Hod. Descend to Yesod around your lower abdomen, and then halt. Remain there with your energy, and then in one swing, move one hand below to Malchut on the bottom, around your lower genitals/feet, while the other hand remains on Tiferet, or chest. Move a light beam of energy between them. This time, imagine an intense red light moving between these two sephirot of Malchut and Tiferet. Breathe into them and feel your entire lower body becoming enflamed with desire. Remain there and focus on this sensation for a few moments; then, slowly and gradually allow your mind and body to relax, remove your hands and place them on your knees or on your sides. Retain normal breathing and gradually open your eyes.

This meditation should be utilized with your partner in order to enhance your intimacy. When practiced with your partner, a slight alteration will be applied. We will practice it in the coming segments.

# Ask and It Is Given

Amidst the intense wave of spirituality that seems to be taking over the world, we hear frequently about the law of attraction, visualization, about simply believing "it is yours" for "it" to tangibly appear, and about asking specifically for what it is your heart desires.

Kabbalistic teachings, albeit viewed as a spiritual practice, hold a very different stance on this matter. Aside from Kabbalah being an actual blueprint of the universe, and thus implementing its wisdom on all cultures, races, religions, backgrounds, orientations, ages, genders, and so forth, its teachings don't support the notion of *asking*—for yourself, that is.

In Kabbalistic practices, the only manner in which your quest is granted to you is by utilizing the light of the Creator via the Seventy-Two Names of God or the Tree of Life for the benefit of others, as particular or as general as one may choose. This means that, simply put, if I aim to be blessed with say, love and prosperity—as these two factors are likely the most sought-after "commodities" on the planet—I shall go about it by emitting a light and intentions (in Hebrew they are called Kavanot) of that profound resource I seek toward a certain person, or the cosmos as a whole. Thus, as a by-product, I will be blessed by the very blessing I bestow, only—and this part is rewarding—I will be graced with this "commodity" *before* others, simply based on my intentions, and my active role in fixing the world (*tikkun olam* in Kabbalah). Now, these "terms" are not a contract written between the Creator and me, and this is a very imperative point to make. We cannot expect these rewards on a timely, earthly, tangible scale because spiritual practices do not relate to the element of time. We also should not base our "bestowing activity" on the expectation of reward—hence the Kavanot, or intentions. If you wrap your head around it, it is rather simple. The universe and the Creator are *not* your valet or your delivery service, and it is definitely not obligated by any means to provide for you. That said, since Kabbalists advocate and fully practice the notion of a benevolent universe caring for divine beings (yes, you included), the principle of trust should remove any anxious discomfort or urgency that may arise.

Sound simple? There's more.

## Maintenance Is Key

Are you a meditator? Do you follow any spiritual or religious practice? Do you practice gratitude on a daily basis? Think of your own actions and possibly examine the actions and choices of people in your realm. Do they act more gratefully upon great fortune that enters their lives? Do you? Is there an extra mile you take after being granted with an unexpected surprise, perhaps such as volunteering or donating? The unfortunate reality is that during hardship or adversity, we tend to "pray and dispense gratitude" much more for the things we wish to arrive in our lives. Yet, when things are going great, we lose sight of the maintenance that is required for things to remain on the up-and-up.

It is an initiative that needs to be thought of, considered, taken into account, and practiced regularly in order to remain in a terrific *living* mode (note that I did not use the term *existence* since it has a completely different purpose in our lives). When we feel terrific or are surprised with great news, or upon "celebrating" an *ordinary*, misfortune-free day, we should give extra thanks to whomever we feel thanks are due. And they are.

Another practice that can be very useful in maintaining the positive things in our lives is streaming light and wellness into the components that we have already. In other words, if I'm blessed with a loving relationship, I need to meditate on one of the Seventy-Two Names of God that relates to relationships, and while doing so, inject this particular sequence with more energy and more strength. This holds a very strong impact on changing and alerting our perspective—yes, on cellular level as well—and, thus, this practice can be supremely beneficial.

The principal is simple: anything that relates to the material realm has a tendency to rise and then descend, deteriorate, and break down, while everything that is related to the spiritual realm tends to ascend and keep ascending, without ever needing to "refuel" or touch the ground—not to mention that it holds no relation to disintegration, but instead to an immense elevation, regularly.

In light if this, we see how a spiritual connection, a mindful practice, or gratitude journaling can elevate our souls *and* bodies—as well as our relationships with ourselves and others—in the most profound manner that we may have never experienced previously.

## Quickstep Meditation

We will return once more to the Seventy-Two Names of God for the sake of this practice. Observe the chart of the Seventy-Two Names of

God before we begin for the purpose of divine blessings of wellness and spiritual wholeness.

We will choose the combination of ההה, a sequence that represents that very intricate and complex choice between ego (selfish) and soul (selfless) on the path to spiritual growth and benevolent bestowal of altruistic wellness to others. The letter ה in particular represents the divine source or creator, whichever is more convenient for you to relate to. But the concept of tripling the force of the divine should tell you enough about the power of this very sequence. When applying this sequence, look deep inside and compare these choices to a broader spectrum of relation; not only the strength it requires to be a giver versus a receiver, but what tremendous change this applied attitude could have on a cosmic, universal level if we distinguish our actual needs from our wants.

Remember that you can digitally scan the letters or gaze at them, visualize them with your eyes closed, or chant them to the sound of HAAH. If you choose the two former options out of the four, you may want to copy this sequence on a small piece of paper that you keep in a safe and respected spot in order to utilize this power. You may also incorporate all four utilization options and switch from one to another as you progress.

Gaze at this sequence for a few minutes before going inside.

Sit in a comfortable position, close your eyes, and take a deep breath through your mouth, all the way up to the top of your lungs. Now, purse your lips and let your breath out slowly as if you're whistling through them. Repeat this three times, and keep a comfortable posture while reverting to normal breathing.

Slowly allow the three-letter sequence of לאו to appear before you and float in your mind's eye.

I like to see these sequences as if they are floating on water in tiny ripples toward me and back, while gazing with my eyes closed. Allow the letters to form and heighten in your memory and breathe "the breath of life" into them. Merge the goal that you have in relation to this sequence and combine it with the energy you create.

It can be a soulful and beautiful connection with a potential soul match, or you can go further and expand into a peaceful existence to all. If you are aiming to unite with your current or hopeful partner in a respectful and harmonious manner, that will definitely and unequivocally serve the greater goal of a harmonious, sacred, and everlasting relationship. You may also alternate or gradually arrive at a higher-level goal as you advance and progress.

When you feel safe and strong in this frequency and the light it emits, gradually allow both your hands to touch the ground, and revert to normal breathing. Gradually and slowly open your eyes. You may want to remain seated in this position for a few moments before getting back on your feet. Drink a glass of water to quench the energy you've emitted.

# Chapter 14
## What's Between Reticence and Sexuality

In our advanced and modern existence and practice, we tend to look at the exchange of sensuality and sexuality as a meager matter. We are exposed to innumerable messages regarding these very practices, and thus, our relation to it is essentially nonchalant and impersonal. As mentioned previously, Kabbalistic teachings stress that there can be nothing more personal than the act of intimacy and soul elevation. To settle this controversy, let us try to dissect this matter through the eyes of Kabbalah. According to the great Kabbalist and Rabbi Moshe Cordovero, the notion of coyness and reticence could be a double-edged sword when serving in the divine practice of sexual exchange.

Cordovero refers to the alleged myth of the "hole in the sheet." The myth tells the tale of assuming orthodox Jews approach the act of intercourse through a "hole in a sheet" in order to minimize the primal pleasure utilized by the sense of vision and touch, while simply practicing the commandment of procreation. Many discussions and assumptions supported that tale as a reality, while others claimed this was merely an "antisemitic" myth that is sourced in an erroneous evaluation of the undergarment orthodox Jews wear called *talit katan*.

For the sake of our discussion, it should be stressed that the immediate dismissal of this "myth" as utter antisemitic hearsay is not 100 percent genuine; in fact, some legitimate sightings prove that practice as rare yet viable in the hands of a few orthodox men in history. Cordovero cites Rabbi Yosef bar Halafta[20] who, for the sake of observing the commandment of Yibum ("donating a seed to a sister in law, if a brother was deceased before the couple sired offspring"[21]), engaged in sheet-separating sexual intercourse on five occasions in order to avoid the physical pleasure of these encounters.

Cordovero presents this *evidence* in utter negation of the Kabbalistic views; the Kabbalah views soul connection as greatly infused by the act of love. The rabbi further cites Genesis 2:24: "Therefore shall a man leave his father and his mother, and shall cleave unto his wife, and they shall be one flesh." In one flesh, Cordovero explains, one refers to the complete nakedness of the partners, where flesh can touch another flesh and become one.

The analogy of this complete and utter union, which is only available and accessible once flesh touches flesh, is an embodiment of the exchange that the Creator can have with his female component, the Shekinah, represented by the tenth sephirah of Malchut.

Many advocates of the coy act and "covered" display propose that the Creator resents exhibition, especially in relation to the act of sex, but Cordovero and his disciples claim that there's a manner in which this notion can be overridden.

A soulful sexual exchange should, by these suggestions, be held in a more dimly lit environment so as to soften the intensity of the visual component of pleasure.

---

20 Schechter, Soloman, and M. Seligsohn. n.d. "JOSE BEN HALAFTA – JewishEncyclopedia.com." www.Jewishencyclopedia.com. Accessed September 8, 2020. http://www.jewishencyclopedia.com/articles/8789-jose-ben-halafta

21 "Jerusalem Talmud Yevamot 1a." n.d. Www.Sefaria.Org. Accessed September 11, 2020. https://www.sefaria.org/Jerusalem_Talmud_Yevamot.1a?lang=bi.

Also, negators claimed a "nonrestricted" act can invite a demonic component into the act (in Hebrew שד), but Cordovero suggests that if the couple integrates a Godly aspect into the sexual union by practicing in a more kind and softly lit environment, they will serve the divine purpose of elevating their souls. (Cordovero suggests adding the divine by placing the letter י after the demonic potential of שד, thus creating a שדי, which translates to "guarding the doors of Israel," and is thus a protective force.)

Cordovero proceeds to share that the practice of the Onah commandment (satisfaction of a woman's conjugal rights) being assigned to the husband toward his future wife upon their sacred nuptials is more imperative and profound than any other commandment. He further explains that there are no other acts of "rule following" that could hold the potential of coming close to merging with the divine than that of sexual union. Cordovero suggests that merging the masculine force of Chochma in the second sephirah with the female component of Binah in the third sephirah can only be generated by the merging of the bottom sephirot, Tiferet and Malchut, on an earthly level. Therefore, this makes the sexual exchange the most significant vehicle in the quest of spiritual enlightenment, more so than any other spiritual devotion, as it allows for the human to be elevated to the theurgist level of the Creator.

# Spiritual Foreplay

Cordovero suggests that the application of certain acts and intentions is essential and prominent in order to create the ground for a sacred sexual union. How does one go about it? Cordovero offers a meditative state that can clear the mind of any negativity. Applying a spiritual "bath" to our hectic "monkey minds" can assist in this task. Cordovero goes to the great length of suggesting certain particular manners that can create the merging between these bottom sephirot for the sake of the upper merging. The male, by these suggestions, should go about hugging his beloved using his left arm under her head first, and only then hug her with his right arm over her head, in order to energetically eliminate the fifth elemental sephirah of Gevurah, which is rigid and judgmental, thus allowing the love to be all-inclusive and held between the left and the right sphere. Cordovero cites the Song of Songs 2:6 in this reference, "Let his left hand be under my head, and his right hand embrace me."

Kissing is the next stage of this "spiritual foreplay," although, according to Cordovero, kisses are not the hors d'oeuvre, but the main course. The Zohar referrs to this connection as the source of the soul and as the breath within the mouth. Thus, upon a loving kiss between the partners, we activate the three upper sephirot in the Tree of Life, equivalating the palate to Chochma, the throat to Binah, and the tongue to Daat. The couple should aim for seven profound kisses with sacred intentions for the coming sexual union to thus elevate the seven bottom sefirot leading to the upper three.

Kabbalistic teachings tell us that even the timing of the sexual union is of great importance. The suggestion is that Friday night is a particularly holy time for it since there's an energetic potential of Malchut (also called Shekinah or Matronit) to unite with the upper Keter of the divine. The claim is that on the weekdays, there's a common unrevealed struggle between the forces of "good and evil" representing the Tree of Knowledge, but on Friday night, this struggle ceases and rests in accordance with the Creator ceasing his work on that day, thus allowing the spiritual strength of the Tree of Life to take over and thus near the soul elevation to a divine level. Kabbalistic teachings suggest another manner in which we can advance this choice of a Friday night sexual union; this upgrade can be attained via the joint chanting/reading of the Song of Songs together or reading the Zoharic text כגוונא.[22]

Cordovero suggests that the heart is the source of this divine connection and is thus where the "fire of the loins" is ignited. In a surprising similarity to the tantric traditions, Kabbalistic teachings also suggest that the intensity of the sexual union holds such profound "fire" that it can elevate the soul on a cosmic level.

___

22 "Kegavna – כגוונא." n.d. Kegavna. Accessed September 8, 2020. http://www.jyrics.com/lyrics/kegavna-%D7%9B%D7%92%D7%95%D7%95%D7%A0%D7%90/.

The Zohar suggests that the divine merging is omnipresent and infinite, but in order to connect the physical and the spiritual divine, the couple must engage in establishing this fire from below in the bottom sephirot. This is emphasized by the following statement: "He who knows not the passion of a woman, could never know and hold the passion to the divine."[23] This statement is based on the Kabbalistic view that in the upper divine sphere, there exists a form of Onah (conjugal rights) need, just as there is on the physical level, and in order to satiate it sufficiently, the Ein Sof needs to draw its strength from the ten sephirot and merge with them, a condition that can only be achieved by the material, physical practice of a passionate, sexual exchange. The passion between the lovers, Cordovero adds, needs to be a true physical fire. That is essential for the divine connection; there should be no regard to the unrelated quest of procreation, because in this sexual union, we are aiming for the divine elevation of the soul, rather than the physical reproduction of offspring. This approach is sensual in nature and looks at the sexual union as the main course, not a means to an end.

Cordovero presents the act of sexual union and Kabbalistic romanticism as a manner in which Malchut can finally reunite with Tiferet, and all ten sephirot can become one once more, after being divided and separated in the physical grind.

## Quickstep Meditation

In this couples' meditation, we will aim to exhibit the actual connection between the upper sephirot of Chochma and Bina by the heat ignited and sourced in the exchange between Tifeeret and Malchut.

Observe the Tree of Life for a few minutes before going inside.

---

23 "Shenei Luchot HaBerit." n.d. Www.Sefaria.Org. Accessed September 11, 2020. https://www.sefaria.org/Shenei_Luchot_HaBerit%2C_Asara_Hillulim%2C_Shaar_HaAhavah?lang=bi.

Sit in a comfortable position opposite your partner and place your hands on your knees or on your sides to start. Later in the meditation, you will have the option of shifting your hands to different locations.

Close your eyes and take a deep breath through your mouth, all the way up to the top of your lungs. Now, purse your lips and let your breath out slowly as if you're whistling through them. Repeat this three times and keep a comfortable posture while reverting to normal breathing.

Start from the top Keter and imagine nothing but a flow of light bouncing from the top, descending down. Place your hands on top of your partner's head. Shift one hand to the right (Chochma) and place it over their right eye. Remain there for a moment, and with your other hand, shift the left to Bina, and place your hand on their left eye.

Remain here and meditate on this exchange between the divine dyad on top. Imagine an intense white light shifting between Chochma and Binah, back and forth. Imagine the two merging together in an erotic harmony. When you feel satisfied with an intense sensual sensation, gather all energy, place your hands back on your knees or on the ground, and shift swiftly below to Daat.

Continue to the right to Chesed and move to the left Gevurah. Keep descending to Tiferet, and place one hand on your lover's chest over their heart, and your other hand on yours.

Take a deep breath. Remain there and start building an intense energy again while breathing more deeply. When you feel satisfied, gather your hands back and move your own energy to the right, Netzach, and swiftly left to Hod. Descend to yesod, and then halt.

Remain there with your energy, and then in one swing, place one hand on your partner's lower abdomen, for Malchut on the bottom, while placing the other hand back on their chest, for Tiferet. Move a light beam of energy between these sephirot. This time imagine an intense red light moving between these two sephirot. Breathe into them and feel your entire lower body becoming enflamed with desire. Remain there and hold this sensation for a few moments, then slowly and gradually allow your mind and body to relax. Remove your hands and place them on your knees or on your sides. Retain normal breathing and gradually open your eyes.

# Tree of Your Fancy

Kabbalistic teachings tell us that every day on this planet, we are making a conscious choice to form "heaven on earth." In the quest of this, we tend to lose ourselves in the cacophony of existence. But we always hold this choice, as official cocreators with the divine.

The Zohar tells us that the allegory depicted in Genesis 3:6, the consumption of the forbidden fruit of the Tree of Knowledge of Good and Evil, should not be taken at face value, but understood as the regal couple's choice to have a "selfish intercourse"—yes, the kind that does not elevate the soul but solely satiates the physical body—with a "divine" yet short-lived satiation.

By Kabbalistic views, the analogy of choosing between the Tree of Life and the Tree of Knowledge is the choice we make between spiritually elevating actions and thoughts versus accepting the uncomfortable existence, such as addiction, less desirable life choices, and otherwise poor decisions, respectively.

Since, similarly to the royal couple, we can derive two options out of the sexual union—one that can be translated into creating life and "heaven on earth" versus disease, pain, and chaos—we have the control and the choice over every single aspect of both our physical and spiritual lives.

By refusing to enhance our spiritual growth and remaining in our "comfort zones," which are more than likely not comfortable at all, we surrender to the "opponents" in our minds that tell us that we have no choice, while in fact, we absolutely do.

This can be applied, as mentioned earlier, to anger, addiction, negative thoughts, ill wishes, overcompensation, not sharing, and so forth.

How do we create this divine union with the divine? The different meditations occupying the Tree of Life system are very efficient, but this connection can be further attained via full awareness of our strengths that we develop and perfect; we can utilize chanting or scanning of the Seventy-Two Names of God, acts of kindness, and different forms of "personal conversations with God" called Hitbodedut (more on this later). The principle of it all is the "*external* wishing and bestowal" versus self-wishing and visualization.

Kabbalistic teachings tell us that the third sephirah of Binah holds the power to free us from our debilitating past no matter what it entails and no matter how many aspects of it we aim to change, while elevating us to a high spiritual existence that will enable the direct connection to the source of creation (sourced in Chochma). Even the mere sound of Binah alludes to its purpose, which is *being*.

We aim to *be* "glued" to the Creator, to join forces with the source, in every action, decision, or thought that visits us in this life.

# Quickstep Meditation

We will choose the combination of,פהל a sequence that represents strengthening our spirituality, in order to overcome addiction. By addiction, we refer to any habitual choice of the past that does us a disservice.

When applying this sequence, look deep inside and compare these choices to a broader spectrum of relation; not only the strength it requires to be a giver versus a receiver, but what tremendous change this applied attitude could have on a cosmic, universal level if we distinguish between habits and acts of soul elevation, which can at times be tricky to decipher.

Remember that you can digitally scan the letters or gaze at them, visualize them with your eyes closed, or chant them to the sound of PAHAL. If you choose the two former options out of the four, you may want to copy this sequence on a small piece of paper that you keep in a safe and respected spot in order to utilize this power. You may also incorporate all four utilization options and switch from one to another as you progress.

Gaze at this sequence for a few minutes before going inside.

Sit in a comfortable position, close your eyes, and take a deep breath through your mouth, all the way up to the top of your lungs. Now, purse your lips and let your breath out slowly as if you're whistling through them. Repeat this three times and keep a comfortable posture while reverting to normal breathing.

Slowly allow the three-letter sequence of פהל to appear before you and float in your mind's eye.

I like to see these sequences as if they are floating on water in tiny ripples toward me and back, while gazing with my eyes closed. Allow the letters to form and heighten in your memory and breathe "the breath of life" into them. Merge the goal that you have in relation to this sequence and combine it with the energy you create.

It can be a soulful and beautiful connection with a potential soul match, or you can go further and expand into a peaceful existence to all. If you are aiming to unite with your current or hopeful partner in a respectful and harmonious manner, that will definitely and unequivocally serve the greater goal of a harmonious, sacred, and everlasting relationship. You may also alternate or gradually arrive at a higher-level goal as you advance and progress.

When you feel safe and strong in this frequency and the light it emits, gradually allow both your hands to touch the ground, and revert to normal breathing. Gradually and slowly open your eyes. You may want to remain seated in this position for a few moments before getting back on your feet. Drink a glass of water to quench the energy you've emitted.

# Chapter 15
## Our Bodies, Our Selves

We tend to observe and evaluate spirituality versus physicality by the occupation of our minds and emotional states, versus our material bodies, respectively.

Kabbalistic teachings, however, see this duality as nonexistent. In fact, the bodily and spiritual practices are so intertwined that there really isn't any physical practice that does not influence our souls and thus our connections to the divine.

The Zohar tells us about the principle of *avodah be'gashmiut*, the teaching that we can serve our divine purposes in and through the physical world, which brings the entire range of human activity into the domain of divine significance. Everything that occupies one's ordinary day becomes a way to (potentially) serve the soul. Although one may assume these practices can be directly related to prayer or meditation, one would be correct, yet not completely so. The reality is that every act of maintenance in which we engage—like eating, moving our bodies, and yes, sexual exchange—can be utilized toward this divine connection and soul elevation.

Take the act of meditation to start. In Genesis 2:7, we are told that "the LORD God formed man from the dust of the earth. He blew into his nostrils the breath of life, and man became a living being." This verse emphasizes the validity and importance of the breath, and its connection to spirituality; in fact, the Latin term *spiritus* simply means breath.

This act of mindfulness, while utilizing the divine-granted, lifegiving breath, allows us to connect to the source of our being on a more profound level.

Begore we examine this, let us take a look at a mundane and necessary act we engage in regularly, like eating. In his book *God in Your Body*, author Jay Michaelson elaborates on how a "simple" act of this form holds the potential of an "invited elevation."

On the physical level, we can even embark on this soul elevation practice as soon as we open our eyes. By feeling our bodies and their sensations, we reconnect with our souls; these are the Kabbalistic "sun salutations" of a sort, which allow the soul to be utilized toward its high purposes, via the carrier, our sensitive bodies. The morning blessing called *Modeh Ani*, or "I am grateful," relates to this concept precisely; that is, gratitude to the creator for re-instilling my body with its soul, or breath, or life, which are the semi-synonymous words of *neshamah* and *neshimah*, respectively.

If we apply a similar principle to the act of love, we are invited to delve into the very core of our divine nature when we practice our sexuality.

Unlike Eastern views of spiritualty, Kabbalistic teachings do not advocate self-segregation, or the utter removal of desires and needs from our systems, in order to incorporate a divine spark and reach this elevation (this self-annihilation is in fact prohibited under Jewish law). We are not propelled to be withdrawn, but rather recognize the fact that "God is in the details." Thus, in these ordinary moments, we can do the most growing through awareness and engagement.

Kabbalists additionally state that having "no desire" is a desire, for that void can never really be achieved, and thus should not be attempted to begin with. The mere truth is that we must have and entertain our desires, but toward a greater good.

# The Shells

In Lurianic Kabbalah, (sources in Issac Luria, the great kabbalist of the sixteenth century) we are enlightened with the concept of *kelipot* ("shells" or "husks") that represent *evil* in the world. Essentially, it is suggested that everything in the physical world contains a spark of goodness, but in many cases, that spark is concealed within a shell that conceals its light. Our job is to find those sparks and elevate them. Of the four kelipot mentioned in the Zohar, three are considered basically impure, while the fourth—the *kelipah nogah* (translated alternately as the "husk of glow" and "shining shell")—can be swayed either toward the impure or toward the pure.

This teaching from the *Tanya*, an early work of Hasidic philosophy by Rabbi Shneur Zalman of Liadi, is composed of five sections that define Hasidic mystical psychology and theology as a handbook for daily spiritual life in Jewish observance. It focuses on how the mundane acts of eating, moving, or corresponding sexually can be a great place to encounter the *kelipah nogah* because we can incline the act either in a serving direction or a disserving direction.

Let us use the sexual act as an example. If we engage in it with our partners in order to strive for soul connection and enlightenment, or for the act of connection and spreading the energy of love, thereby utilizing the upper sephirot of the divine via the activation of the primal, physical sephirot mergence, we serve this purpose in a positive direction. Conversely, if we relate to this sacred act as an act of vengeance, power, control, or humiliation, we achieve quite the opposite, and in so doing, descend our soul.

Satiation should thus not be the goal, but a sense of indulgence for a higher purpose. Similarly to food consumption, one can gorge on a meal until the stomach can no longer digest, or he can alternatively enjoy the most indulging sustenance only to a point of satisfaction and vigor.

In other words, if I root my consumption in the desire to solely to satisfy my body, without awareness or good intentions, then I tip the shell surrounding that act in a disserving direction, and thus the opportunity for holiness is lost.

Physical acts like eating, interacting sexually, or moving our bodies through dance, exercise, or the like, aren't inherently positive or negative, and thus the moral valance arises through our mindfulness and our intention to serve.

# Quickstep Meditation

We will choose the combination of אכא , a sequence that represents bringing order to our lives by connecting to the soul through the very vehicle that enables its purpose here on earth, the body. When applying this sequence, look deep inside and compare these choices to a broader spectrum of relation; not only the strength it requires to avoid habitual action that may not serve you anymore while avoiding the erroneous separation of physical and spiritual acts, but the consideration of what tremendous change this applied attitude could have on a cosmic, universal level if we distinguish between habits and acts of soul elevation.

Remember that you can digitally scan the letters or gaze at them, visualize them with your eyes closed, or chant them to the sound of AKA. If you choose the two former options out of the four, you may want to copy this sequence on a small piece of paper that you keep in a safe and respected spot in order to utilize this power. You may also incorporate all four utilization options and switch from one to another as you progress.

Gaze at this sequence for a few minutes before going inside.

Sit in a comfortable position, close your eyes, and take a deep breath through your mouth, all the way up to the top of your lungs. Now, purse your lips and let your breath out slowly as if you're whistling through them. Repeat this three times and keep a comfortable posture while reverting to normal breathing.

Slowly allow the three-letter sequence of אכא to appear before you and float in your mind's eye.

I like to see these sequences as if they are floating on water in tiny ripples toward me and back, while gazing with my eyes closed. Allow the letters to form and heighten in your memory and breathe "the breath of life" into them. Merge the goal that you have in relation to this sequence and combine it with the energy you create.

It can be a soulful and beautiful connection with a potential soul match, or you can go further and expand into a peaceful existence to all. If you are aiming to unite with your current or hopeful partner in a respectful and harmonious manner, that will definitely and unequivocally serve the greater goal of a harmonious, sacred, and everlasting relationship. You may also alternate or gradually arrive at a higher-level goal as you advance and progress.

When you feel safe and strong in this frequency and the light it emits, gradually allow both your hands to touch the ground, and revert to normal breathing. Gradually and slowly open your eyes. You may want to remain seated in this position for a few moments before getting back on your feet. Drink a glass of water to quench the energy you've emitted.

# Who's on Top

We are living entities in this universe, and as such, we understand that no life is lived in a vacuum. In other words, we are a product of certain cultural, civil, religious, and philosophical spheres that facilitate or debilitate our thoughts and actions. In this climate, one can assume that a number of revolutions, in particular the women's movement, enabled a space or sphere in which the principal of equality is a given. Along these lines, we may investigate the presence of hierarchy or dominance in the committed relationship. Does the egalitarianism that we experience in our modern societies apply to marriages? And if it does, is it beneficial? This topic may be vast and can expand even further, but going back to the relevance of it, it is important to understand that the Kabbalistic notions of male and female energies, and the feminine aspect of the divine that strives to merge completely with the divine male, is utterly unrelated to rights, laws, or any other practices, and does not view anyone as superior, other than in comparison to the Creator himself.

Kabbalistic teachings dig deep into the cosmic notion of the divine, interacting with the "human" attributes we exhibit here on earth. It is worth mentioning that the chewed up idiom "I'm only human" isn't applicable in this doctrine because we all encompass sparks of the Creator, and thus are able, and in fact, propelled, to carry on the divine goal of creating a better reality for humanity as a whole (*tikkun olam*), and within the human material existence—the body, in particular.

In a collection of Kabbalistic traditions inscribed at the end of the fifteenth century,[24] we find a clear expression between delight and pleasure on one hand, and the divine on the other: "The lower entities leave an imprint on the supernal one by their actions, and this is the reason why each man should delight, because of the delight of the King and the Queen. And whoever adds to this delight, it is better."

The "regal" pair referred to in the quote above is compounded of the sephirot Tiferet and Malchut—that is to say, the male and the female divine manifestations, respectively. Their erotic union is considered to be of paramount importance for the state of harmony in the higher and lower worlds. Their exchange of pleasure depends upon the human performance here below on earth, and hence, by indulging in physical delight, a person induces an addition of delight on higher realms of the divine.

A delight on/ in? *high* by means of human pleasure (Taanug in Hebrew), is understood as a divine activity.

According to another view of the Baal Shem Tov (Besht for short), the alternation between coming closer to the godly action and retreating from it is intended to continuously recreate the feeling of delight that is "the quintessence of the worship of our divine nature, and the Creator."

It is important to emphasize the affinity between the delight that is encompassed in the sexual act, and the penis.

---

24 Sefer Shushan Sodot, fol. 77b, par. 473. On the possibility that this collection of traditions has been influential on Hasidism, see Margolin, The Human Temple, 262, 311, 315–317 (Hebrew). On Sabbath and theurgy see also Idel, "Sabbath," 74–79.

Though it is the worship of the Creator that is explicitly invoked as generating the delight, its occurrence is placed in the immediate conceptual vicinity of the "sign of Covenant"—a widespread term for circumcision. This *localized sphere*, referring to the ninth sephirah of Yesod, does not leave any place for ambiguity about the fact that the two concepts—delight and the phallus—are directly related.

In the quote below, we can comprehend the dual nature of all creatures that encompasses the feminine and masculine, but more typically, in the Kabbalistic aspect of this union, we gather the position of emanator versus receiver, which qualifies the quality of feminine versus masculine, sans official gender.

> Everything in the world necessarily possesses aspects of male and female. This is especially true in the case of the worshiper of the creator, who has to possess the aspects of male and female, namely that of emanator and recipient. The male aspect means, for example, that which is always emanating by dint of his holiness and great cleaving, and the purity of his thought, he emanates a spiritual delight into the supernal lights, worlds and attributes. And he has also a female aspect, namely that which is the recipient and draws down to the lower worlds the influx from the supernal worlds.[25]

The recipient of delight is therefore defined by the very quality of receptivity, as female, independent of any question of gender or sex, as we know it socially.

This approach, reminiscent of Jung's views of male and female as two qualities found in both men and women, is here part of the redefining of the hierarchical relationship and the gender of the factors involved in the experience.

---

25 R. Abraham Joshua Heschel of Apta, Ohev Israel, fol. 81cd. On delight see also ibid., fols. 80cd, 81ab, 83cd, 85b. Compare also to R. Asher Tzevi of Ostraha, Maayan okhmah, fol. 93b.

R. Nachman of Breslov depicts the notion of femininity versus masculinity in an interesting fashion when he states, "It is known that the recipient of delight from someone else is called a female ... Therefore, when the Holy One ... receives delight from the prayer of Israel [Israel being humanity, rather than the actual nation or religion] it is as if He becomes a female in relation to Israel."[26]

This explains why acts of a joint dyad—by the sacred act of sex that can be perceived as prayer—are widely understood as having a real impact on the divine. It induces delight and generates a state in the divine world, that may be understood as feminine; erotic delight emerges as the result of a specific ritual act that induces delight. This entity constitutes a form of relationship between the human and the divine.

Likewise, the two aspects of the righteous—male and female—do not pertain to sex or gender. Among the main interpretations of this model is the erotic one that emphasizes the importance of inducing delight as its initial stage.

# Scent of a Woman

The story of Lilith is one to take to account when discussing these very topics. Lilith's story emerges precisely out of a struggle over domination in marriage. The story of Lilith has been bubbling up in Jewish circles for over four thousand years.

Esteemed authors like Jessica Benjamin in her book *The Bonds of Love*, states that love cannot coexist with domination. Love and domination are not a reversible, dualistic pair, and so love emerges only in an "intersubjective realm—that space in which the mutual recognition of subjects can compete with the reversible relationship of domination."

Lilith's roots are in Sumerian mythology, where she is a powerful goddess. In the scripts, she's depicted as an owl dwelling among waste places (Isa. 34:14). In the rabbinic mind, she takes further shape as the first wife of Adam, a figure who helps to explain (among many

---

26 Liqqutei Moharan, Mahadura Qamma, no. 73.

alternative options), why there are two creation stories in Genesis. In the first creation story, it is written, "Male and female he created them" (Gen. 1:27), while in the second, more fleshed-out story, "the LORD God fashioned the rib that He had taken from the man into a woman" (Gen. 2:22). By the time that this second woman, Eve, was created, the first woman, who was to become Lilith, had disappeared. These aspects of the creation story are, of course, another commentary of a sort, as we formerly mentioned that the dual creation story can be analyzed as the dual faced and gendered creature initially placed in the Garden only to be separated by the Creator into two-parted entities, entertaining opposing genders and personalities.

For the sake of this section, we will assume the Lilith version of the dual creation stories. The goddess's disappearance is first explained in full in the tenth century text, *The Alphabet of ben Sirah*.

In this text, Adam and Lilith were created at the same time, presumably with the possibility of equality between them. We first encounter them, however, locked in an intimacy dispute, represented as a quarrel over sexual positions. Adam insists that he is to be on top, signifying domination, but Lilith refuses and instead pronounces the unspoken name of God, which allows her to flee the Garden. She ends up on the shores of the Red Sea, where she mates with the king of demons, Samael, producing legions of demon offspring. Adam, meanwhile, complaining to God of his loneliness, persuades God to dispatch three angels to bring Lilith back to him. The angels find a reluctant Lilith, yet are able to extract from her the promise that she will not kidnap the unborn fetuses of gestating women as long as they wear an amulet containing the names of the three angels during childbirth.

In the Zohar, Lilith is a highly charged sexual figure. Within the human world, she is thought to be the Queen of Sheba, and alternatively one of the two prostitutes who come to Solomon for judgment. Within the cosmic world of angels, demons, and God, she functions as Queen of the Demons, and in the fallen world, she is symbolized by the destruction of the temple. She is "the slave woman," consort to God, until the time of the Messiah, when God could reunite with the exiled feminine.

As a mythic figure, Lilith satisfies an important need for both men and women. Serving the fears of both men and women, and their anxiety relating to each other's sexuality, Lilith serves as a release valve for emotions that need to find concrete expression.

Howard Schwartz in his book *Lilith's Cave* compares Eve and Lilith to the mermaid and the siren respectively, two kinds of mythological creatures of the sea; one that helps sailors through the rocky shoals, the other that lures them, entranced, to their deaths. To identify with the one at the expense of the other poses a danger to contemporary Jewish feminism, Schwartz claims. He states that, "The myths of Lilith and Eve cry out for recognition of their polar nature within a single woman, as do the myths of Jacob and Esau in every man.... To deny one side or the other is to deny the wholeness of the self."

In the Lurianic Kabbalistic views of the Lilith story, the plot thickens and becomes much more mystical and profound in the tikkun, or karmatic, level.

Lurianic Kabbalah states that the soul of Lilith is reincarnated in a number of iconic leading women in the bible, thus reclaiming her place, even upon paying a physical price, allows one to be elevated to a higher spiritual realm. Kabbalistic teachings tell us that in this reincarnation of Lilith's soul (*gilgul* means "reincarnation" in Hebrew), Lilith appears as Leah in the triangle of Jacob, Leah, and Rachel, as the latter represents Eve, and Jacob stands for Adam's reincarnation.[27] In this sense, there's a redemption to a degree, as the last woman standing out of these dyads is actually Leah (Lilith) over Rachel (Eve). In another mentioning of a potential reincarnation of Lilith, it is suggested that Dinah is being physically compromised in the story of her rape (Genesis 34) but is then redeemed by her brothers and gains the upgraded title of "Jacob's daughter" rather than Leah's.

---

27 *Window of the Soul: The Teachings of Rabbi Isaac Luria* edited by James David Dunn; *Lilith: a Rereading of Feminine Shadow* by Ohad Ezrachi and Marc Gafni found on the website:kabalove.org/articles/Lilith-2nd-gate.

To conclude this point for now and drive it home, we should revert to the initial question of egalitarianism—or rather lack of dominion—in the committed relationship, and in sexual exchange in particular.

In a psychoanalytical notion, to dissect this very intricate and charged factor, we should assume that a certain parity strives in the sensual exchange for the cosmic structure of things to remain everlasting. In other words, should this parity evaporate completely, the cosmic charge—or draw between the feminine and the masculine energies of the Tree of Life, represented by Malchut for feminine and Tiferet for masculine—may fail to be achieved and attained, thus jeopardizing the upper root of divine connection between Chochma (male) and Binah (female).

# Chapter 16
## Divine Entanglement

We concluded the prior chapter with the profound understanding of the unquestionable correlation between pleasure attained in the world of Assiyah (action/earth) and the divine realm of Atzilut (emanation/God).

For the sake of this union, we will engage a specific dyadic meditation that enables this connection.

## Quickstep Meditation

In this meditation, we will aim to exhibit the actual connection between Tiferet and Malchut via Yesod, the latter acting as the active source of masculine energy.

Observe the Tree of Life for a few minutes before going inside.

Sit in a comfortable position facing your partner, and place your hands on your knees or on your sides to start. Later in the meditation, you will have the option to move your hands to different locations.

Close your eyes and take a deep breath through your mouth, all the way up to the top of your lungs. Now, purse your lips and let your breath out slowly as if you're whistling through them. Repeat this three times, and keep a comfortable posture while reverting to normal breathing.

We will avoid any emphasis on other parts of the Tree aside from the dynamic between these three sephirot.

Sit in a comfortable position, allowing your feet to be placed close to your body.

Place one hand on your heart or chest area, and the other around your feet.

The hand positioned on your chest represents Tiferet. Start feeling the heat of this hand while imagining a strong lavender light intensifying and humming through your body with every minute that passes.

Take a deep breath.

Remain there and start building an intense energy again while breathing more deeply. Begin building the sensation of heat and intensity around the hand near your feet or thighs, which represents Malchut. Imagine a bright blue light emanating from this area and warming this region and your overall energy sphere.

Stay there for a few moments, then begin moving your heart-positioned hand down while moving the feet-positioned hand up and place them one on top of the other, around your lower abdomen, representing Yesod. Begin circling your hands around your abdomen, building heat and energy. Imagine a bright orange light like a fire, burning your inner truth and energy, emitting pure sexual source, and generating it up to the divine spheres.

Begin moving the upper hand up and down, from chest to abdomen, and the bottom hand up and down, from the feet to the abdomen. Repeat it a number of times, and in between, place your hands on your abdomen again, and circle around. You may feel inclined to shift in your seat, or move your waist. This is normal and logical; your body is only following your spiritual inclination.

Stay in this sensation and gradually retain normal breathing and position.

When you feel satisfied, take a deep breath, and open your eyes slowly and gently.

# The Language of Love

According to Jewish tradition, the Hebrew language has a divine origin. In Genesis 1, the Creator creates the world by pronouncing his will; hence, language has the ultimate creative potential. This view forms the starting point for most mystical and magical traditions, from antiquity right up to present times. The Kabbalistic *Book of Formation* (*Sefer Yetzirah* in Hebrew)—one of the earliest Jewish mystical texts of Hellenistic provenance, dated by scholars somewhere between the second and seventh centuries CE—describes the process of formation as taking place through the twenty-two letters of the Hebrew language, and alongside the ten sephirot. In this book, we find hidden details regarding the formation of "something new out of something present" in a somewhat similar manner to that of the Creator's initial plan for creating the universe. Subtleties are key, and thus the book is a book of *formation*, rather than *creation*, as the only one who can create "something out of nothing" is the Creator himself.

In a sense, these Hebrew letters, and uttering a combination of letters and numbers, holds the potential to become *godlike* to the degree that one may be able to form a creature out of the ground—though we are still only sparks of the Creator, rather than *the Creator*, as we form, rather than create, out of an existing substance that was initially present solely due to the Creator's craft.

Regardless, in this course of possible action, we understand the power of words, letters, and speech. Letters hold power in three dimensions—namely, their shape, their numeric value, and their pronunciation. We are constantly reminded that the tongue holds such power over enlivening and destroying, a principle that should definitely be applied to our relationships.

# Whisper in My Ear

When we dig deep into Kabbalistic teachings, we are encouraged not only to view or scan letters and words in our mind, but also to utter them, simply due to the fact that this is the preferred method of the Creator, who "spoke" this universe into tangible manifestation.

If we borrow this model and apply it to our relationships, we will rediscover the ancient concept of an open dialogue.

Many couples complain about the other party "not understanding them" or acting wrongly when they should "know better." The lesson out of this Kabbalistic offering is that this notion should not even play a role in a healthy exchange.

Similar to praying or chanting our wishes and aspirations, we must present our wishes, wants, and preferences to our partner. We should strive to make ourselves be heard; we should avoid keeping silent for the sake of status quo.

A real, vital relational exchange nourishes a healthy dynamic.

In the spirit of understanding this ancient advice, we also need to take into account the way this speech is used in our dyadic exchanges.

The Zohar tells us that we should relate to the verbal exchange with our partner in a similar manner to the conversations we have with the Creator upon praying, mediating, or chanting.

We are told that we should speak softly, almost in a whisper when possible, as if our partners' ears are right next to our lips. And that is exactly how our conversations with the Creator are conducted; note that chanting and prayers, although verbally uttered, are far from loud, and thus our relational, physical exchanges here on earth and with our beloveds should hold the same characteristics.

## An Ongoing Process

As a creation, matter needs to have a source, a beginning. Kabbalah teaches us that the Creator "spoke" the world into existence. This means that the Creator's "speech" created our reality—the trees, rocks, water, and everything that we see and take for granted.

However, there is a fundamental difference between what the Creator creates and what man forms. What man forms is, in fact, only a change of status of preexisting material properties, so every component in your "brilliant" computer is taken from something that was already created by the Creator.

The Baal Shem Tov teaches that we will never cease to discover benefits from the amazing myriad of natural metals and minerals that our Creator placed within the earth's crust.

The earth, including all that is within it, did not exist prior to creation. Therefore, the earth must continually be *recreated* in order for it to exist.

# Never-Ending Story

Quantum physics established theories that were long discussed and published many lifetimes prior. If quantum physics teaches us that as long as you look at a particle, it exists, but as soon as you cease giving it eye contact or attention, it ceases to exist, then we are constantly required to keep it tangible. The particle doesn't exist in this physical world without our acknowledgment. So, anything that doesn't inherently exist needs another creative force to continuously create it in order for it to continuously exist.

Every atom ever created needs to be continuously *spoken* into existence. Although we are given the ability to manufacture almost anything, it does not change the fact that continuous creation is necessary for these secondary products to exist. For without the raw atoms constantly being spoken into existence, there would be no material to form by-products.

Sound like magic? It simply is! In fact, the words *abra cadabrah* come from the two Hebrew/Aramaic words, *ibarah c'dabrah* or *avra kadavra*, meaning, "it will be created in my words."

Showing gratitude to the Creator by means of prayer, acts of kindness, and so forth, is a well-known tool that solidifies our spiritual connection and allows us to feel at ease with our great fortunate existence. In a similar manner, we must always feel grateful for our relational exchanges, being that it keeps on being formed every moment that passes us by.

When we are aware of these constant gifts, we begin to realize that we are loved and provided for unconditionally, with no ties to reciprocate, but what *we* feel is serving of our remarkable life conditions.

# Maintenance Task

Asking is internal, but uttering gratitude is external, and it is key.

Write a list of all the fortunate things in your life—all the things you would miss if you no longer had them—then list the things that you want, but do not yet possess.

The Baal Shem Tov explains that we may ask for what we "lack" in a different fashion. We should ask for what "is best for us" rather than our wishes, as the divine source knows better and has a much broader view of the plans for our lives, and our beneficial desires. In that sense, one may utter: "Thank you for the blessings you have given me. Please bless me with what is most suitable for my path."

Why is the recreation necessary? Isn't the divine infinite and capable on maintaining things as they are? As discussed previously, of course the divine source can create a reality that is maintenance free, yet as Rabbi Menachem Mendel Schneersohn (The Lubavitcher Rebbe) explains, the Creator chose continuous creation so that we could feel grateful for this great gift of life every day we are granted with it, for gratitude equates to happiness.

# Quickstep Meditation

We will choose the combination of לוו, a sequence that represents removing our ego or egotistic self from the relational equation, thus allowing our prayers to be answered in the fashion in which they will be most beneficial to our divine soul quests. When applying this sequence, look deep inside and compare these choices to a broader spectrum of relation; not only the strength it requires to be a one-time giver, but what tremendous change this applied attitude of always recreating and removing selfish acts for the greatest good of all, our selves included, can have on a cosmic, universal level.

Remember that you can digitally scan the letters or gaze at them, visualize them with your eyes closed, or chant them to the sound of LAVAV. If you choose the two former options out of the four, you may want to copy this sequence on a small piece of paper that you keep in a safe and respected spot in order to utilize this power. You may also incorporate all four utilization options and switch from one to another as you progress.

Gaze at this sequence for a few minutes before going inside.

Sit in a comfortable position, close your eyes, and take a deep breath through your mouth, all the way up to the top of your lungs. Now, purse your lips and let your breath out slowly as if you're whistling through them. Repeat this three times, and keep a comfortable posture while reverting to normal breathing.

Slowly allow the three-letter sequence of לו to appear before you and float in your mind's eye.

I like to see these sequences as if they are floating on water in tiny ripples toward me and back, while gazing with my eyes closed. Allow the letters to form and heighten in your memory, and breathe "the breath of life" into them. Merge the goal that you have in relation to this sequence, and combine it with the energy you create.

It can be a soulful and beautiful connection with a potential soul match, or you can go further and expand into a peaceful existence to all. If you are aiming to unite with your current or hopeful partner in a respectful and harmonious manner, that will definitely and unequivocally serve the greater goal of a harmonious, sacred, and everlasting relationship. You may also alternate or gradually arrive at a higher-level goal as you advance and progress.

When you feel safe and strong in this frequency and the light it emits, gradually allow both your hands to touch the ground, and revert to normal breathing. Gradually and slowly open your eyes. You may want to remain seated in this position for a few moments before getting back on your feet. Drink a glass of water to quench the energy you've emitted.

# Chapter 17
## Divine Destiny

In the writings of The Baal Shem Tov, we understand that what comes to us from the Creator is actually a reflection of our own state of mind. The very concept of metaphysical views, which are more popular today, of *thoughts creating reality* and "think your way into health and wealth" are sourced in these principals precisely. By this logic, if we are blissful, kind to others, merciful, and compassionate, then the Creator/universe is bound to bestow joy, kindness, mercy, and compassion upon us.

The principle of Kabbalistic teachings is that the mere source of accomplishing soul elevation in this world is by employing intention (Kavanah) into it; this applies to all life aspects in general, and to relationships and intimacy in particular.

Why is our state of mind so imperative? Simple. By keeping a positive stance, we subconsciously affirm our trust in the cosmos and the Creator to provide us with all that we strive for, and more. Here, too, as mentioned previously, it is important to truly trust rather than pretend to trust until things fail to go your way and then immediately terminate your structured beliefs and certainties. By remaining despondent, we are essentially saying, "The world is a negative place and I believe my needs will not be met." Kabbalistic teachings tell us that if you struggle financially, but pause and take heed to anything charitable (it does not have to be a financial commitment, there are many ways to give that are not monetary), the very act of this choice will send a vibrational message to the divine that you trust your financial betterment is in fact coming, not from the unrewarding job you hold, but rather from your conviction that you can donate your time, effort, or even financial resources, because more is always generated for you.

The Zohar teaches us that man can be controlled by one of three "organs": brain/mind, heart/emotions, and liver/ego.

Rabbi Josef Isaac Schneersohn teaches that in a similar manner to which one can sense a certain part of the body more significantly only when it is sore or in pain, so does one's ego strive to make itself heard only upon a "soreness" of one's self esteem, or the lack of it.

# Love and Educate

Needless to say, in the mere action of loving, we are already bestowing a form of knowledge and awareness to our love interests.

An important point that should be made here is that if we aim to educate another because we think we know better, feel better, or are better overall, then the concept of bestowing good is completely eliminated. The desire in our heart for betterment should always, without fail, stem from a light and happy heart that wishes to give and enhance the well-being of others, near or far.

Kabbalistic teachings say that there are two primary (yet opposing) emotions that govern our lives: love and fear. The former creates closeness and attraction, while the latter emits distance and retraction.

Every thought we have, everything we say, and everything we do, is either a product of love for someone or something, or due to a fear from someone or something. The part of the brain that controls fear, mainly the amygdala, is a part that overrides rational thought, literally bypassing the source of our rational mind, thereby shifting our ability to process only through instinctive reactions. In other words, if you are in a "state of fear" (i.e., worried, anxious, or stressed) you *cannot* be in a "state of love."

Rabbi Bechya, in his brilliant *Duties of the Heart*, writes, "The human heart cannot hold both fear and love at the same time."[28]

This applies to say that in our fear or pain we cannot see the "other side of love;" we are simply oblivious to it. Should we aim to shift to a state of love, we first must begin with the awareness of a divine plan that is by far more incredible and beneficial than *any* best-case scenario that we could ever imagine or wish for.

Let us take a common occurrence relevant to this discussion and to long term relationships, in essence. In Kabbalistic terms, thinking about being unfaithful or lusting over an attractive person our eyes happen to catch does not apply as adultery, because adultery is not about the desire in the heart, but rather about the action of the body. Even if a person doesn't *desire* to be charitable, yet gives charity anyway, that person has then successfully engaged in a good deed! To a large extent, it is a divine quest that we should be challenged by the negative opponent inside us, thus allowing the Creator and ourselves the moral satisfaction of conquering it.

The Lubavitcher Rebbe elaborates about how incomparable the pleasure a farmer would get from the produce reaped out of a perfect field in the perfect climate to the satisfaction he would get if he managed to take a barren dessert and give it life.

## Soul Elevation through Sexual Union

By Kabbalistic teachings, if one follows a sincere and altruistic notion of the sexual union, one embeds the intention of advancing to higher levels of the divine connection by merging the lower (tangible) sephirot, while also providing one's partner with physical relief from perhaps muscle tension, pain, or discomfort that may accompany the sexual buildup the body carries. Yes, we are divine sparks of the Creator, but we are

---

28 Kaufmann Kohler and Isaac Broydé (1901–1906). "Bahya ben Joseph ibn Pakuda". In Singer, Isidore; et al. (eds.). *The Jewish Encyclopedia*. New York: Funk & Wagnalls.

still carrying that energy within a physical body that holds limitations on one hand, and bountiful potential for divine emulation on the other. This kind of a true, intention-based mutual dedication encompassed in sexual unity is one that holds the potential to elevate our souls into the supreme level of emanation (Atzilut).

How is the sexual union applicable to this elevation, per se?

We are well aware of the logic behind religious laws and rituals regarding conjugal rights—when, how and how often, along with the times we should avoid it. Yet, more important than that, on the spiritual rather than religious level, we should come to the understanding that in every sexual union we are create a "spiritual offspring." This energy that is emitted and transmitted is profound, and it holds the power to elevate us as a couple, as well as each one of us individually, into a higher soul connection with the divine. In other words, the fact that no "tangible" result—such as conception—comes out of a sexual union that isn't planned as a means to an end, we need to remain aware that as carriers of divine sparks, our interpersonal exchanges—and in particular, this most primal and essential one of sexual unity—are a platform for so much more. This is the reason for the very particular laws the Zohar gives in regard to keeping the frequency and practice of this engagement as the number one "commandment" for a committed married couple.

Another aspect of the sexual union lies in the verbal or grammatical source of this engagement. As mentioned previously, one of three obligations a husband has toward his wife upon nuptials, by Jewish law, is the commitment to keep her satisfied and provided for, concerning her physical pleasure, on a regular basis. This obligation is called *onah*, or her "time," if translated from Hebrew. Yet, Kabbalistic teachings add a layer to this principle, and state that in the root of this Hebrew term lies the word *laanot*, which means to "reply" or "answer," that is, to provide a response to the wife's need or request. This stands to suggest that the sexual union is so imperative that its absence may suggest a lack of communication or "solution" to a request presented by the wife to her husband. If we examine it at face value, we often hear about the female's endless "headache" and the male's incessant need, yet in realty, the situation can be quite different, and at times, completely opposite.

# Quickstep Meditation

We will choose the combination of כוק, a sequence that represents a spiritual connection so strong that it ignites the sexual energy, which is the vehicle to the divine emanation. In essence, the כוק Name of God is unique because it provides a circular deliverance of a spiritual connection.

First, it emits the spiritual connection necessary for the sexual exchange, and then the sexual exchange ignites the spiritual union with the Creator. If this energetic combination is practiced with an open heart and trust, it can be one of the most profound combinations among the Seventy-Two Names of God and overall Kabbalistic practice.

When applying this sequence,[29] look deep inside and compare these choices to a broader spectrum of relation; not only the strength it requires to be a one-time connector to your partner and the divine, but what tremendous change the applied attitude of this circular energy can have on a cosmic, universal level.

Remember that you can digitally scan the letters or gaze at them, visualize them with your eyes closed, or chant them to the sound of KOK If you choose the two former options out of the four, you may want to copy this sequence on a small piece of paper that you keep in a safe and respected spot in order to utilize this power. You may also incorporate all four utilization options and switch from one to another as you progress.

Gaze at this sequence for a few minutes before going inside.

Sit in a comfortable position, close your eyes, and take a deep breath through your mouth, all the way up to the top of your lungs. Now, purse your lips and let your breath out slowly as if you're whistling through

29 Note: a similar meditation can be practiced together alongside your partner or facing one another. If you choose to practice together, you may follow the same routine, but begin and end with holding each other's hands while breathing and meditating. Alternatively, lean against a wall and allow the other to relax against your chest, while closing hands together on the leaning partner's heart/chest area.

them. Repeat this three times, and keep a comfortable posture while reverting to normal breathing.

Slowly allow the three-letter sequence of כוק to appear before you and float in your mind's eye.

I like to see these sequences as if they are floating on water in tiny ripples toward me and back, while gazing with my eyes closed. Allow the letters to form and heighten in your memory and breathe "the breath of life" into them. Merge the goal that you have in relation to this sequence and combine it with the energy you create.

It can be a soulful and beautiful connection with a potential soul match, or you can go further and expand into a peaceful existence to all. If you are aiming to unite with your current or hopeful partner in a respectful and harmonious manner, that will definitely and unequivocally serve the greater goal of a harmonious, sacred, and everlasting relationship. You may also alternate or gradually arrive at a higher-level goal as you advance and progress.

When you feel safe and strong in this frequency and the light it emits, gradually allow both your hands to touch the ground, and revert to normal breathing. Gradually and slowly open your eyes. You may want to remain seated in this position for a few moments before getting back on your feet. Drink a glass of water to quench the energy you've emitted.

## Androgyny

Kabbalistic views of the upper sephirah of Binah versus the bottom sephirah of Malchut, represent two aspects of the feminine attributes of the divine connection. The upper Binah represents the feminine mother, while the bottom Malchut represents the spouse or partner and uses the erotic feminine aspects of the same representation.

Kabbalistic teachings tell us that although the upper Binah is the epitome of the mother, the nurturer, and the caretaker, conversely to the erotic Malchut, both of them still represent the procreation of offspring. The upper sephirah may be responsible for the tangibility of this continuance, while the bottom sephirah is responsible for everything that exists externally to the soul level of Atzilut, or emanation. This role is exceptionally imperative, as nothing can exist without Malchut giving spiritual birth to it in its own sensual manner.

Binah, in this structure, is viewed as the tongue, while Malchut is viewed as the mouth.

Interestingly enough, the Kabbalistic teachings in regard to the sephirot relate both aspects of masculinity and femininity to all of them in a more fluid and flowing manner, rather than a distinct separation between the two genders and their representations within the Tree of Life. Thus, Binah as an example, is also related to as עלמא דדוכרא, which is Aramaic for the "male world." In this perspective, Binah holds both feminine and masculine facets where the masculine side is the nurturer and creator of abundance, while the feminine side of Binah is the one responsible for the orderly structure, thereby driving this abundance to all lower sefirot.

In the same fashion, Malchut as the daughter in this mother–offspring relationship with Binah as the matriarch is being related to as the "guardian angel" in its masculine facet. Here, Malchut holds both roles of the angel—when she's the masculine, she's sending blessings as the embodiment of these blessings, and when she's the feminine, she holds the jurisdiction of driving these blessings into the world by being their carrier who was impregnated with them by the masculine side beforehand.

Overall in the Tree, feminine and masculine aspects of the sephirot aren't represented solely by who's topping whom; Malchut, as an example, is below Binah, and thus feminine due to its location, but Malchut is also on top of the world of souls in the lower level, thus gaining the position of the masculine.

The mere accurate representation of these two aspects is represented by the dichotomy of the influencer and the influenced.

In other words, the focal point isn't how I relate to someone else, but rather how I relate to myself upon seeing myself in another, and not as two different entities. Practically speaking, whenever there's difficulty, the most efficient way to solve it is to look within and adjust particular factors, thus turning these difficulties into understandings.

Emotions have the tendency to grow a life of their own that is entirely unrelated to the source that initiated that sensation. This concept is called *yenikah*, which means drawing sustenance from a source, as in the sense of breastfeeding.

The principle of oneness versus separateness is the perception that one and the other are essentially the same thing. The Zohar tells us that any love that is dependent on something isn't going to last; but what kind of love is it if it isn't dependent on something? It's more of a recognition that you and the other share a commonality that is greater than any particular feature. This relates to the story of creation in Genesis. In some commentaries, the creation of Eve out of Adam's rib isn't an accurate depiction. In Hebrew, the word for rib that is used in this story is *tzela*, which translates as "side." Thus, Eve was created from an aspect or a side of Adam, which means they are essentially one person, rather than two separate entities.

The fundamental value of us as humans is that we are an *extension* of divinity; a person isn't composed of their actions! A human is significant because he simply is the spark of the divine without ever doing anything. And thus, it can be influential to look at our relationships in this fashion. Nonetheless, the only way we manifest and utilize this point of simply being is if we practice this intrinsic positivity with our choices and behaviors, and the way we relate to other people, our partners in particular.

# Chapter 18
## The Magic of Temporary Abstinence

Jewish and Kabbalistic teachings tell us about the sanctity of marriage (the law of Niddah mentioned previously). The obligation to abstain from sexual exchange around a woman's menstruation, suggests an erotic separation for two weeks out of the month, around the woman's menstruating days, and a week after, leading to fourteen days of no sexual exchange. The principle behind this law is the ability to maintain the fire in the relationship and allow for the couple to indulge in a mini honeymoon every month when they finally reunite. Is it a guarantee for a successful long-term sexual and romantic dyad? Not always, but if this practice is applied, in addition to other actions and choices that allow our exchange to remain respectful and fluid, these suggestions may well assist in the maintenance of a sublime sensual life.

## Quickstep Meditation

We will choose the combination of עַרִי , a sequence that represents an absolute certainty in the light force of the Creator—a spiritual connection so strong that it ignites the sexual energy as a vehicle to divine emanation. In essence, the עךיִ Name of God is extraordinary since it provides a circular deliverance of the creation source, which was one creature made of different "sides" (the word "rib," or *tzela* in Hebrew). עךיִ represents reverting to it with the understanding that we are essentially one and should utilize goodly sparks in order to once more establish a divine unity with our partner.

If this energetic combination is practiced with an open heart and trust, it can be very helpful for our well-being and fresh sensual exchange.

When applying this sequence, look deep inside and compare these choices to a broader spectrum of relation; not only the strength it requires to connect to your partner and the divine, but what tremendous change the applied attitude of this circular energy can have on a cosmic, universal level.

Remember that you can digitally scan the letters or gaze at them, visualize them with your eyes closed, or chant them to the sound of ARY. If you choose the two former options out of the four, you may want to copy this sequence on a small piece of paper that you keep in a safe and respected spot in order to utilize this power. You may also incorporate all four utilization options and switch from one to another as you progress.

Gaze at this sequence for a few minutes before going inside.

Sit in a comfortable position, close your eyes, and take a deep breath through your mouth, all the way up to the top of your lungs. Now, purse your lips and let your breath out slowly as if you're whistling through them. Repeat this three times, and keep a comfortable posture while reverting to normal breathing.

Slowly allow the three-letter sequence of כוק to appear before you and float in your mind's eye.

I like to see these sequences as if they are floating on water in tiny ripples toward me and back, while gazing with my eyes closed. Allow the letters to form and heighten in your memory and breathe "the breath of life" into them. Merge the goal that you have in relation to this sequence and combine it with the energy you create.

It can be a soulful and beautiful connection with a potential soul match, or you can go further and expand into a peaceful existence to all. If you are aiming to unite with your current or hopeful partner in a respectful and harmonious manner, that will definitely and unequivocally serve the greater goal of a harmonious, sacred, and everlasting relationship. You may also alternate or gradually arrive at a higher-level goal as you advance and progress.

When you feel safe and strong in this frequency and the light it emits, gradually allow both your hands to touch the ground, and revert to normal breathing. Gradually and slowly open your eyes. You may want to remain seated in this position for a few moments before getting back on your feet. Drink a glass of water to quench the energy you've emitted.

# Chapter 19
## Renewing Sacred Unity Regularly

If the Creator is "perfect," what prompted Him to create the universe? What void was he seeking to fill?

Kabbalistic teachings tell us that what the Creator sought was the sacred union: marriage. A committed relationship of this form necessitates the existence of someone distinct from yourself, with whom to share your life, the union of husband and wife. The Creator chose humanity as the perfect partner he desires to merge with.

In that sense, we are definitely not his children, but his spouse.

That said, this desired union has been a form of a roller coaster, to say the least, between the human and divine entities, and that is an immediate reflection of the soul unity between a man and a woman. Truly, a life that is lived and shared will always encounter obstacles, loss of faith, disbelief, dysphoria, and disappointments. Yes, very similarly to the divine-human dyad, if one desires the reshaping of this exchange and its maintenance, no matter what it takes, one will find a way.

Is there a factor of self-control in this godly–human equation and its earthly counterpart?

Kabbalistic teachings say it is in fact a mandatory requirement; a person who lacks self-control can never live up to one's own standards. In other words, one is well aware of what the correct conduct is yet fails to pursue it for various unsatisfactory reasons. Rabbinical teachings shed a more profound light on this notion by stating that our inept God-given nature embeds the ability to "order ourselves" toward certain obligations. Due to that source in particular, we can attain self-control on a larger scale, which can be applied in many areas of our lives, and in romantic relationships in particular.

The Zohar emphasizes the physical/instinctual pull versus the strength of the soul's desires. The unbalance between these two can determine your soul growth forward, or potentially cause it to remain static or revert backward.

Ironically, although it appears to us that our physical/instinctual draw is by far stronger, the practice of self-control enables a balancing act of these opponents and a renewed stamina to "do the right thing."

Kabbalah calls our wicked tendencies *yetzer hara*, or the "evil inclination." By this notion, we are taught that the most efficient manner to combat this wickedness is to practice joy. By being happy, you give yourself the energy, motivation, and will to fight. However, if you are despondent, it will be very easy for the yetzer hara to beat you, in his constant vigilance, by tricking you toward poor choices, which will precede a sense of guilt. From that point on, the battle is over, and the evil twin won; it is by far easier for that opponent to attain the upper hand if one feels less worthy, even temporarily and circumstantially.

## What's Love Got to Do with It?

This most ancient and yet unsatisfactorily replied-to inquiry always rises to challenge our artificial status quo with nature. If we look at scientific and biological reasoning, yes, we strive to fall in love so we can procreate and thus maintain the human species. Yet, could this truly be it? Be it *the* largest aim, it may still leave us unsatisfied and bewildered as to the intricate values of love and intimacy.

The Kabbalistic conception of human love and sexuality is completely different. By this notion, we are driven to search for our divine images for our quintessential selves.

In the original story of creation in Genesis, we are told that man was originally created as a "two-sided" being: "Male and female He created them, and He called their name 'man.'" The Creator then split this two-sided creature into two, and ever since, the divided halves of the divine image seek and yearn for one another. It is imperative to mention here that commentaries stress that procreation was not an issue in this strange androgynous state, and thus was not the reason for the "do over" and final separation of the two. This reflects on procreation being a non-entity in the quest of "love and romance," contrary to the biological suggestion.

The two-faced creature did not contain half individuals; man is a full-fledged personality and woman is a full-fledged personality, independently. But there are elements in their transcendental persona that remain incomplete if they don't find one another. There's something missing in each of them; they were once a part of a greater whole.

The human race is, in essence, one entity: a male–female singularity. When man and woman come together and unite in a sensual union, they recreate the divine image in which they were both formed as one.

The teachings of Kabbalah take this a step further, seeing the male–female dynamic not just as two genders within a species, but rather two forms of energy: an internal energy and a projective energy. Feminine energy and masculine energy coexist in every person, and in every part of nature.

Divine energy, in fact, is interchangeably described in the feminine and in the masculine. Contrary to the common perception of the "patriarchal" creator in Biblical scripts, many of the divine attributes are feminine, such as the Shekinah.

What we thus experience is a separation of two energies, and a yearning to become one whole once again via sensual union.

This attraction, which manifests itself in many physical sensations, is essentially the desire to become a complete, divine whole, connecting to our source in the Creator. This yearning and longing does not suggest that we were ever truly disconnected, yet we may go off on our own individual, narcissistic, even selfish, paths. And here, there's a voice inside us saying, *I yearn for something greater*, or *something is missing*. When a man is attracted to a woman, or a woman to a man, it may seem to be a very biological urge, but from a Kabbalistic stance, it's just a physical manifestation of a very deep, spiritual attraction.

In and of itself, the unity of male and female is a divine act—a divine experience—regardless of any notions of procreation or survival forces.

## Attachment and Long-Term Relationships

The British psychologist John Bowlby introduced his attachment theory in the '50s. He suggested that children are innately predisposed with one of three attachments styles, namely, secure or insecure, and the latter encompassing two other styles, avoidant or anxious. These tendencies, which Bowlby exemplified in his research and later via "the strange situation" experiment carried out by his assistant Mary Ainsworth, are so embedded in the young child that without any intervention or the mere understanding of their mechanisms, they will impact one's overall ability to successfully attain, sustain, and maintain an adult relationship.

Let us now shift this theory into our Kabbalistic discussion and its relation to interpersonal exchange.

When we look at a communication between two partners that can hold one tendency or another in their blueprint, we are propelled to see and understand how challenging a true soul connection may become.

Kabbalistic teachings, nonetheless, add a layer to this preconceived notion that is utterly comprehensible in other facets. The former tells us that in order to attain and maintain soul connection and a sacred exchange—overall and in the sensual arena, per se—we need to recognize these tendencies and diffuse them as a prerequisite of this union. Conversely to the more common psychological approach of this engagement, in Kabbalistic teachings, we do not suggest the acquisition of a partner who may fit our attachment styles. We have designated soul mates and we are connected to their souls, rather than their earthly tendencies or features. And so, we are simply prompted to accept these features as present; nonetheless, we are encouraged to promptly address them in a fashion that can only be accomplished by a significant other. As an interjection, one may benefit from consulting a professional in the field of relationships when applying these altera-tion methods; but, these, regardless, can be achieved and pursued by the couple independently, without any external help. As we keep being reminded, we encompass the divine spark within us; these sparks are a beacon, and thus we simply cannot fail to lead our sacred relationships into a safe haven if a genuine intention (Kavanah) is applied.

What does it take? It can vary, but as an example, let us suggest that the husband is an avoidant styled individual, while the wife is anxious. In a general view of this relationship, we will see a very clingy, haunted female who goes to great lengths in order to get attention and affec-tion from a closed-up and supremely nonchalant male. Now, these are surface presentations of a much deeper challenge both partners pos-sess. Yet, if we break it down to the fundamental basics, we will find that both are reacting in these allegedly opposing manners due to the same fear: the fear of rejection. The avoidant husband was conditioned further in this direction by a non-relating mother, while the clingy wife was overly showered with unhealthy attention and anxiety in her early, impressionable years; but they are both afraid of being left in a void, or lack that life vest they so seek. In Kabbalist views, right there is the anchor to their redemption. If both acknowledge and make valid effort to react in a less individually typical fashion upon any trigger, they will jointly transition into a more secure style in their attachment, and from there, the sky is the limit.

## Quickstep Meditation

We will choose the combination of הרה , a sequence that represents cutting off the umbilical cord of past experience. In the relational sphere, we are often overwhelmed with what is expected of us but using this sequence can allow us to activate the power of our primordial, divine essences, unrelated to the shape and features we were provided with in this lifetime.

When applying this sequence,[30] look deep inside and compare these choices to a broader spectrum of relation; not only the strength it requires to overcome your tendencies on occasion, but acknowledging the tremendous satisfaction and change the applied attitude of this energy can have on a cosmic, universal level.

Remember that you can digitally scan the letters or gaze at them, visualize them with your eyes closed, or chant them to the sound of HARACH. If you choose the two former options out of the four, you may want to copy this sequence on a small piece of paper that you keep in a safe and respected spot in order to utilize this power. You may also incorporate all four utilization options and switch from one to another as you progress.

Gaze at this sequence for a few minutes before going inside.

Sit in a comfortable position, close your eyes, and take a deep breath through your mouth, all the way up to the top of your lungs. Now, purse your lips and let your breath out slowly as if you're whistling through them. Repeat this three times and keep a comfortable posture while reverting to normal breathing.

Slowly allow the three-letter sequence of הרה to appear before you and float in your mind's eye.

I like to see these sequences as if they are floating on water in tiny ripples toward me and back, while gazing with my eyes closed. Allow the letters to form and heighten in your memory and breathe "the breath of life" into them. Merge the goal that you have in relation to this sequence and combine it with the energy you create.

---

30 Note: a similar meditation can be practiced together alongside your partner or facing one another. If you choose to practice together, you may follow the same routine, but begin and end with holding each other's hands while breathing and meditating. Alternatively, lean against a wall and allow the other to relax against your chest, while closing hands together on the leaning partner's heart/chest area.

It can be a soulful and beautiful connection with a potential soul match, or you can go further and expand into a peaceful existence to all. If you are aiming to unite with your current or hopeful partner in a respectful and harmonious manner, that will definitely and unequivocally serve the greater goal of a harmonious, sacred, and everlasting relationship. You may also alternate or gradually arrive at a higher-level goal as you advance and progress.

When you feel safe and strong in this frequency and the light it emits, gradually allow both your hands to touch the ground, and revert to normal breathing. Gradually and slowly open your eyes. You may want to remain seated in this position for a few moments before getting back on your feet. Drink a glass of water to quench the energy you've emitted.

# Chapter 20
## The Love Tank: Gas up Your Relationship

In the reality we live in today, we tend to enter a relationship in a non-chalant fashion, regarding its need for maintenance. In other words, we fail to relate to the parts of our lives that come after the couple rides gently into the sunset and the credits run smoothly on our TV screens, at the end of this fantastic scenario.

In reality, that phase that we are never exposed to in the romance novel feature will come, and we should aim to be prepared.

Sure, it is a great gift of sheer bliss to indulge in the novelty of a zesty relationship. You're walking on air, no care in the world, you can almost hear the cartoon blue bird tweeting a perfect song in your ear as you caress the ground with your feet, barely touching it.

This phase is phenomenal, and whether it is felt as the most extreme levels of joy, or simply managed cerebrally, it has a shelf life. Now, that does not mean that we are bound to fall out of a magnificent love after the conclusion of this phase. It only means that we should train our minds to compare to our relationships to a very luxurious, sexy, brand new car. That car holds the potential to either take us anywhere and have our minds blown and overwhelmed with bliss over the new sights and experiences we could be exposed to, or conversely, to come to a complete halt in the road and have us stranded and frustrated over the breakdown of our remarkable vehicle.

What do these two polarities lean on? They lean on one single component: the precious and **correct** gas we fill the car with.

In our great minds, we can come up with solutions to almost every single problem or difficulty under the sun, yet when it comes to more simplistic steps that may be required in our personal, relational, love life, we become numb, uncreative, and paralyzed.

In the spirit of this analogy, the gas we invest in is supremely imperative. Even if we "gas up" the car, but choose the wrong octane, we will pay an even bigger price, potentially, because our romantic exchanges are fragile and unique.

The main component that will lead this affair in the right direction and toward the correct gas pipe in the virtual gas station of life is the elimination of selfness; it should be gradually geared and transitioned into otherness, at least to a 50 percent degree of action. What could this mean? Simple. It means putting our desires and wants on the back burner, while getting involved in the vitality of the "**us**." Note that I did not say "the other's" desires and quests. This is for two major reasons. First, there is no other; we are a single unit that simply appears divided under falsely apparent physical separation. We are not really separate, but the restriction our bodies place on the tangible appearance of our souls and energies makes this a challenge to disregard.

The second reason for the "**us**" versus "**them**" rationale is that if we both try to only give, there will be a void in our "sacred container," namely our "half full/half empty" glass. Essentially, this means that there's no real altered view of life between the pessimistic **half empty** and the optimistic **half full**. In Kabbalistic terms, we are a full range "product" of divinity that encompasses both parts of this glass, and thus need to conduct ourselves and our partners to integrate as a single unit. The "us" is always greater than its components in this view, and thus should always be nurtured and tended to.

Conversely to other esoteric teachings, Kabbalah does not suggest self-annihilation, but claims that we should strive for the unity and prosperous existence of the single relational unit, and more important, in this lifetime, here and now, on earth, the world of action. There's no suggestion of self-deprivation or elimination of ego in this common practice. Yes, we are advised to utilize these egotistic tendencies toward the process of soul elevation, but not to dismiss the self, per se, body or mind.

Do these "love fuels" tend to allow our dyadic experiences to run better in different stages of our relationships? And what are these stages? We will expand on this topic even further as we progress in this journey, but the simple answer to this question is, "Yes!"

## Methodologies:

Words of affirmation: Verbal. It is crucial that your partner receives affirmations from *you*, regardless of anyone else. One can receive a hundred accolades from others and still feel self-conscious in the absence of a partner's reassurance.

Gift giving: Action. If your partner is one who feels reassured by this kind of love fluid, make certain your gift is suitable and rewarding to your partner; in other words, avoid rewarding your partner with a "gift" that benefits you more than them.

Attention and time: Action. This is an important octane, because nothing can replace your personal attention and surrender to the special time together with your partner.

Acts of kindness: Action. It is of no importance who the more "prominent" partner in the relationship is or how much they "do." If your partner needs your help with something, there shouldn't be anything that is of higher importance to you than accommodating their peace of mind.

Romantic time: Action. Placing your physical bodies in the same location is not applicable as quality time spent together. This should be a time that both partners feel is rewarding and rejuvenating to the relationship or mutual dedication to this unity. Keep in mind that although we are in fact spiritual divine beings who encompass sparks of the Creator, we are still placed in physical bodies in order to carry out these spiritual practices. Romantic bestowing can be applied to erotic time spent together, caressing, holding, kissing, and reassuring one another's "bodies" with the affirmations and strength that only a romantic unity can provide.

A side note of these practices: It is important to keep in mind that the specific "charge" you're entertaining via a specific *gas of choice* might be different from your partner's choice at the same stage. If this is related to and addressed, a more successful flow in the relationship can be achieved, no matter what stage or length of the exchange.

## Male and Female Energies

Many schools of thought and theories posit the core essentiality of male and female energies. In our Kabbalistic sphere, we can refer to them as the male and female souls or sources, which are inevitably gearing toward an essence reunion into one complete and divine soul connection. In this discussion, we encounter a variety of methodologies that may shift toward a unification, but what potentially differentiates Kabbalah from other spiritual practices is the fact that in the former, we don't see these entities as separate to begin with. Yes, on a tangible level they may appear so by being embodied in a characteristically female or male bodies, yet on a spiritual level, they have no separate existence. Let us use a more comprehensible example that is also true conceptually in relation to Kabbalistic wisdom. By this perception, we look at the act of inhaling breath as self-preservation, a receiving mode—the feminine. And we look at exhaling breath as a giving mode—masculine. We are literally affecting creation. It is externally bound, as mentioned in Genesis 2:7: "Then the LORD God formed man of the dust of the ground, and breathed into his nostrils the breath of life; and man became a living soul."

This *alleged* dichotomy is the mere essence of creation, but no inhalation is independent from its following exhalation as long as there's the breath of life in the living being.

When we observe the Tree of Life in this sense, we can divide the ten sephirot into a number of faculties that can help us better integrate the masculine right side of the Tree with the feminine left side of it harmoniously, or at least with less friction.

# Gendered Language

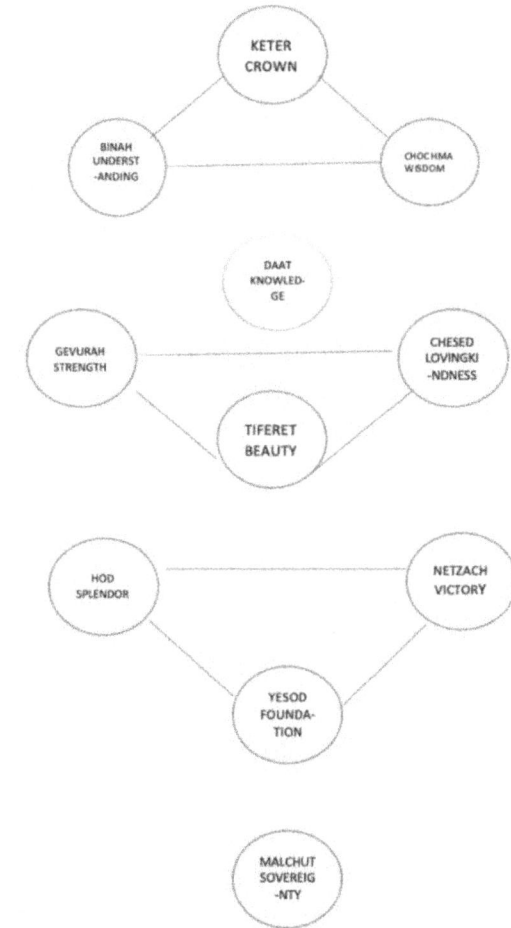

KETER
CROWN

BINAH
UNDERST
-ANDING

CHOCHMA
WISDOM

DAAT
KNOWLED-
GE

GEVURAH
STRENGTH

CHESED
LOVINGKI
-NDNESS

TIFERET
BEAUTY

HOD
SPLENDOR

NETZACH
VICTORY

YESOD
FOUNDA-
TION

MALCHUT
SOVEREIG
-NTY

The importance of language, utterance, and verbality were mentioned previously as divine tools of creation. We discussed the importance of speech and how, in Kabbalistic terms, this universe was created by the godly pronunciation of specific verbal combinations.

In this fashion, it is imperative to keep in mind that the two parts of the soul, namely the feminine and masculine, use their verbal skills in different ways, and thus at times come across as an actual lack of communication or misunderstanding based solely on these differences.

The masculine energy tends to use its verbality in order to "dominate" a situation, or provide a solution. We can often witness males argue harshly simply to make a point of having the "upper hand." In feminine energy, conversely, the use of utterance is different. It is used as a reward; communication itself is rewarding to females, thus the application of the "silent treatment" is far more prevalently used by females, even though it may not hold a threat to their partner, and at times, it may be considered a reward.

The three upper faculties are cognitive; we observe the differences between these energies in the realm of thought.

Chochma, being the male realm, relates to an idea, like having the feeling of a "light bulb" switched on overhead.

In order to develop the idea that emerges, in comes Binah, the feminine, to propel its development.

Daat is not a formal sephirah, but as the mediator, it propels the idea that was founded and developed into a real action mode.

The word Daat has its imperative significance in the sense of pure action. If we go back to the scripts and look at the initial act of intimacy between Adam and Eve in Genesis 4:1: "And the man knew Eve his wife; and she conceived and bore Cain, and said: 'I have gotten a man with the help of the LORD,'" we witness its strength.

The concept of *knowing* is the true dual act of creation and intimacy, and the word *Daat* translates as "knowledge."

The notion of Daat is the fusion between masculine and feminine energies in the very manner in which it was first carried out in the Garden of Eden.

The next three faculties in the Tree are personality traits. Chesed, the masculine, is emitted in benevolence and transcendence. It is the will to provide and give independently of a methodical examination of its service to the other. Conversely, Gevurah, the feminine, is disciplinary, meticulous restraint, and challenging choices. It may sound very disadvantageous, but if you take an example of a couple walking down the street who encounter a beggar, the Chesed tendency may be driving them to give the person some change, but the charity bestowed might be used to support an addiction or misbehavior. The Gevurah tendency, however, will likely choose to not give away currency, but may choose to purchase food for this person or help with shelter.

Here as well, the mitigator Tiferet may influence both side's ability to see things mutually. It may propel the masculine to strive to make his counterpart blissful in the way that *she* views bliss, and this may equivalently allow the feminine to avoid the need to critique her counterpart, such as in daily occurrences of, "This should be done *my* way." Tiferet can help with accepting the other's way of doing things and becoming more lenient.

The last three faculties of the Tree are functional or practical. While Netazch allows the masculine to move forward and push progression, the Hod component is prone to follow, be consistent, diligent, and complement the masculinity of Netazch.

Yesod comes to mediate by supporting the masculine in his need for achievement, while allowing the feminine Hod to feel at ease and calm about the choices that are made in the pursuit of that achievement or success. We often see men feeling suffocated over the need to be responsible and support the family, while longing for a different path. Yesod can be utilized to find the middle ground between that pursuit and the feminine need for stability by providing a more mediating and long-term solution. It also enables the sustainability of supporting one another's "dreams" for a longer period than the "honeymoon period." We often refer to this period as unrealistic or unpractical, but if we utilize Yesod in the quest of grounding, we can marry a carefree flare that is seasoned with stability at the same time. It does require thinking out of the box and a mutual effort toward this goal, just as with all acquisitions of a true spiritual connection.

# Chapter 21
## What Do We Love?

Kabbalistic teachings tell us this definition is not about someone's features, their status, their qualities, or even their "goodness," but rather their "*godness*." This may sound entirely esoteric and unclear, but if you place it in tangible terms, it may be quite comprehensible. The Kabbalah equates love to "godness" or divine substance, so essentially, this element of soul is the same element in all of us—it is simply dispensed into different bodies and restricted by the container, or the vessel. Yet, the souls inside our bodies, which are the essence of love, strive to reunite with the same element placed in another body, synonymous with the manner in which water drops tends to be "drawn" to one another and form a joint stream.

In our lives, we are placed in tangible, physical bodies in order to carry out a soul mission, yet the soul inside always wants to reunite with its counterparts, and thus our bodies experience that longing and craving, which translates as the sensation of love.

## Why Divorce Is Necessary

Looking at the status of relational commitment in today's world, we can solemnly declare that the institute of marriage is standing on its last legs. That said, we witness an opposing phenomenon that perhaps has always been present, but in our world of globalization and social media, has become even grander and more profound. I'm referring to the wedding planning industry. Yes, young girls have always dreamed of their wedding days, essentially in the most fairytale-like notions that include the fairest prince, the prettiest dress, and the most exquisite "forever after" future. But, within the insurmountable exposure of social media, bigger is not only better, it can never be big enough. And so, this industry has created a reality in which your desired outcome should be flawless, over the top, and clearly unrealistic, especially in light of the realization that what happens after you say "I do" is far more challenging, yet imperative to the survival of your committed relationship.

Kabbalistic teachings tell us that the concept of divorce is essential to the success of marriage. In fact, it is referred to as a product of chaos, which was the initial state of creation, before the Creator decided to put things in order, and thus, it is a part of the divine whole.

According to Kabbalah, this chaos resulted from the aggressive and assertive divine energies that filled the primordial world. Each energy focused exclusively on its task, unable to accommodate the others. They operated with independence and disregard, which resulted in chaos. We are created as independent and fierce individuals who long for connection and warmth on one hand, while being excruciatingly rigid in our need for independence and space on the other. These dual forces stand for a committed relationship, namely marriage, versus a divorce, repectively.

It is logical, therefore, that the human—a product of both worlds—is an amalgam of both assertion and accommodation. We are fiercely independent, yet we yearn earnestly to be touched by others. Marriage is a product of our accommodating side, whereas divorce is a product of our assertiveness and need for independence.

When we finally find our soul connection or the match to our spiritual quest, we revel in our bond greatly; then, slowly, the realization dawns that gaining love requires the surrender of a significant portion of independence. We are no longer able to choose *as we please* and do *as we feel.* We must now take another into account and do only what is right for both parties.

If we forgo our independence in favor of love, we grow resentful of those we love. If we jealously guard our independence, we risk alienating the ones we love. There must be a happy medium that enables us to retain our independence and our love.

Our point of origin, our transcendental selves, is our humanity. When we accommodate each other, we transcend the outer shell of our particular differences and engage our core humanity. Thus, rather than confining us, accommodation can be a transcendental and liberating experience, an opportunity to engage our truest state of being.

However, this is only true when we *choose* to accommodate. When accommodation is forced on us, we don't transcend our differences and engage our common humanity. We remain confined to our outer shells of differences, and we are forced by others to give, nonetheless. Rather than opening us to our true state of being, such giving restricts our freedom, drains our vitality, and shuts us off from our very selves.

Kabbalistic teachings remind us that the mention of a committed unity in the scriptures is immediately followed by the laws of divorce, clearly not for non-associative reasons. It says in Deuteronomy 24:1: "When a man taketh a wife, and marrieth her, then it cometh to pass, if she find no favour in his eyes, because he hath found some unseemly thing in her, that he writeth her a bill of divorcement, and giveth it in her hand, and sendeth her out of his house."

This choice to state the laws of nuptials and divorce, one after the other, in such proximity, carries a potent lesson. It reminds us that marriage and its attendant compromises are not foisted on us. They are a choice we make freely, every day.

The option to end a marriage is always available, and if we remain in our marriage, it is out of our own choosing. In other words, the claim that some may make regarding the "ball and chain" does not apply in Kabbalistic views of the sacred unity. Here, it is strictly a choice, and it is made on a daily basis by both parties.

This awareness is the bridge that allows us to retain our independence alongside our need to connect; it is the ingredient that can save a marriage. If, when making compromises in marriage, we feel set upon and compelled, the marriage can drain our sense of self and well-being. Alternatively, if we remember that marriage is a choice and that in it, we choose freely to give of ourselves, it actually reinforces our sense of self and independence, because the choice to give can be made only when we are independent enough to make choices.

## Quickstep Meditation

We will choose the combination of הזי, a sequence that represents accessing divine energies to invite order rather than chaos into our lives in general, and our relational lives in particular. When applying this sequence, look deep inside and compare these choices to a broader spectrum of relation; not only the strength it requires to see your choice to make your relational dyad sustainable and blissful, but what this choice and the ability to ascend into the higher spheres of existence above chaos can have on a cosmic, universal level.

Remember that you can digitally scan the letters or gaze at them, visualize them with your eyes closed, or chant them to the sound of HAAZY. If you choose the two former options out of the four, you may want to copy this sequence on a small piece of paper that you keep in a safe and respected spot in order to utilize this power. You may also incorporate all four utilization options and switch from one to another as you progress.

Gaze at this sequence for a few minutes before going inside.

Sit in a comfortable position, close your eyes, and take a deep breath through your mouth, all the way up to the top of your lungs. Now, purse your lips and let your breath out slowly as if you're whistling through them. Repeat this three times and keep a comfortable posture while reverting to normal breathing.

Slowly allow the three-letter sequence of הזי to appear before you and float in your mind's eye.

I like to see these sequences as if they are floating on water in tiny ripples toward me and back, while gazing with my eyes closed. Allow the letters to form and heighten in your memory and breathe "the breath of life" into them. Merge the goal that you have in relation to this sequence and combine it with the energy you create.

It can be a soulful and beautiful connection with a potential soul match, or you can go further and expand into a peaceful existence to all. If you are aiming to unite with your current or hopeful partner in a respectful and harmonious manner, that will definitely and unequivocally serve the greater goal of a harmonious, sacred, and everlasting relationship. You may also alternate or gradually arrive at a higher-level goal as you advance and progress.

When you feel safe and strong in this frequency and the light it emits, gradually allow both your hands to touch the ground, and revert to normal breathing. Gradually and slowly open your eyes. You may want to remain seated in this position for a few moments before getting back on your feet. Drink a glass of water to quench the energy you've emitted.

# Chapter 22
## The Feminine Mystique

Kabbalistic teachings are very particular about the higher terrain in which the feminine soul walks. Conversely to many religious scripts, in Kabbalah, we observe a very lenient and even adoring and fascinated view of the feminine.

Simply by the embodiment of a feminine soul, the Kabbalists tell us, one is exempt from many ritualistic requirements, prayers, and other forms of worship. Kabbalah goes to great lengths to emphasize the greatness of the feminine soul and its multifaceted function by stating that it does not require reincarnation, because at a core state, it is flawless.

The sages tell us that the subconscious male quest of femaleness is based on that perfection that the masculine aims to attain.

The Kabbalistic term *alma de nukba* can be translated from Aramaic as "the feminine world," a world that the Kabbalists were utterly fascinated by. The female is viewed as a form of higher specimen, and the Kabbalists took awe in her form, her blood, her womb, and her beauty.

Kabbalistic teachings relate to the tenth sephirah of Malchut as the representation of Shekinah, the female counterpart of godliness. Malchut's representation of the Shekinah is multifaceted; not only is she the only form of channel or connection between human and divine interaction via the Tree of Life, but she's also a representation of the shift to the form of every woman in society—leading women in particular—while playing the double role of head to lower soul levels, and bottom to higher ones, in the different realms of soul existence.

```
        AK
     ATZILUT
      BRIAH
    YETZIRAH
     ASSIYAH
```

The above triangle represents the levels of soul. In this manner, if a soul is in the level of Briah, which is the third level of soul, then Malchut overheads Keter on the lower level of Yetzirah while being the bottom component to the world of Briah, and overheads Briah's Keter from the upper level of Atzilut.

Going back to the feminine place in this fascinating realm, in his mystical work Sha'arey Orah (Gates of Light), Rabbi Joseph Gikatilla relates to the feminine representations of the Shekinah as personified in our foremothers.

Gikatilla states that, "The Shekinah, in the time of Abraham our forefather, is Sarah, in the time of Yitzhak our forefather is Rivkah, and in the time of Ya'akov our forefather is called Rachel…"

The Zohar reflects a similar perspective on this notion stating that, "All of the females in the world share in her knowledge of the divine secret." (II Zohar105b)

The Shekinah holds a very active role in continuance to the higher value of the feminine contribution. The Zohar refers to this extreme contribution by her playing a rescuer's role to humanity in the negotiations with the divine.

"It is like a man who was in love with a woman who lived in the street of the tanners. If she had not been there, he would never have set foot in the place; but because she was there, it seemed to him like the street of the spice merchants, where all the finest scents in the world could be found." (III Zohar 115b)

As mentioned previously, the upper "feminine counterpart" to Malchut is Binah, which is viewed as the nurturing mother, and as the older, responsible provider; while the lower Malchut is viewed as the lover and the erotic, sexy component, but also as the daughter, the one who needs to be guided by the older feminine above.

As we discussed, letters, sequences, and words in the Hebrew alphabet are considered sacred and hold the power of creation. Along these lines, Kabbalistic teachings elaborate even more about the roles of Rachel and Leah in the relational, erotic triangle with Jacob.

By these teachings, the ten sephirot are aligned with the sacred name of God: י.ה.ו.ה

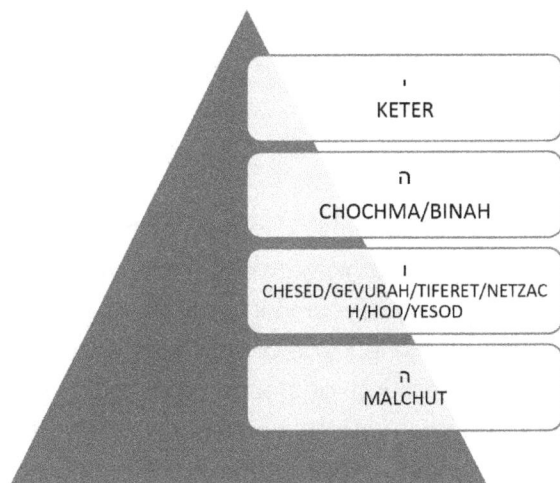

As presented in the chart, the upper ה is represented by Chochma/Binah, and the lower ה is represented by the quality of Malchut. Under these terms, Leah is considered the motherly, less erotic function represented by Binah or the upper ה, while Rachel, who's referred to as a

lower spiritual realm, is depicted in the lower sephirah of Malchut and takes the place of the lower ה in this equation. Both matriarchs are considered a depiction of the Shekinah and have their unique place, but as stated previously, the early perish of Rachel emerged, by Kabbalistic views, from Jacob's ascension to the name Israel, and by his soul elevation, that required a new order and his sole occupation of a "higher realm" soul mate, Leah.

# Quickstep Meditation

In this meditation we will aim to exhibit the actual connection between Binah and Malchut.

Observe the Tree of Life for a few minutes before going inside.

Sit in a comfortable position opposite your partner and place your hands on your knees or on your sides to start. Later in the meditation, it will be suggested that you move your hands to different locations.

Close your eyes and take a deep breath through your mouth, all the way up to the top of your lungs. Now, purse your lips and let your breath out slowly, as if you're whistling through them. Repeat this three times and keep a comfortable posture while reverting to normal breathing.

We will avoid any emphasis on other parts of the Tree and will immediately aim for the dynamic between these two sephirot.

Sit in a position that allows your feet to be placed close to your body.

Place one hand on the left side of your face, and the other where your body touches the ground, or around your feet.

The hand positioned on your face represents Binah. Start feeling the heat generated by this hand, while imagining a strong green light intensifying and humming through your body with every minute that passes.

Take a deep breath. Remain there and start building an intense energy again while breathing more deeply. Begin building the sensation of heat and intensity in the hand located near your feet, which represents Malchut. Imagine a bright blue light emanating from this area and warming up this region and your overall energy sphere.

Stay there for a few moments, then begin moving your face-positioned hand downward, while moving your feet-positioned hand upward, placing them one on top of the other over your heart. Begin circling your hands around your heart, building heat and energy. Imagine a bright blue and green light, like a yellowish combined fire, burning your inner truth and energy, emitting pure energetic force, and generating it up to the divine spheres.

You may feel inclined to shift in your seat, or move your waist. This is normal and logical; your body is only following your spiritual inclination.

Stay in this sensation and gradually retain normal breathing and position.

When you feel satisfied, take a deep breath, and open your eyes slowly and gently.

# Finding Balance

We are told that a true spiritual quest involves a complete emotional and internal transformation. We are bombarded with the notion of seclusion, with distancing ourselves from others and from our desires, with becoming frugal, with sharing only love and compassion to others with a form of self-annihilation.

Kabbalistic teachings tell us a completely different story, but let us discuss the basic *give and take* of the human dyad to begin.

A relationship is often a challenging terrain that can present us with obstacles, challenges, miscommunications, disagreements, and so forth. It is imperative for us to understand that these are natural components in a long and committed relationship. Although not presented in the Hollywood version of "our lives," in reality, this is more prevalent than the ride toward the sunset. It truly starts and ends with our commitment to the relationship, and the commitment to ourselves, to keep a truthful observation of each situation as it emerges, and dedicate ourselves to finding a reasonable solution that can appease all parties to a manageable degree.

Let us discuss a crude injustice that is unfortunately common within long-term relationships. Infidelity is a problematic one, but let's assume we are highly dedicated to the promotion of a social cause, and our partner decides to support another—perhaps even an opposing cause— for the moment.

This kind of disagreement may create an unprecedented explosion within our exchange; it may even feel like a direct hit, and a very intentional assault, to our dear sets of beliefs.

All of these feelings and emotions are suitable, correct, and maybe justifiable, but if there's a part of us at least that values the relationship more than its components, which are transitory, we will look at the bigger picture and strive to find a solution.

The biblical story of the sons of Jacob selling their brother Joseph to slavery in Egypt is one that can be used here to make this point. To shorten the story, at the tail end of this fiasco, Joseph becomes the Pharaoh's viceroy when the brothers are sent by their despaired father Jacob to solve the famine that crawled up to the land due to Egypt's harsh regulations. Jacob sends his sons, excluding the only one he has left from his beloved Rachel, the young Benjamin. The plot thickens down in Egypt when Joseph, unrecognizable to his brothers and viewed as a leading man in Egypt's royalty now, demands the presence of his youngest brother. The sons are forced to go and get Benjamin but encounter a very fearful and weak Jacob who tells them that if this son, who is all he has left of Rachel, fails to return to him, he'll surely perish. The brothers persuade Jacob and travel back to the land of Egypt, accompanied by young Benjamin, only to be faced with the very thing they most feared: the capturing and enslavement of Benjamin. Now, the brothers are a group of stubborn men who care more about themselves than their father, excluding Judah, who feels utterly responsible for his father's well-being—in a sense he places the "relationship" (his father's lifeline) before his own discomfort and anger (the social cause of disagreement, in our example). What does he do? He pleads with Joseph in a very unconventional manner, one that throws Joseph through a change of heart. We read in Genesis 44:18: "Then Judah came near unto him, and said: 'Oh my lord, let thy servant, I pray thee, speak a word in my lord's ears, and let not thine anger burn against thy servant; for thou art even as Pharaoh." A few verses later he adds: "Now therefore when I come to thy servant my father, and the lad is not with us; seeing that his soul is bound up with the lad's soul; it will come to pass, when he seeth that the lad is not with us, that he will die; and thy servants will bring down the gray hairs of thy servant our father, with sorrow, to the grave."

To conclude this theme, Joseph breaks down in tears in awe of his candid and caring brother Judah and reveals his identity. He ends up changing the entire faith of the children of Israel and their dire straits.

Going back to our discussion and this analogy, we always have a choice. We can keep our positions, regardless of their validity, and remain focused on being "right," or we can see the relationship as a greater goal than any other obstacle that may reveal itself along the way.

Kabbalistic teachings, unlike other esoteric practices, also do not promote full surrender and complete self-annihilation, as mentioned earlier. It does, nonetheless, suggest a common sense and an objective analysis of the situation. We are told that "the one who is lenient when needs to be firm, will be firm when needs to be lenient."[31] Simply put, it advises us that we need to measure our positions in different situations, and try to reflect it in our actions in order to promote the sustainability of a relationship, rather than choose the surrendering or dismissive act toward self in the *service* of the relationship, which may end up not being of any service at all.

## Quickstep Meditation

We will choose the combination of חהו, a sequence that represents resisting enslavement to jealousy and physical matter.

With this sequence, we are able to see the bigger picture and allow the truth to seep into our relational lives, rather than remaining stuck in

---

31 "Kohelet Rabbah 7:16." n.d. Www.Sefaria.Org. Accessed September 8, 2020. https://www.sefaria.org/Kohelet_Rabbah.7.16?lang=he.

our heads over a certain occurrence. When applying this sequence, look deep inside, and compare these choices to a broader spectrum; not only the strength it requires to see your choice to make your relational dyad sustainable and blissful, but what this choice to ascend into the higher spheres of existence above petty matters can have on a cosmic, universal level.

Remember that you can digitally scan the letters or gaze at them, visualize them with your eyes closed, or chant them to the sound of CHAHU. If you choose the two former options out of the four, you may want to copy this sequence on a small piece of paper that you keep in a safe and respected spot in order to utilize this power. You may also incorporate all four utilization options and switch from one to another as you progress.

Gaze at this sequence for a few minutes before going inside.

Sit in a comfortable position, close your eyes, and take a deep breath through your mouth, all the way up to the top of your lungs. Now, purse your lips and let your breath out slowly as if you're whistling through them. Repeat this three times and keep a comfortable posture while reverting to normal breathing.

Slowly allow the three-letter sequence of חהו to appear before you and float in your mind's eye.

I like to see these sequences as if they are floating on water in tiny ripples toward me and back, while gazing with my eyes closed. Allow the letters to form and heighten in your memory and breathe "the breath of life" into them. Merge the goal that you have in relation to this sequence and combine it with the energy you create.

It can be a soulful and beautiful connection with a potential soul match, or you can go further and expand into a peaceful existence to all. If you are aiming to unite with your current or hopeful partner in a respectful and harmonious manner, that will definitely and unequivocally serve the greater goal of a harmonious, sacred, and everlasting relationship. You may also alternate or gradually arrive at a higher-level goal as you advance and progress.

When you feel safe and strong in this frequency and the light it emits, gradually allow both your hands to touch the ground, and revert to normal breathing. Gradually and slowly open your eyes. You may want to remain seated in this position for a few moments before getting back on your feet. Drink a glass of water to quench the energy you've emitted.

# Marriage

What a strange concept marriage is. We quest to find another, who seems to complement our alleged values on some level, and then we proceed to bind our lives together in this unnatural manner in which we may misplace, not to say lose, some sense of self, space, independence, and overall mind—and we do it avidly, possibly a few times in our lifespans.

Kabbalistic teachings tell us that there is no way that this kind of unrealistic notion could emerge from the human mind. If someone had to conjure up a plan of this sort, it would be the divine creator. And why is that? These teachings tell us that only under the circumstances of a sacred marriage are we able to finally marvel in the true differences between genders.

Let us explore further. We see these differences everywhere we look; in our parents, our siblings, and our friends. But only in a marriage do we encounter the opportunity to appreciate and enjoy these differences. What you made fun of in your female classmate, you may adore about your wife; and the things that made your upstairs neighbor terribly obnoxious, could turn a husband into the man you love.

But what is it that makes us different? Is it just social conditioning that makes a man a man and a woman a woman? Is it innate? Is femininity based on a hormonal balance or a specific upbringing? Are men trained to be masculine, or do they innately know how to be, naturally?

In the works of Kabbalah, the question is dealt with extensively. The Kabbalistic approach is both unique and revolutionary. It says that the source of male/female identity is beyond both nature and nurture. *It is embedded in our very souls.* Men and women encompass different souls, which is the core source of this disparity.

In Kabbalistic terms, men's souls come from *divine transcendence* while women's souls come from the divine *immanence. Immanence* roughly refers to the idea of "the divine" being present in the world we inhabit—the world of action, or Assiyah. *Transcendence* refers to the idea of divinity that is wholly separate from our tangible universe and its universal laws.[32]

Transcendence covers all realms of the glorious beyond. It is the divine quality of being beyond; immanence, conversely, dwells on being present. These are the male and female aspects of the divine, and they are reflected in man and woman respectively, down here in the human realm.

Although every individual is unique and we don't all fit into oversimplified definitions, in a general sense, there is a clear distinction between male and female spiritual postures.

Their diverse soul-sources translate into two very different personas, and in fact, in cases where a female soul is "erroneously placed" in a male body, this particular individual will need to undergo a very spiritually elated transformation in order to enable a "soul shift" into the adherent gender; otherwise they may encounter an ongoing resistance to engage in a sacred relationship.

We are told the story of our forefather Isaac who encompassed a female soul and only upon the pre-sacrificial encounter in the hands of his father Abraham, which was abolished last minute by the divine order, experienced a soul shift into a male soul. This enabled his immediate quest of Rebecca, his *designated* soul mate. The "birth" of Rebecca, as well as the sparing of Isaac as a sacrifice, are mentioned in the same chapter in Genesis 22, only separated by a few verses in order to emphasize the relationship between the "upgraded" Isaac and the validity of his match.

---

32 Lomas, Christopher. 2019. "What Is the Difference between the Words 'immanence' and 'Transcendence'? – Quora." Quora.Com. 2019. https://www.quora.com/What-is-the-difference-between-the-words-immanence-and-transcendence.

To make this even clearer: Men are seen as *removed* souls; male souls are designed to provide the *direction* in the relationship. Women are *involved* souls; their souls implement the divine *presence* in the relationship. If we account the sephirot into it, we are looking at Chochma for the directional masculine, and Malchut for the Shekinah, or feminine presence. In fact, the Hebrew word Shekinah comes from the root "to dwell," or "be present" (*lishkhon*).

This disparity in our soul substance, or soul component, needs not be a hindrance to the relationship. In fact, as we exemplified in the Isaac and Rebecca story, this very difference is what made the relationship possible; yet, with the modern quest of egalitarianism in every aspect of life, including a romantic, soul felt relationship, we are misled to believe that its absence is problematic when nothing is more harmful to desire and passion than parity, in its nonproductive sense. In other words, yes, we should agree on a set of beliefs, plans, and practices in our joint lives, but we can only keep things fresh and inspirational on an erotic level if the element of surprise and unexpectedness is present.

We don't all fit exactly into typical molds. In fact, we each have elements of both gender groups—our male and female sides. But in a general way, there is a male and a female attitude. The male is more aloof. The female is more involved.

There is nothing wrong with either attitude. Each has its advantages and disadvantages. Sometimes it's good to be removed. When it comes to seeing things in context and making judgments, objectivity is beneficial and essential. You can only see things for what they really are when you remain outside of them; once you are involved, you can no longer see *the big picture*. This is the strength of the male soul—distance, which allows for objectivity.

But objectivity has its downsides, too. You'll get nowhere if you stay on the sidelines of life and remain a spectator. To truly live and experience means getting involved, and to do this, you need to come down out of the world of theory and immerse yourself in the moment. This is where the female element comes in. It is her sense of involvement and presence that gives life its unique personality. It is the woman who makes life real and vibrant, who takes things from the analytical to the experiential, from theory to practice.

Marriage is the ultimate partnership between the two worlds of immanence and transcendence. The man leads the woman, the woman guides the man. Man gives perspective, the woman gives experience. One without the other is an incomplete puzzle. Together, they form a unit that has the best of both worlds.

It is no small feat to unite man and woman—two opposites as diverse as heaven and earth, heart and mind, theory and practice; after the wedding, we have a lifetime to learn how to work together and discover the wonder and beauty of two worlds becoming one.

# Chapter 23
## A Pretty Wild Idea. A Pretty Good One, Too.

### Kabbalistic Teachings and Eastern Methodologies

In the course of this book, we have encountered many occasions in which Kabbalistic teachings, which are considered esoteric and alternative, differ from other likeminded methodologies, mainly originating in the Eastern spheres.

Kabbalah teaches us that although this disparity is correct and legitimate, we still share the same universe, and the divine nature of it is mutual. Therefore, there are more angles that reflect the resemblance, rather than the separation, between these approaches.

### Reiki and Kabbalah

Reiki is a Japanese healing method that is considered an alternative practice. Reiki practitioners use a technique called *palm healing* or *hands-on healing*, through which a "universal energy" is said to be transferred through the palms of the practitioner and onto the patient in order to encourage emotional or physical healing.

The Japanese word *reiki* is compounded of the words *rei*, meaning "spirit, miraculous, or divine," and *ki* or *qi*, meaning "vital energy, breath of life, or consciousness."

In this sense, as well as others that we will discuss shortly, Kabbalah is similar to Reiki, as the core principle of the Kabbalistic approach is the "divine breath of life," or אל חי, in Hebrew. The principle of hands and fingers being the tip of the iceberg to innate energy that the human being encompasses is also a related and shared principle. Kabbalistic teachings tell us that we are sparks of the divine, and as such, hold the power to heal ourselves and others; in Kabbalistic terms, this action is called *tikkun olam*, or "healing the world."

The significance of the numerical value of five is an additional point of similarity. Reiki holds five principles sacred; these are:

1. Just for today, I will not worry.
2. Just for today, I will not be angry.
3. Just for today, I will do my work honestly.
4. Just for today, I will give thanks for my many blessings.
5. Just for today, I will be kind to my neighbor and every living thing.

These principles are strictly common sense, yet not so easy to follow. In a sense, these are *simple*, but not *easy*. The Reiki principles are immediately applicable to everyday living, as well as any highest spiritual pursuit. This means that one does not have to follow a certain religion or spiritual path in order to follow them, which is very similar to the Kabbalistic principles being advocated as the blueprint of the universal wisdom. In relation to the principle of five, the five fingers on each palm are the ones viewed by Reiki practitioners as the source of the healing energy. In the Kabbalistic view, we look at the tree of life as divided into two sides of the body—simply for practical or tangible purposes—where one is the feminine side (left) and the other is the masculine side (right), each encompassing five out of the ten complete sephirot. If we observe the specific sephirot, we can divide the masculine sephirot as Keter, Chochma, Chesed, Netazch and Yesod, while the feminine sephirot are Binah, Gevurah, Tiferet, Hod and Malchut, the feminine Shekinah.

KETER
CROWN

BINAH
UNDERST
-ANDING

CHOCHMA
WISDOM

DAAT
KNOWLED-
GE

GEVURAH
STRENGTH

CHESED
LOVINGKI
-NDNESS

TIFERET
BEAUTY

HOD
SPLENDOR

NETZACH
VICTORY

YESOD
FOUNDA-
TION

MALCHUT
SOVEREIG
-NTY

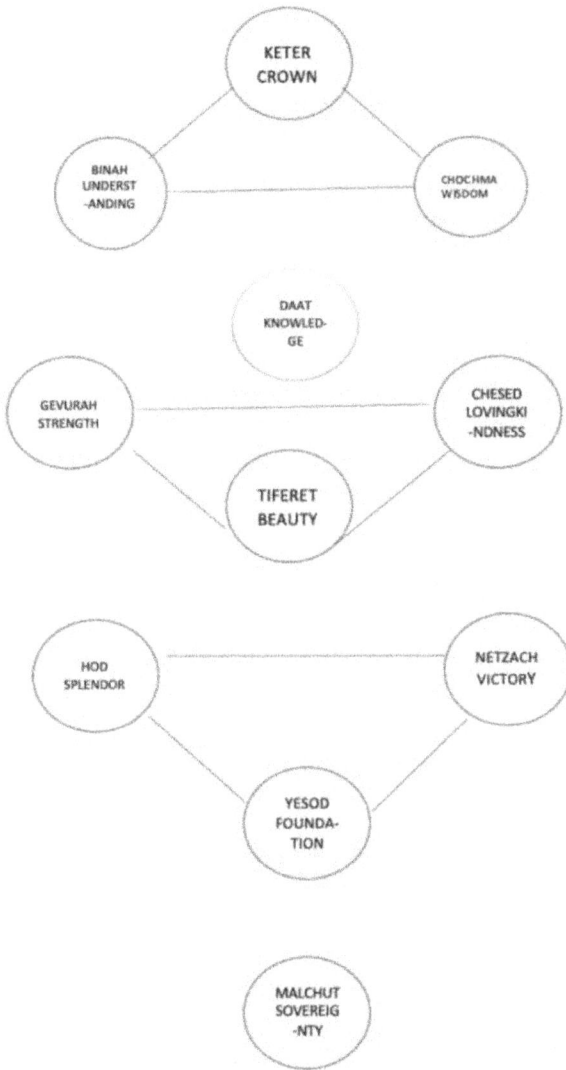

Taking this a tad further, we can equate the Tree of Life's ten sephirot to the chakra system. In Sanskrit, *chakra* means "wheel" or "circle," which is presented similarly in the sephirot mode.

The concept of the chakra system is found in the early traditions of Hinduism. Beliefs differ between the Indian religions, with many Buddhist texts consistently mentioning five chakras, while Hindu sources offer six or even seven,[33] in relation to the significance of five. Early Sanskrit texts speak of them both as meditative visualizations, combining flowers and mantras, and as physical entities in the body.[7] Some modern interpreters speak of them as complexes of the electromagnetic variety, the precise degree and variety of which directly arise from a synthetic average of all positive and negative so-called fields, thus eventuating the complex *nadi*, which is the pipe or channel through which the divine energy is delivered. If we look at the ten sephirot, not only do they share similar functions or even titles (like crown and Keter is similar in both), but the Kabbalistic view of the ten sephirot suggests that there are six "mid-body" sephirot that are aligned with the principle of chakras in the physical location and in relation to certain energy centers in the body, while the remaining four represent the extremities, which are the source light emitted into the midsection.

By this definition, the six sephirot encompassing the aligned chakras are Keter, Chochma, Binah, and semi-sephirah Daat, which align one on top of the other and become one. Then Tiferet, Yesod, and Malchut align together in a similar fashion, while Chesed and Gevurah represent the upper limbs (as they're referred to during meditation and hand placement), and Netzach and Hod represent the lower limbs.

## Quickstep Meditation

In this meditation, we will aim to exhibit the actual connection between all the midsection sephirot, while allowing the light to be emitted from the upper extremities and the lower extremities, at once.

Observe the Tree of Life for a few minutes before going inside.

Sit in a comfortable position opposite your partner, or alternatively on your own, and place your hands on your knees or on your sides, to start. Later in the meditation, it will be suggested that you roam your hands to different locations.

---

33 Heilijgers-Seelen, Dory. 1994. *The System of Five Cakras in Kubjikāmatatantra 14-16*. Groningen: Forsten.

Close your eyes and take a deep breath through your mouth, all the way up to the top of your lungs. Now, purse your lips and let your breath out slowly as if you're whistling through them. Repeat this three times and keep a comfortable posture while reverting to normal breathing.

Sit in a comfortable position allowing your legs to be placed close to your body.

Place your hand on top of your head, inviting the sublime divine energy of Keter, and the other hand on your feet close to your body, relating to Malchut's divine energy.

Begin feeling the heat of your hands while imagining a strong light intensifying and humming through your body with every minute that passes.

Take a deep breath. Remain there and start building an intense energy again while breathing more deeply. Begin building the sensation of heat and intensity in the hand located near your feet. Imagine a bright light emanating from this area, warming up this region and your overall energy sphere.

Stay there in that assuredness for a few moments. Then begin moving your head-positioned hand downward to your shoulders, while moving the feet-positioned hand upward toward your thighs. Begin circling your hands, one going down starting at your throat, descending to the heart and forward, while the bottom hand ascends to the reproductive area, then the abdomen and forward, ascending to the heart. Remain around your heart, building heat and energy. Imagine a bright blue and green light, like a yellowish combined fire, burning your inner truth and energy, emitting pure energetic force, and generating it up to the divine spheres.

You may feel inclined to shift in your seat or move your waist. This is normal and logical; your body is only following your spiritual inclination.

Stay in this sensation and gradually retain normal breathing and position.

When you feel satisfied, take a deep breath, retract your hands back slowly to their original positions, the upper hand ascending to the throat, face, and head, while the lower one to the abdomen, sexual organs, and feet. Remain here for a few moments, then open your eyes slowly and gently.

# Beings of Divinity

A lot has been said about the divine sparks that are encompassed by each and every one of us, the sparks that grant us with the miraculous ability of formation and guide our spiritual journeys thorough the ultra-specific soul levels mentioned earlier. There are many manners in which the Kabbalistic text analyzes the story of creation and the primordial "sin," depending on the source of commentary, different schools of thought, and personal views. Rabbi Yitzchak Luria, the great Kabbalist referred to as the Arizal, speaks of the godly existence of the first human creation, namely Adam, in the enchanting book *Apples from the Orchard*. Luria states that prior to the primordial sin, Adam did not possess a physical form. We have discussed the Genesis 3:21 "garments of skin" that the Creator gave Adam and Eve post-sin, yet it is imperative to mention again that the idea of two primordial creatures being attired in a Tarzan-and-Jane-like outfits is far from the situation we should imagine. Many renowned commentaries[34] suggest that the couple was amorphic and airy; the skin garments they were given referred to in Genesis 3 are the very forms we recognize today as our human bodies.

Luria adds that Adam was clothed in light, and he encompassed all the spiritual worlds together. According to the Ari's teachings, Adam's head was in Atzilut, the world of emanation; his torso, which corresponds with the second triad of the sephirot—Chesed, Gevurah, Tiferet—dwelled in the world of Briah, or creation; his lower extremities correspond to the bottom triad of sephirot—Netzach, Hod, Yesod—and were in the world of Yetzirah or creation; and finally, the crown of Adam's sexual organ was just tipping, hovering above the world of Asiyah (action), where we spend our days here on earth.

You may note that leaves Malchut as an abandoned and unoccupied sephirah. I'm delighted you noticed since this specific sephirah is saved for the female sexual organs, which are positioned separately and

---

34 "Bereishit Rabbah 20:12." n.d. Www.Sefaria.Org. Accessed September 11, 2020. https://www.sefaria.org/Bereishit_Rabbah.20.12?lang=bi&with=all&lang2=bi.

below the male sexual organ, as we mentioned previously, in relation to the Kabbalistic view of preferred sexual position for soul elevation. The Arizal goes even further in his teachings and refers to the primordial sin not as an actual fruit consumption from a forbidden tree, regardless of what that fruit may be, but as a "soulless" act of sexual lust between Adam and Eve. The Arizal states that Adam's sin encompasses three cardinal sins within it, which may explain the very explosive divine reaction to this seemingly benign action. The sins the Arizal cites are idolatry, sexual aberration, and murder.

Why murder? The elimination of the souls that left Adam's body upon his seminal emissions. The sages compare intentional seminal emission to murder since the individual is squandering his potential to bring life into the world.

The sin of idolatry is mentioned because he caused the sparks of holiness to cling to the forces of evil. Giving power to the forces of evil is serving them, which is idolatry.

And sexual aberration is suggested even without a specific mentioning of which soulless act of sex the royal couple engaged in. The Arizal states that the souls who left Adam as seminal emissions returned as the generation of the flood. The Creator sought to wipe out the generation of the flood "for all flesh had corrupted its way on earth," meaning that they engaged in various kinds of sexual aberrations.

What can we do with this insightful information?

One suggestion is to implement these commentaries into our everyday relational lives by examining where we are, what we are, and how we operate in our relational choices. Simply put, we must relate to ourselves as a universe on a micro level. As such, we encompass the four levels of soul inside our body, restricted and small as it may appear. If we break down the soul levels again, we can see that emanation–spiritual is the highest level, creation–intellectual is the level below, formation–emotional is beneath that, and finally, the world of action–physical is on the bottom.

The higher (or rather deeper) one goes in the spiritual quest and surrender, the more stable and servicing their choices are.

emanation-spiritual

creation-
intellectual

formation-
emotional

action-
physical

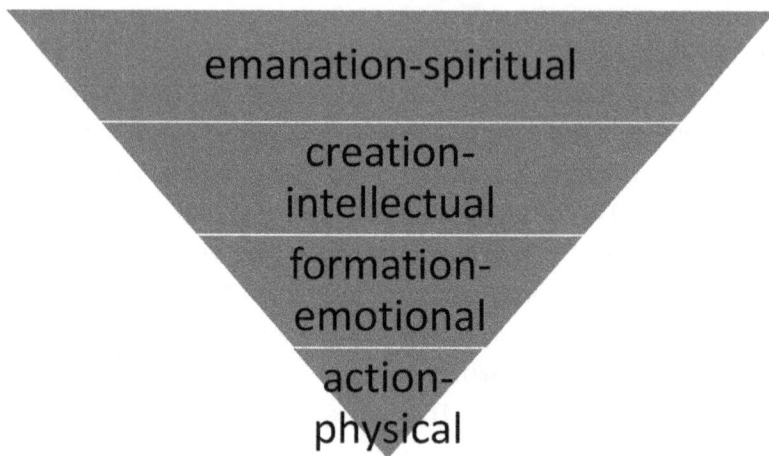

Alas, in our general lives, we tend to operate and attempt to balance our entire world of relations on a foundation that is very unstable. It may look like the graph above in which the physical attraction or physical compatibility component is very weak and unstable, yet we tend to base our entire relational choices on this "parity." This does not stand to say that we should attempt to be in a relationship with a partner who we find appalling, this only stand to address the large emphasis that this component has in our lives. Yes, we should aspire to have a partner to whom we feel physically drawn, but what Kabbalistic teachings tell us is that if we aim to locate a mutual spiritual ground—such as essential beliefs, practices, and life choices—and perhaps add the component of an intellectual ground that can encompass our philosophical aspirations and inspirations, we may just find the physical aspect of our partner much more appealing had it not played the initial, most crucial role in the prospective dyad.

## Quickstep Meditation

We will choose the combination of ילי, a sequence that represents returning to our embryonic, primordial knowing in order to recapture parts of our souls and resisting slavery to jealousy and physical matter.

With this sequence, we are able to see the bigger picture and allow the truth to seep into our relational lives, rather than dwell in the shallow waters of life's dictation led by ego and the absence of connectedness. When applying this sequence, look deep inside and compare these choices to a broader spectrum of relation; not only the strength it requires to see your choice of a partner or to see your current partner for their higher soul level, rather than their upside-down pinnacle, but rather what this choice and our ability to ascend into the higher spheres of existence, above petty matters, can have on a cosmic, universal level.

Remember that you can digitally scan the letters or gaze at them, visualize with your eyes closed, or chant them to the sound of YALLY. If you choose the two former options out of the four, you may want to copy this sequence on a small piece of paper that you keep in a safe and respected spot in order to utilize this power. You may also incorporate all four utilization options and switch from one to another as you progress.

Gaze at this sequence for a few minutes before going inside.

Sit in a comfortable position, close your eyes, and take a deep breath through your mouth, all the way up to the top of your lungs. Now, purse your lips and let your breath out slowly as if you're whistling through them. Repeat this three times and keep a comfortable posture while reverting to normal breathing.

Slowly allow the three-letter sequence of ילי to appear before you and float in your mind's eye.

I like to see these sequences as if they are floating on water in tiny ripples toward me and back, while gazing with my eyes closed. Allow the letters to form and heighten in your memory and breathe "the breath of life" into them. Merge the goal that you have in relation to this sequence and combine it with the energy you create.

It can be a soulful and beautiful connection with a potential soul match, or you can go further and expand into a peaceful existence to all. If you are aiming to unite with your current or hopeful partner in a respectful and harmonious manner, that will definitely and unequivocally serve the greater goal of a harmonious, sacred, and everlasting relation-ship. You may also alternate or gradually arrive at a higher-level goal as you advance and progress.

When you feel safe and strong in this frequency and the light it emits, gradually allow both your hands to touch the ground, and revert to nor-mal breathing. Gradually and slowly open your eyes. You may want to remain seated in this position for a few moments before getting back on your feet. Drink a glass of water to quench the energy you've emitted.

# Chapter 24
## Learning Sexual Intelligence

Common sense may lead us to believe that sexuality or the practice of intimacy is a natural instinct. Birds and bees do it, so what could be challenging? It's a very innate human activity; it's what happens between partners, and all we need to do is relax and enjoy it, right?

Kabbalistic teachings suggest otherwise. Sure, all species in nature engage in the act of procreation. Bonobos and related primates even utilize this tool for kinship, friendship, the exchange of power, and shelter—yes, very much like us humans—but is it considered intimacy? To be intimate means to go into a sacred and very profound place; even the pronunciation of the word sounds like "into me," and in fact, the word intima by definition is the very core membrane of an organ or body part. We should take into account the depth of this profound offering that is so deeply embedded in us.

In the world that we dwell in, by Kabbalistic terms the world of Assiyah, we deal with the mundane, the ordinary, and the earthly. This illusion of separation from the worlds above us—the world of Yeztira, which is sacred and profound, as well the world above it, the world of Briah—is what leads us to the misunderstanding of our function, and our choices. Sure, we have the world of creation that is holy and unreachable for our soul level, but in between, we have the world of formation; this world is, metaphorically, hovering on top of our mundane physicality's crown, if we relate it to the top sephirah in the Tree of Life. The fact that the top of our heads touch this elevated soul level means that we have access to it, but what does it take to actually access it?

First, we need to comprehend that the sacred is that which is holier than the ordinary, but not so holy as to become unattainable. Sacredness, therefore, is something in between what we have and what we cannot have, literally.

So, where do intimacy and healthy sexual exchange fit in? By their very nature—not by divine decree—sexuality and intimacy belong to the arena of the sacred. We experience it, but we cannot own it; we are allowed to indulge our bodies, but we must integrate our souls; we can be sexual, but we cannot possess our own (or others') sexuality. The reason for it is very natural and basic. To be intimate means one person enters into the private, sacred part of another human being's existence.

You cannot own another person's intimacy. It's not available. Even if the person chooses to give ownership, it is not theirs to offer. It's not sharable. It's one of those things in life that are lent to us simply because we encompass a body that can indulge by using our five senses, but we can never possess it.

Well, if it's that unavailable, if I can't possess it, then what connection, what relationship do I have with it?

This is where sanctity steps in. We can experience intimacy, but we cannot own it. It is also where the sublime pleasure of sexuality, in comparison to other earthly pleasures, is sourced. Our cravings for food are delightful, but they are noncomparable to the sexual impulse, because we consume food and then it's gone—we possess and eliminate it. Sexuality is always there and can never be (or shouldn't be) consumed and eliminated.

The pleasure of sexuality is sourced in the combination of having and not having. It's something that you are granted, but that you cannot own and possess. When you experience this duality, the pleasure of being in another person's intimate space while at the same time remembering that your presence there is a divine privilege, and is what makes sexuality different.

The key word is familiarity. With the sacred, you cannot afford to become overly familiar. With the truly divine, there's no danger. It's out of our reach, we need not worry about your godly aspirations. But with the sacred, we are challenged with these fine subtleties: When does familiarity breed contempt? When is familiarity really destructive and unwelcome? In sanctity. If you become familiar, too familiar, with the intimacy of another person's life, whether physical, emotional, or mental, then you've compromised the sanctity of this dyad.

## Unhealthy Closeness

We are told the unfortunate story of King David's children and half siblings, Amnon and Tamar. Amnon was utterly infatuated with the beautiful Tamar. He lusted and pined for her in the most earthly, bestial, and primordial manner.

Since his desire was all-consuming, he was given the terrible advice of faking an illness in order to be granted with fair Tamar's caring presence and nurturing. This advice backfired when his burning desire overtook Amnon, and in a split moment of disregard to the sanctity of an intimate engagement, he raped Tamar to satisfy his longing. We are told that a minute after he concluded the offensive act, he could not stand her presence: "Then Amnon hated her with exceeding great hatred; for the hatred wherewith he hated her was greater than the love wherewith he had loved her. And Amnon said unto her: 'Arise, be gone.'"[35]

An act that is inconsiderate of another's sensual space, and of course one that is unnaturally forced and based solely on a physical aspect, is not only unsacred but harmful, both to the initiator and, of course, the recipient.

The principle of less familiarity, or adding soul to our physical arousal, is ancient, but in our current reality, we are pushed to be familiar and "own" our sexuality, and that of others. To be less familiar can mean

---

35 Samuel 2:13-15 KJV

respecting the boundaries of the other; to be less familiar could be "sacrificing" your own pleasure for the sake of another.

Less familiarity is a known factor that we exercise in many realms and avenues in our lives. As an example, certain sacred names, like using the respectful parental terms rather than our parents' given names when we refer to them, and other practices that we take for granted, are all sourced from the same fountain of sacred practice; to be less familiar, respect the unknown, and avoid trying to own what is only lent to your precious and temporary caring.

# Quickstep Meditation

We will choose the combination of,עַנָו a sequence that represents the appreciation of the holy, encompassing humility, and gratitude toward the gifts you were granted with, for the time being.

With this sequence, we are able to see the bigger picture and allow the truth to seep into our relational lives, rather than dwelling in the shallow waters of life's dictation led by ego, and the human need to possess and conquer.

When applying this sequence, look deep inside and compare these choices to a broader spectrum of relation; not only the strength it requires to see your practices as serving a higher goal, but to view what this choice and our ability to ascend into the advanced spheres of existence above immediate earthly needs can serve on a cosmic, universal level.

Remember that you can digitally scan the letters or gaze at them, visualize them with your eyes closed, or chant them to the sound of ANAV. If you choose the two former options out of the four, you may want to copy this sequence on a small piece of paper that you keep in a safe and respected spot in order to utilize this power. You may also incorporate all four utilization options and switch from one to another as you progress.

Gaze at this sequence for a few minutes before going inside.

Sit in a comfortable position, close your eyes, and take a deep breath through your mouth, all the way up to the top of your lungs. Now, purse your lips and let your breath out slowly as if you're whistling through them. Repeat this three times and keep a comfortable posture while reverting to normal breathing.

Slowly allow the three-letter sequence of ענו to appear before you and float in your mind's eye.

I like to see these sequences as if they are floating on water in tiny ripples toward me and back, while gazing with my eyes closed. Allow the letters to form and heighten in your memory and breathe "the breath of life" into them. Merge the goal that you have in relation to this sequence and combine it with the energy you create.

It can be a soulful and beautiful connection with a potential soul match, or you can go further and expand into a peaceful existence to all. If you are aiming to unite with your current or hopeful partner in a respectful and harmonious manner, that will definitely and unequivocally serve the greater goal of a harmonious, sacred, and everlasting relationship. You may also alternate or gradually arrive at a higher-level goal as you advance and progress.

When you feel safe and strong in this frequency and the light it emits, gradually allow both your hands to touch the ground, and revert to normal breathing. Gradually and slowly open your eyes. You may want to remain seated in this position for a few moments before getting back on your feet. Drink a glass of water to quench the energy you've emitted.

## Mindfulness and Sexuality

*Mindfulness*, the practice of going within, has vastly become the trend of this decade. We are surrounded with inspirational slogans and quotes from world renowned gurus, yogis, and spiritual teachers regarding the imperative place of mindfulness in our daily function, whether it is with colleagues, friends, spouses, children, or generally anyone we communicate with. Yet, the influence of mindfulness on our functional love lives has been limited.

It could be due to the fact that esoteric modalities, especially those that are Eastern sourced, see the body as an "intrusion," as a non-entity, or perhaps one that is best deprived and reduced in importance, when compared to the place of our mental state. Here again, Kabbalistic teachings tell us otherwise.

Let us roll back to the story of the Noah and the flood in order to understand the relevance of these teachings when it comes to sexual function. Kabbalah tells us that the Genesis 9 story of Noah being chosen to literally carry the destiny of humankind on his shoulders was a story of self-connectedness and preservation, which is a key component to healthy relations with others, including on an erotic level.

Now, the plot thickens, as it always does, when humble Noah, just existing the ark, needed a break from his weary mind—an understandable quest for a man who's about to embark on the reconstruction of the world per se, and chooses to go for the closest liquor cabinet: a vineyard.

The thought of removing yourself from a conscious state, and perhaps numbing yourself via substances or other distractions, cannot be beneficial for any task at hand, let alone one that is relational in nature.

We are told that Noah chose to take a break from his role as world hero by getting intoxicated, but that "absence of mindfulness" only led to an unexpected evolvement, which would have massive global consequences for generations to come. The mentioning of the particular event—being exposed in his nakedness to his son, Ham—in such detail, stands to educate us about the connection between self-awareness and sensual bodily functions.

The sages state that "there is no erection without Daat." This statement refers to the fact that in order for procreation to occur, Yesod, which is related to the male organ, must be infused with at least some level of consciousness. Without this presence of mentality, the organ is flaccid, or, in the terminology of Kabbalah, *dead*.

It is likely that if a man or woman is challenged with a sexual dysfunction or discomfort, we would look to the medical or physical contribution relating to this challenge. Yet, here we are told that the entire ability to function is directly related to our ability to connect to our consciousness, to our mindfulness. The reason you're reading this very suggestion is based on a scientific implication, and so a number of studies have been released in the past decade regarding this particular correlation of functionality that is based on mindfulness.

In her fascinating study and following book, Dr. Lori Brotto of the university of British Columbia exemplifies how the component of mindfulness plays a significant role in that functionality.[36] In a 2007 paper, Brotto et al. discuss the use of mindfulness in the treatment of women with sexual dysfunctions. The paper elaborates on a trial of a women's study group that illustrates how mindfulness was effective in improving their sexuality and quality of life. Brotto concluded that though the findings were preliminary, they suggest that mindfulness may have a place in the treatment of sexual concerns.

In an additional study from 2013,[37] researchers decided to pilot test the feasibility, acceptability, and potential effect of a group-based, sensorimotor intervention, with a strong mindfulness component, on women's sexual health. These results were implicated to the women's partners and the dyad based functionality after the study. Compared with pre-intervention scores, researchers found that overall mindfulness and functionality scores significantly improved following the intervention. Cofounders of this research concluded that the qualitative data indicated that the intervention had an impact on both body awareness and dyadic connection.

These results can help us deduce the great connection between body and mind, but that is a "given" in the views of many; nonetheless, when it comes to official solutions for physically manifested dysfunctions, we

---

36 Brotto, Lori A., and Julia R. Heiman. 2007. "Mindfulness in Sex Therapy: Applications for Women with Sexual Difficulties Following Gynecologic Cancer." *Sexual and Relationship Therapy* 22 (1): 3–11. https://doi.org/10.1080/14681990601153298.

37 Mize, Sara J.S., and Alex Iantaffi. 2013. "The Place of Mindfulness in a Sensorimotor Psychotherapy Intervention to Improve Women's Sexual Health." *Sexual and Relationship Therapy* 28 (1–2): 63–76. https://doi.org/10.1080/14681994.2013.770144.

should really look deeper inside into the soul connection that Kabbalistic teachings tell us about.

# I'm Not My Body

In continuance to the Eastern notion that one's body is less important than one's mental state, we see that Kabbalistic teachings negate that very core principal. We are put here on earth to function *within* these "skin garments," and thus we should regard these physical bodies of ours as significant and important. Kabbalah also looks at the body as serving the quest of the soul, as its kind chauffeur, in the pursuit of collecting divine sparks *in* this world, rather than in anticipation of some future existence.

We are told that within this principle of achieving godliness here and now, we are granted with our bodies, along with our very functional and gratifying five senses, in order to pursue this goal to the best of our ability. So, when we are told by neighboring esoteric modalities that we are not our bodies, it is a partial truth, at best. We *are* our bodies, because our souls were placed in them, and thus we have the responsibility to nurture them and care for them in the best way possible. This notion does not advocate hedonism in any shape or form; if anything, Kabbalistic teachings are laced with principles of fasting, curbing needs, and so forth.

But we are told that this body holds a divine purpose, and as such, it should be maintained and cared for. In this regard, our sexual needs also serve a divine purpose, but they can only attain that purpose or service if the physical interpretation of desire and pleasure is not limited to the tangible sphere alone. We are told that when our bodies are no longer present on this planet, our closest level of soul, called *nefesh*, is restless and continuously rotates between the place of the body's burial, and the physical environment that body used to occupy—at least until the upper souls find their paths (which will be discussed in later segments).

The reason for this restlessness is the strong connection between the vessel and the inhabitant—the body and soul—as they are joined by the divine spark and remain connected for essentially eternity.

Abraham used the intoxication to harmonize soul and body upon his self-circumcision at the age of ninety; Adam used it to gain awareness of body; and Noah utilized that potential to lose sense of tangibility and evaporate. Needless to say, the only manner in which this could be beneficial is Abraham's choice of harmonizing the two.

# Chapter 25

## Why Do We Fall in Love?

Gazing into a loved one's eyes across a candlelit table for two, one may think that he or she has risen above a survival-of-the-fittest mode of existence, but, in truth, this "rising higher" is just nature's way of packaging that primordial drive. By the same token, the accoutrements of human courtship—the romance, the flowers, the music, the moonlight—are really just nature's way of getting two people together.

The teachings of Kabbalah take this to a different angle; it views the male–female dynamic not just as two genders within a species, but rather two forms of energy: an internal energy and a projective energy. Feminine energy and masculine energy coexist in every person, and in every part of nature.

Even the divine source wears both masculine and feminine faces. In the Kabbalistic scripts, the Zohar speaks mainly of the Shekinah, mentioned throughout the book, as the feminine aspect of God.

So, what we have here is a split of two energies and a yearning to become one whole. This attraction, which manifests itself in many physical sensations, is essentially the desire to become a complete, divine whole, connecting to our divine source. Not that we've ever been completely disconnected, but consciously or unconsciously, we can go off on our own individual, narcissistic, even selfish, paths. And here, there's a voice inside us saying, "I yearn for something greater."

An attraction between two individuals may seem to be a very biological urge, but from a Kabbalistic perspective, it's just a physical manifestation of a much deeper, spiritual attraction.

## The Honeymoon Phase

Terminology matters, and so looking at this topic to begin with raises a number of questions, especially in regard to the idea of *falling* in love. Kabbalistic teachings remind us that everything is designed in perfect synergy with the challenges and gifts that life and this universe can offer us, based on our actions and essential understanding of our purpose here on this earth.

Kabbalah tells us that even the notion of "falling" in love is meant to be felt, experienced, or sensed in this fashion because the Creator gives us a glimpse, a sneak peek, into the hall of fame and love and devotion. In essence, we are getting a glimpse of what is in store for us, and then, pretty swiftly as we can all attest from life experience, we are brought back to the ground; at times we land gently, and at times we crash, which marks the onset of the divine force's message that essentially says, "There you are. Did you enjoy it? Now you try." "Try what?" you may defensively ask. Try to build this same wonderful synergetic sensation and full body experience from the tools and logic you were given. Try creating a harmonious relationship. Try negotiating a wonderful dyadic life. Try to experiment with formation, not creation, but formation. Since we are in fact a mini universe encompassing these sparks of divinity, this should be attainable for us.

Now, the notion of "falling" is also well calculated, because falling means this just landed into our hearts, heads, and souls. but we all know that real sacred relationships that are nurturing and nourishing take a lot more than a chance or a fluke. Life has the tendency to educate us about these illusions, if we slip into them. Kabbalistic teachings tell us that the top intellectual sephirah of Chochma represents our creativity, and thus can be utilized to concoct the right manner in which this desirable relationship can be attainted and maintained.

We know that the "devil is in the details," but "God is in the ordinary." In other words, we should utilize our godly strengths every day and everywhere. This can be related to a beautiful Kabbalistic term called חכם לב, which means "wise at heart." Sure, we think and process with our minds, but to be wise at heart, one needs to utilize all these divine sources in order to be attentive, aware, and conscious from the heart.

Now, this isn't a new or different notion; we hear about the heart–mind connection everywhere we turn, but in this sphere, it goes even deeper. As we said, terminology, letters, sequences, and numbers matter, so in the Hebrew scripts, we are told that the one who can find bliss in life on all levels, including the relational sphere, of course, is one who encompasses what the acronym מלך stands for, which is mind (מוח) heart (לב) and liver (כבד). The word encompassing these three also means "king," by unelated definition. But of course, all is related, and the idea behind this principle is that a person who handles life regally, like a king, is one who integrates the important components of one's mind for intellectual reasoning, heart for compassion and kindness, and liver for the fortitude to see things in the manner they should be, a rightful manner, not by whims or desires.

Kabbalah tells us that this integration between mind, heart, and liver is "negotiated" by a narrow vessel, the neck and throat. This narrow vessel is in charge of transferring the imperative information between these two, and at times of discomfort, stress, depression, or lack of self-trust, we tend to clench this vessel and disable the flow of energy between these functional spheres.

What is a kind and benevolent person to do in order to unblock this channel?

Kabbalistic teachings tell us that upon adversity, we are most likely to unclog this channel because a "broken heart" is an open one, open to receive. The thirteenth century poet Rumi ruminated on this notion quite often, and said, "The wound is the place where the Light enters you."

Nonetheless, Kabbalah assures us that we need not await misfortune in order to open the channels between our energy centers. According to this wisdom, what a person is to do is dwell on his imperfections via meditation, chanting, prayer, or any other act of mindfulness, one that enables the soul to be fully open to "criticism." This act of meditating on our imperfections is not meant for self-deprecation, but rather the understanding that we are a full "glass" of water, rather than a full half versus an empty half. We are the universe in its entirety, and thus need to get connected to our imperfections, because that is where the light enters, that is where our vulnerability shines, that is precisely where we are willing to welcome our desired partners into our lives.

What is *Tzimtzum* according to Kabbalah, and how is it relevant to our relationships?

*Tzimtzum*, or "constriction," is a Kabbalistic narrative explaining how an infinite divine source "made room" for the emanation of finite forms and created beings. This idea was first articulated by the Arizal (Rabbi Isaac Luria, 1534–1572) and transcribed by his foremost student, Rabbi Chaim Vital (1543–1620), in the book *Etz Chaim*. In this text, and in others, tzimtzum is described in metaphorical terms that would normally describe a physical event located in time and space.

In the tzimtzum narrative, which describes three general phases in the unfolding of the divine relationship with creation, the image of light plays a central role. Before we start taking the concepts apart, it is important to get the different phases of the narrative clear.

Phase one: "Before" the tzimtzum, "there was a celestial and simple light that filled all existence, and there was no empty room. Rather, all was filled with simple infinite light, which did not have either beginning or end, ergo infinite and boundaryless, Kabbalistic teachings call this infinite light (*Or Ein Sof*)."

Phase two: Then, this light was contracted (*tzimtzum* is the Hebrew word for contraction) and drawn aside, leaving an empty, hollow space, *chlalal*, in Hebrew. After this tzimtzum, there was now space where emanations and creations could have the potential to be formed.

Phase three: Then, straight from the infinite light, there was a single straight line (*kav*), drawn down from the surrounding light, successively descending into the hollow space that permitted it now. The top of this line is drawn from the infinite light itself and bottoms it, while through this line the infinite light is drawn and spread out below. Thus, in that hollow space, all the realms were emanated, created, and made.

The resemblance between physical light that we experience as humans and the divine light (*or ein sof*) is that both of them reveal their source—the luminary or the divine essence (called *Atzmut*). In the original revelation, not only could nothing other than the Creator exist, even the Creator could not be manifest in any feasible or conceivable way, as wise, kind, or just. *Tzimtzum, thus,* refers to the constriction of this infinite manifestation of the divine self, providing a "space" in which the divine self could be manifest in a more finite form, and ultimately, in the creation of finite beings.

Confused? Stay focused, it becomes clearer. Let us remain here for the time being and try to make some sense of all this, and find the implications of these exclusive experiences, and their relevance to our relationships.

## Go Small or Go Home

Given that we are divine sparks or all-encompassing mini universes, how can we manifest that similar act of creation? By enabling a specific space where a divine and sacred hollow can be formatted (note that I haven't said created) out of our own magnitude.

By Kabbalistic views, the way we can go about this challenging task is by first acknowledging the smallness, yet greatness, of our existence. We are a single spark on a macro level, yet a whole universe on a micro level; in reflection to the potential dyadic exchange, we must take the light of our existence and allow a certain place in this space for a small sprout to begin its growth. How can we attempt this? A good place to start is by practicing humility. Every time we are reminded of the fact that, unlike the divine, we are forming, not creating, and that none of this, albeit tangible, is ours to keep or own, then we can allow for a space to open where relational bliss can flourish.

Once we practice this on a regular basis, and it becomes a form of a second nature, we are ready to enable another human being to occupy this space in our hearts and souls by connecting to their "beams" and starting a joint powerhouse that holds the potential for a soulful relationship. If at any point we fail to recall our purpose, we hold a dangerous strength to "burn this space down to ashes" with the magnitude of our original light. Ego, in particular, is a culprit that may leave torched terrain in areas where a garden bed previously prospered. The lesson here is both the awareness aspect of our existence as well as the practice of humility and kindness; not in a superficial condescending sense, but in a real, truthful manner, one that can yield actual life.

# Quickstep Meditation

We will choose the combination of אני, a sequence that represents grasping the bigger picture behind our limited views and obstacles. This sequence also stands for the Hebrew definition of "me," which is very relatable since we are discussing the very notion of overcoming the ego for the better good of all.

When applying this sequence, look deep inside and compare these choices to a broader spectrum of relation; not only the strength it requires to be a humble and enabling partner, but what this choice and our ability to curb our blinding light holds for the entire global benefit, and even our *selfish* wish for a "helpmate."

Remember that you can digitally scan the letters or gaze at them, visualize them with your eyes closed, or chant them to the sound of ANI; if you choose the two former options out of the four, you may want to copy this sequence on a small piece of paper that you keep in a safe and respected spot in order to utilize this power. You may also incorporate all four utilization options and switch from one to another as you progress.

Gaze at this sequence for a few minutes before going inside.

Sit in a comfortable position, close your eyes, and take a deep breath through your mouth, all the way up to the top of your lungs. Now, purse your lips and let your breath out slowly as if you're whistling through them. Repeat this three times, and keep a comfortable posture while reverting to normal breathing.

Slowly allow the three-letter sequence of אני to appear before you and float in your mind's eye.

I like to see these sequences as if they are floating on water in tiny ripples toward me and back, while gazing with my eyes closed. Allow the letters to form and heighten in your memory and breathe "the breath of life" into them. Merge the goal that you have in relation to this sequence and combine it with the energy you create.

It can be a soulful and beautiful connection with a potential soul match, or you can go further and expand into a peaceful existence to all. If you are aiming to unite with your current or hopeful partner in a respectful and harmonious manner, that will definitely and unequivocally serve the greater goal of a harmonious, sacred, and everlasting relationship. You may also alternate or gradually arrive at a higher-level goal as you advance and progress.

When you feel safe and strong in this frequency and the light it emits, gradually allow both your hands to touch the ground, and revert to normal breathing. Gradually and slowly open your eyes. You may want to remain seated in this position for a few moments before getting back on your feet. Drink a glass of water to quench the energy you've emitted.

# A Friendly Deviance

What do we think, know, and think we know about the concept of infidelity?

The very moment this concept is presented, our minds are filled with sultry encounters, sexy movie scenes, painful movie scenes, wine, lingerie, and red lipstick on white collars. We are constantly reminded that this is the oldest and most primal human need, that we are not built for monogamy or any formed relationship (one can stray on numerous partners, if that is the choice), that lust has a short shelf life, that we are programmed and conditioned this way, that our chimp and bonobo ancestors fancy this activity, and so on. All these claims and potential reasonings are applicable, and some were even examined scientifically, but we have indeed revolutionized, and we are a thinking, living, conscious creature with a pulse and judgment; what is there to do with this notion, and why do we keep struggling to avoid it and pursue committed relationships if that is an innate determinism for us? Author Shirly Glass in her remarkable book *Not "Just Friends"* reveals some profound ideas and theories regarding this topic, and not in the chewed-up sense of it.[38]

In principle, the data is less important; you can look up the statistics for infidelity in less than a minute online, but what Glass presents is very aligned with the Kabbalistic view of soul connection. To simplify, this means that we are responsible for the *awareness* of our role in the sacred, committed dyad.

That awareness should tell us in a crystal-clear manner what belongs in this exchange and what stands outside of it, jeopardizing its very core, way before it actually does. Glass offers many perspectives that are gender based and may shed light on our relational conduct. Her data states that women who have affairs often consciously detach from their marriages *before* getting involved. In contrast, Glass adds, men more often withdraw from their marriages as a *consequence* of extramarital involvement.

This piece of data alone is very imperative to the way we observe our relationships; for one, both partners should be aware of the feminine detachment factor in a committed relationship. If you're a woman in the relationship and feel more and more estranged from your partner, that is a sign that the friendly engagement you're carrying on at work is risking the core of your relational stability. If you're the husband in this dyad, your role is to pay attention to these shifts in behavior and address them promptly and efficiently.

Glass offers the flip side of this coin and states, that for both genders, the inconceivability of alternatives is a sign of dedication to their marriage partner. Dedicated couples are as protective of their relationships

38 "Dr. Shirley Glass – Introduction – NOT 'Just Friends.'" n.d. Www. Shirleyglass.Com. Accessed September 8, 2020. http://www.shirley-glass.com/introduction.htm.

as couples who've just fallen in love, which can create a form of shield from the dreaded "shelf life" we are constantly reminded of.

Glass offers a unique theory she calls Walls and Windows" In her view, many affairs grow from mere "benign" friendships, unbeknownst to both partners in this extramarital exchange, but boundaries shift slowly, and observing these boundaries at any given moment can bring both friendship and marriage into sharp focus. Glass suggests that the way to determine whether a particular friendship is jeopardizing the formal relationship is to ask, "Where are the walls and where are the windows?" This is a useful metaphor for clarifying boundary issues in extramarital triangles.

According to this theory, a committed couple constructs a wall that shields them from any outside forces that hold a threat. They look at the world outside their relationship through a shared window of openness and honesty. The couple is a unit, and an affair erodes their carefully constructed security system. It erects an interior wall of secrecy between the committed partners at the same time that it opens a window of intimacy between the philandering partners. When this transition launches, the committed couple is no longer a unit. This shift brought the external partner *inside* the sacred realm and pushed the marital partner *outside* of it.

Glass suggests that asking oneself about the placement of walls and windows can help decipher when an external relationship has moved beyond friendship into an extramarital relationship. When a friend knows more about your marriage than a spouse knows about your friendship, you have already compromised the healthy status quo of your sacred dyad.

Glass elaborates about the relevance of "coming clean" even before any "formal" action is taken. The idea is that if one even entertains the thought of *running off* with another (this is in regards to a real-life potential partner that is tangible and reachable. You may still fantasize about a weekend in Aruba with Brad Pitt, that'll be safe enough!), the wise step would be to share these thoughts and challenges with your partner. I know what you're thinking, you don't want to alarm/hurt/bother/be ridiculed/start a fight, fill in the blank.

But data shows that the sharing of this information alleviates the fear and allows any wall to be immediately knocked down to the ground, while opening a new wide window within the committed relationship. In an instant, the guilt and fear can turn into a reunion and a form of strength in the relationship. Now, if your partner is deprecating, lacks understanding, or is judgmental or aggressive, you're dealing with a different challenge in your relationship that does not concern infidelity, yet it should be addressed promptly as it does not belong in a healthy, nurturing relationship.

Glass brings up another point that relates to post affair assumptions and misconceptions. When this kind of secret is revealed publicly, outside observers may speculate unfairly and ignorantly that the philanderer's wife must have been reluctant or inadequate in the bedroom, or that the husband of an unfaithful wife was spending too much time at work, as a rationale to the affair.

Glass calls this the Prevention Myth, which states that a loving partner and a good marriage will prevent affairs. This isn't supported by research and should be completely disregarded. It is imperative to point out the correlation between Kabbalah and Glass's theory here, in the sense that attraction is normal, but just because you experience it, doesn't mean you have to act on it. Similarly, the *evil inclination* is embedded, but you have free will! Your divine sparks should provide you with the tools to overcome temptation.

Glass mentions a few "don'ts" that should be taken into account on the path toward a healthy long-lasting exchange. These are nicely aligned with Kabbalistic teachings.

One of the measures of true commitment is to not allow yourself to be pulled away from priorities by distractions. Don't let yourself fantasize about what it would be like to be with that other person. Affairs begin in the mind. In Jewish views, we refer to the serpent in the Garden by its original Hebrew name *nachash*, which means "to speculate." Similarly, once Eve was drawn into the speculation of another, better life, the perfect relationship with Adam shattered.

Glass also warns the devoted partner about flirting with others. Looking is human, but flirting signals that you are available. You've sent out an invitation of receptivity and are ready to see who says yes. Not to mention the discomfort and insult it imposes on your partner. In the equivalence to Kabbalistic views, we are told about *shmirat einayim*, which translates as "monitored gaze." In other words, you are welcome to see, but avoid a long stare or gaze for all the reasons listed above.

# Chapter 26
## The Four Worlds

We have discussed the principal of soul levels through which this world was created, by Kabbalistic views. Only after applying the principle of timztum (constriction) did it become at all "feasible" for the divine source to apply anything into the finite world of creation in the space that was made available. To make it more comprehensible in a tangible sense, we can compare these worlds to four stages of a project.

Let us examine a scenario: you're planning the vacation of your dreams, one that encompasses all of the spectacular and indulgent variables that you have ever imagined. You sit with your loving partner and start to work out a plan toward this spectacular goal.

Delineating this spectacular process can evolve somewhere along these lines:

First, the two of you come up with the idea of the vacation, the concept of it. This is the world of emanation, the top notch, where everything is still pretty much conceptual and has no tangible foundation.

After toying with this idea for a while, running special scenarios in your minds, perhaps even playing with it further as a tool for a sexy intimate moment, you decide to move along and progress to the next stage of the planning.

This stage is the broadening of the basic plan. In Kabbalistic views, this will evolve into the world of creation, right below the top emanation, where you were upon conceptualizing the notion of taking a vacation.

In this world, you start entering valid points that should be encompassed in the dreamy vacation plan; what activities should take place, where you should stay, what amenities should be encompassed in these facilities, activities that you would indulge in, and so forth.

The plot starts to thicken when you move to the next stage. This is the stage of emotional involvement with the plan and putting the pieces into place. This all starts to materialize in the world of formation and enables the actual placement of components, such as making reservations, booking activities, and purchasing the most flattering bikini that will make all heads turn at the beach.

Things are getting ultra-exciting in the world of action when this whole planning manifests. You're finally lying on that beach, you finally raise a glass to the greatest vacation ever, you finally feel the pristine white sand between your toes: you've arrived.

In the higher worlds, one is blinded somewhat by rays of the "Divine Light" (*giluyim*, in Hebrew). The higher one goes, the more sublime the revelation and the more blinding the light. Yet, from the world of action—earth—we can appreciate the sun in a far greater manner. It is specifically in this realm where there is a total eclipse of the divine Light, during which the observer can actually come into contact with *it*, himself.

Though the divine source stands far beyond comprehension, one can observe creation and realize that this can only be the work of the divine.

| Yud | Atzilut (emanation) | Chochmah (wisdom) | Initial Inspiration |
|---|---|---|---|
| Hei | Beriah (creation) | Binah (understanding) | Broadening of Concept |
| Vav | Yetzirah (formation) | Chessed (kindness) through Yesod (foundation) | Emotional Involvement in Plans |
| Hei | Assiyah (action) | Malchut (kingship) | Building of Project |

Applying this sequence to the Kabbalistic premise, we now see how the final and most exciting stage in our finite human eyes is simply the least evolved stage on a spiritual level, in terms of divine force. The actualization of things might be the end goal, but the means are more imperative and require a very unique set of planning from the Creator. In that very manner, Kabbalah tells us that almost everything that we engage with in this world that is so suitably titled "action" is goal oriented. If we could go about our lives healthy and functional without the need to sleep, would we ever spend years of our lives on this activity? If we could maintain a healthy and athletic body without ever moving it or nourishing it correctly, would we ever bother with the gym or the health food market? The answer is a strong no.

Yet, Kabbalah tells us that we *can*, regardless, live our lives in a divine manner in which every single action can integrate Godliness. We can eat in a godly manner, which involves being mindful of what we consume, how we consume it or how much of it, and we will take steps to follow a set of "guidelines" that are suggested by our spiritual, religious, or ideological paths. We can make love consciously and involve the sacred presence in it, which will integrate a strong connection with our partners, a caring for every aspect of the act and around it, a strong tendency to detail, and a profound interest and a dedication to the other's pleasure and well-being—not as a means to an end, that they may feel grateful or reciprocate, but just for the sake of the end goal, caring for another, not as means to our pleasure.

This can be applied to every aspect of life, and if experienced mindfully, holds promise to a miraculous dyadic exchange, one we have only dreamed about, until now.

## Quickstep Meditation

We will choose the combination of היי, a sequence that represents prophetic abilities due to the acknowledgment of meager self versus grand divinity, and thus the creation of intuitive transformation of consciousness.

Returning to our embryonic, primordial knowing in order to recapture parts of our souls; resisting slavery to jealousy and physical matter.

With this sequence, we are able to see the bigger picture and allow the truth to seep into our relational lives, rather than dwelling in the shallow waters of life's dictation, led by ego, and the absence of connectedness.

When applying this sequence, look deep inside and compare these choices to a broader spectrum of relation; not only the practice of this sequence and the awareness it brings, which enables us to live in purposeful manner toward every single act or engagement in this world of action, but also that we are also able to influence a ripple of acknowledgment that may elevate the whole human consciousness toward a higher and a more appreciative realm on a cosmic, universal level.

Remember that you can digitally scan the letters or gaze at them, visualize them with your eyes closed, or chant them to the sound of HEYY. If you choose the two former options out of the four, you may want to copy this sequence on a small piece of paper that you keep in a safe and respected spot in order to utilize this power. You may also incorporate all four utilization options and switch from one to another as you progress.

Gaze at this sequence for a few minutes before going inside.

Sit in a comfortable position, close your eyes, and take a deep breath through your mouth, all the way up to the top of your lungs. Now, purse your lips and let your breath out slowly as if you're whistling through them. Repeat this three times, and keep a comfortable posture while reverting to normal breathing.

Slowly allow the three-letter sequence of היי to appear before you and float in your mind's eye.

I like to see these sequences as if they are floating on water in tiny ripples toward me and back, while gazing with my eyes closed. Allow the letters to form and heighten in your memory and breathe "the breath of life" into them. Merge the goal that you have in relation to this sequence and combine it with the energy you create.

It can be a soulful and beautiful connection with a potential soul match, or you can go further and expand into a peaceful existence to all. If you are aiming to unite with your current or hopeful partner in a respectful and harmonious manner, that will definitely and unequivocally serve the greater goal of a harmonious, sacred, and everlasting relationship. You may also alternate or gradually arrive at a higher-level goal as you advance and progress.

When you feel safe and strong in this frequency and the light it emits, gradually allow both your hands to touch the ground, and revert to normal breathing. Gradually and slowly open your eyes. You may want to remain seated in this position for a few moments before getting back on your feet. Drink a glass of water to quench the energy you've emitted.

# Overindulgence

We live in a world that appears to offer everything for the taking: the right partner, the big bucks, the right fashion, the perfect home, the great success, public admiration, and so on. Yet, alongside the immediacy and "accessibility" of it all, we are thrown into a constant rabbit hole of chasing and accomplishing. If you want the house, you have to work seventy hours a week; if you want the lover, you have to accumulate fortune, fame, and a physical upgrade; if you want the admiration, you have to sacrifice dignity; you get the picture. In the midst of it all, we can't help but notice glimpses of other paths and terrains that appear as if on a *Matrix* TV screen, in our rearview mirrors, or right in front of us, disturbing the frequencies of our driven, weary minds.

These glimpses cause us to look within, to slow down, to focus! Some will call it enlightenment, others will call it self-discovery, or simply ignore it, but the Kabbalistic views of this very familiar experience have a different explanation and suggestion. Kabbalah tells us that our world of Assiyah, the world of action, is in the realm of the lower letter Hey in the unspoken name of the Creator. That letter is familiar to you by now, and it looks like this: ה.

Kabbalistic teachings tell us that when our overindulgences cover our awareness of our true purpose, this letter alters itself into a different letter called Chet, which looks like this ח; in plain observation, you can see these are similar—only the space between the roof of the letter Hey and its left pillar is now closed, in the letter Chet.

Not only do these teachings mean that we are clogged and locked up by our disserving life choices and endless pursuits, but the very meaning of the word *chet* (it's a letter as well as a word in Hebrew) is "sin."

Now, this notion of observing our overindulgences carefully, and treading forward lightly, is not a self-frugality principal, as we suggested that aspect of self is very different in Kabbalistic views versus other esoteric practices. Instead, the need to observe and *recalculate route* here is sourced in the understanding that the process of tzimzum (constriction) is what creates that subconscious sensation of a void, when in fact, the infinite divine light is everywhere, only not genuinely apparent because there's no tangible life in the presence of all this light.

The illusion of this void is what stands behind two very familiar experiences. First, the sensation of being utterly alone and separate, and not a part of a group, cause, nation, or life. And second, the sensation of never having enough, always needing more, worrying about being deprived.

Every human being experiences these essential sensations. Sometimes we're not aware of them at all, and sometimes the awareness is profound. But whatever the case, it's always there. It's part of the plan of creation.

This core illusion of aloneness and solidity is what allows us to exist as separate and unique human beings. In its raw, unrectified state, it cuts us off from the truth. But ultimately, we are destined to see through the walls, transcend the illusion, and fulfill our potential as uniquely magnificent expressions of the divine.

## The Sound of the Void

The illusion is powerful, but not all-inclusive. If we were totally cut off from an awareness of what lies beyond, chances are that we would be perfectly content. There would be no reason to question ourselves or our existence, no drive to continuously experience more.

But we are not cut off completely. A glimmer of the infinite light from before creation surrounds and permeates each person who walks this earth. This light is what gives us the profound sense that there is something else out there. Only the something doesn't always feel like an actual something. It often feels like *something missing*—the void.

This void, this *missing*, hovers at the edge of our consciousness, threatening our comfortable sense of solidity and bringing with it an essential longing for ... well, for something. Something more.

This sensation of *something missing*, is actually the glimmer of something too vast and amazing to be perceived by our ordinary senses. But being physical beings in a physical world, we are not naturally inclined to relate to it in this esoteric way. In fact, the non-physical all too often makes us feel vulnerable and uncomfortable. So, instead of slowly allowing our eyes to adjust to this more subtle light, we avoid the experience altogether, or seek to fill the void with physical things. In comes addiction, or overindulgence, if you will.

The void pulls us relentlessly toward the next high, the next success, the more exciting relationship, the bigger, flashier toy. The feelings it triggers—like sadness, depression, anxiety, or dissatisfaction—drive us to eat too much, drink too much, work too hard and long, hoard more; in short, whatever it takes to avoid facing the threatening insubstantiality of it all.

But, as uncomfortable and threatening as it can feel, if we are willing to face the discomfort, to stop running and start getting attuned, we can begin to explore the secret of the void, and to expand our ability to see and hear things that lie outside your normal range.

## A Deeper Level of Life

The message is simple. In being willing to embrace the vulnerability, to stop running or chasing and instead strive to expand our ability to *see*, we may begin to reconnect with what has been concealed, the part of us that is most truly and infinitely alive.

Kabbalah explains that this alleged darkness is really a much vaster and more brilliant form of light—one that's simply too great for our senses to acknowledge. As physical beings, we are primed to seek (the illusion of) permanence and stability. But the bad news—the paradoxical news—is that physical things are inherently unstable and impermanent.

Coming face-to-face with this fact can be overwhelming. It can feel, indeed, like hovering over a dark and formless void.

Many of us spend our lives attempting to avoid facing any of these notions, to avoid the darkness within ourselves, or to create stability and solidity out of things that are intrinsically unstable. This is why we are constantly in quest of a new plaything, a new relationship, a new adventure. This pursuit, nonetheless, does nothing to brighten the darkness, nor to expand our capacity to see. We remain trapped in a world of struggle and illusion. But if, instead, we train our eyes, bit by bit, to see the concealed light, to notice the subtle undertones, we can begin our emancipation.

What is it that you escape to? Maybe you eat or drink or work or sleep too much. Or maybe you take solace in having very strong opinions, in making yourself feel bigger and more solid by being right, criticizing, blaming, or complaining. Maybe you try to lose yourself in a relationship, or maybe you avoid the vulnerability that intimate relationships bring.

Whatever it is that you do, Kabbalah tells us, if we attempt an occasional let go and avoid these habitual tendencies, you will embark on this revelation and soul release. Instead of choosing the habitual notion, let yourself be open to something—anything—that challenges the way you've seen things up to this point. Going without that extra cookie, that glass of wine, or arguing to always be right could bring up feelings or perceptions that have something important to tell you. Giving up a protective habit is one of the most powerful ways to expand your capacity to see and hear.

Maybe you can let yourself be vulnerable to someone else, where you'd normally be defensive. Perhaps you can take an hour away from work to sit with your children or loved ones without any agenda of accomplishment at all. Take a few minutes to open your heart to your creator. These things bring more divine light into the darkness and help to illuminate the void.

Whatever you choose to do, if you do it consciously, listening intently for what you haven't been willing to hear before, it will almost certainly help you expand beyond the limitations of who you've known yourself to be. It will help you to embrace a new level of yourself, a new level of being alive.

# Chapter 27
## Connectedness

We encounter the Shekinah time and again in the Kabbalistic text; so far we understood that she's represented in the sephirah of Malchut, that she's the feminine component of the divine, and that she's a pretty "tough cookie" when attempting to align us humans in the quest of our divine sparks. It's imperative to keep in mind that in this ongoing relationship between us and the Creator, Shekinah is encompassing us all in her femininity, vis-à-vis the Creator's masculinity. In other words, we are all a part of that receiving entity, the feminine Shekinah.

By the very nature of things, femininity encompasses the *being*, while masculinity encompasses the *doing*, the performance. This is the source of motherly love, which is based on just the existence of the child, while paternal love leans on what the child does, his tangible choices, the way he performs. Regardless, both genders encompass attributes of both in one. Finding the divine within is led by the feminine attributes, hence the Zohar's vast engagement with the Shekinah.

Kabbalistic views add that the masculine divine is found in the *garments* of the soul, such as thoughts, speech, and actions; humans dwell in the being, the action. In comes Shekinah, whose garment is made of sacred and divine scripts, enabling her to shine over the world, take us under her wing (on many occasions, the Shekinah is symbolized by a dove), and allow us to dwell in the quest of our divine parts.

Shekinah is also a skilled warrior since she was sent here into what Kabbalistic teachings call *tohu*, "empty mess," or the lowest of worlds, the world of action, earth. This is the world of total otherness, a world where the majority of inhabitants hold no sense of anything else other than this world. Some even sense that they themselves are the masters of this world, or even that nothing else exists other than themselves.

So in an objective view, the Shekinah is given the most excruciating job of getting in this haystack and trying to make some sense of it all, while looking for these divine sparks where her masculine counterpart, the Creator, claimed they were located. The Shekinah is to rescue them from their shells of darkness and reconnect them to their source above so that they become once again meaningful and divine—all through *us*.

Like the Shekinah, our soul is not here for its own sake—the soul is perfect before her descent below. It comes here, as does the Shekinah, to redeem the sparks of the body in which it is infused, of the personality it is given, and of the portion of this world, to which it is assigned. Everything is planned to the last detail, perfectly.

Kabbalistic teachings call this process *birrur*, or "sorting out." *Birrur* means to sort out the good from the bad, the desirable from the waste; as we struggle to discard the bad, the ugly, and the deceptions that surround us, seeking out all the divine sparks they contain, we are acting as the Shekinah's foot soldiers, locating value wherever it can be found.

Birrur can be performed only when wisdom is the master; as the Zohar says, "With wisdom they will be purified." The wisdom to which the Zohar refers is a higher vision, one that permits us to transcend our own personal desires and surrender to a higher truth. A wisdom that allows us to see beyond the mud—mostly our own mud—to recognize the gold that is there, embrace it, and distinguish it from its dirty shell.

After we dwell in the process of Birrur, we are free to be elevated into the next spiritual task; this task is the *tikkun*, when the divine spark is connected to its proper place. At this point, it sheds its outer, muddy crust, and begins to glow through the shell that shrouded it, so that the shell itself is transformed to become divine.

Wherever your feet lead you, they are directed from above to bring you into proximity to those divine sparks that belong to your soul alone. It may manifest in any which way possible; a relationship that must be healed, an aching heart that needs mending, a cause you're passionate about.

With you as the Shekinah's agent, this soul of yours can pursue this divine plan. By now, all our souls have been recycled many times. What your soul accomplished in previous descents, and what is left to be accomplished—all that is of necessity hidden from you. As Rabbi Moshe Cordovero wrote, "Those who know do not say, and those who say do not know." For if we would know, we would accomplish without struggle. And it is the struggle itself that brings out the innermost powers, the powers of redemption.

As with the sparks, the further the soul descends, the greater will be its ultimate ascent. Indeed, there is only ascent. For the descent itself, in retrospect, is the active stage that powers the ascension.

It is important to understand that in order to redeem, one must be present; birur, tikkun—these cannot happen from afar. This world cannot be healed and transformed, except by those who dwell within it. Tikkun means keeping the world standing while repairing from within. The ultimate tikkun is a harmony of a world that can contain infinite light and yet remain a world.

To do that requires full involvement and not "for others" but *with* others. If you plan to offer your help to someone in need, the only way this soul connection and ascension can be accomplished is by acknowledging the understanding that you were put there in order to experience this situation. You're not an external observer that is only there by "choice."

That is the process of tikkun. We are left with many questions while contemplating these profound Kabbalistic ideas. We may ask, "But why would the Creator need our help? And why are we sent on this horrific chore if the Creator can manifest this in a 'heartbeat'?" The answer is that there is no answer. The very cause of looking and questing is the lack of firm answer. Grasping the answer would sabotage the mission.

# What's on a Man's Mind

The Talmud, the important body of Jewish ceremonial law, states that, "To match couples together is as difficult as the splitting of the Sea of Reeds." This refers, by Kabbalistic views, to second or third marriages, rather than the first and hopefully infinite nuptial. Trying to match a couple where both partners have suffered a loss of a sort in a prior commitment can be challenging, because as humans we tend to slowly lose faith one ounce at a time. But the reason this strange analogy is used in relation to such a beautiful and profound goal is deeper than what may appear on the surface. Kabbalistic teachings shed light on this subject by explaining what we already know regarding the two planes this world is composed of, namely land and sea. Kabbalah tells us that just as the dry land is exposed and naked to the eye of the beholder who occupies it, so are our conscious minds; we manage them daily, and by our actions and choices, we exhibit layers of our minds to our environment. Yet, the important and concealed part of our existence, namely the subconscious, is not observed by others, nor do we ourselves hold a great familiarity with it. The subconscious mind is equated to the sea. Why is that important?

Kabbalah tells us that the mere glimpse into our hidden subconscious can expose us to many facets that are not quite appealing or inviting. We can discover shame, fear, guilt, pain, insecurity, an urge to destroy, to survive, to dominate, a cry for love; we can find the truthfulness in Freud's libido, Jung's collective unconscious, or perhaps Adler's search for power, but all these are mere manifestations to the core of it all, what Kabbalah calls *man's quest for oneness with the divine*.

In fact, the founder of the Chabad movement and author of many books like the Tanya equated the element of fire with the soul. Basing his statement on the beautiful verse in Proverbs 20:27, "The spirit of man is the lamp of the LORD, searching all the inward parts," meaning that like the flame that holds the dancing light within the lamp, a man's soul is flickering and vibrating, aspiring to connect and finally be reunited with the Creator. In fact, as mentioned earlier, and as greatly appropriate for the use of the fire element, relationships and intimacy are expressed in the Hebrew terms for man and woman—*Ish* (איש ) and *Isha* (אשה))—both contain the Hebrew word for fire, *Esh* (אש) . They also each contain one more letter—a *yud* (י) and a *hei*(ה) respectively—which when combined, makes up one of the most used divine names, יה. The significance of this is profound. Man without woman, and woman without man, lack the fullness of God's name. When they unite, the two half images of the divine within them also unite. The fire and passion drawing them to each other is their yearning to recreate the full name of God between them.

Going back to that difficult stretch one needs to make in order to reestablish a true sacred connection, the quest for a relationship with the divine is manifested in our search for relationships with our twin flame here on earth, in the world of action.

To drive this point all the way home, we can observe that in a Jewish wedding ceremony, a part of the blessing that is recited states, "Who created the human being in His image ..." in relation to the divine force, of course. The reason for this choice of blessing upon this specific occasion is that only through union of man and woman is the image of God is most closely reflected; through marriage, man and woman return to their true natural state, a single being reflecting God, each in his and her own unique way. Marriage allows wife and husband to discover their full and complete self, a self made up of masculine and feminine energy that comprises the divine essence.

Why does this "trivial" conclusion that should be comprehensible to all deserve a place of importance? When we view the surface self, selfishness is easier than selflessness; isolation more natural than relationship; solitude more innate than love and commitment.

If we take this principle and apply it to everyday life, wronging our partner is only understood on the reciprocal end of it, as if the same is being done unto us. In other words, the answer to the question, "Does it matter if I wrong my partner if I don't really mean it, or if I correct it later?" is yes, it matters, because we are divine beings and thus hold a divine power and spark, which should be accounted for.

Would you accept a misfortune if the Creator claimed it wasn't personal, or stated that you may receive a compensation at a later time? The answer will likely be no. Only when we "split our sea," when we discover the depth of our souls, the subtle vibrations of our subconscious, do we discover that oneness satisfies our deepest core; that love is the most natural expression of our most profound selves.

# Quickstep Meditation

We will choose the combination of נמם, a sequence that represents removing limitations to make it across your personal Sea of Reeds.

Returning to our primordial knowing, in order to recapture parts of our souls, resist slavery to the tangible, and allow a true soul connection, we must acknowledge the divine space between our partners and us—the earthly as well as the godly.

With this sequence, we are able to see the bigger picture and allow the truth to seep into our relational lives, rather than dwell in the shallow waters of life's dictation led by ego and the absence of connectedness. When applying this sequence, look deep inside and compare these choices to a broader spectrum of relation; not only the practice of this sequence and the awareness it brings, which enables us to live in a purposeful manner toward every single act or engagement in this world of action, but also that we are able to influence a ripple of acknowledgment that may elevate the whole human consciousness toward a higher realm, and a more appreciative one, on a cosmic, universal level.

Remember that you can digitally scan the letters or gaze at them, visualize them with your eyes closed, or chant them to the sound of *NAMAM*. If you choose the two former options out of the four, you may want to copy this sequence on a small piece of paper that you keep in a safe and respected spot in order to utilize this power. You may also incorporate all four utilization options and switch from one to another as you progress.

Gaze at this sequence for a few minutes before going inside.

Sit in a comfortable position, close your eyes, and take a deep breath through your mouth, all the way up to the top of your lungs. Now, purse your lips and let your breath out slowly as if you're whistling through them. Repeat this three times and keep a comfortable posture while reverting to normal breathing.

Slowly allow the three-letter sequence of נמם to appear before you and float in your mind's eye.

I like to see these sequences as if they are floating on water in tiny ripples toward me and back, while gazing with my eyes closed. Allow the letters to form and heighten in your memory and breathe "the breath of life" into them. Merge the goal that you have in relation to this sequence and combine it with the energy you create.

It can be a soulful and beautiful connection with a potential soul match, or you can go further and expand into a peaceful existence to all. If you are aiming to unite with your current or hopeful partner in a respectful and harmonious manner, that will definitely and unequivocally serve the greater goal of a harmonious, sacred, and everlasting relationship. You may also alternate or gradually arrive at a higher-level goal as you advance and progress.

When you feel safe and strong in this frequency and the light it emits, gradually allow both your hands to touch the ground, and revert to normal breathing. Gradually and slowly open your eyes. You may want to remain seated in this position for a few moments before getting back on your feet. Drink a glass of water to quench the energy you've emitted.

# Chapter 28

## Trust

In 1 Samuel, chapter 17, we are introduced to who will later become God's most uplifted and admired king of Israel, David. We are told about the smaller figured young teenager whose main occupation was herding sheep. We are told that unlike his siblings, young David was not even destined to go and join the battle led by king Saul, and that his presence in the battlefield was circumstantial as his father asked him to go and bring supplies to his brothers and check up on their well-being. Why is this story interesting and important for our own view of soulful strength?

Kabbalistic teachings tell us that this prospect can be derived from the King David story in a multifaceted manner. Let's start with the idea if individuation. David, even prior to the battle with Goliath and the following unquestionable reign, was unique and an individualist.[39] His dualistic and unique nature was portrayed accurately in his unordinary appearance of a fiery red mane and kind eyes. David was the epitome of kindness and holiness, mixed within a sublime and tenacious warrior who takes what he wants and can defeat a lion and a bear with his

---

39 Gottlieb, Mel. 2012. "King David's Individuation Process Seen through a Kabbalistic Lens." *Psychological Perspectives* 55 (2): 182–204. https://doi.org/10.1080/00332925.2012.677638.

bare hands, not to mention a giant combat machine like Goliath, but at the same time, can spend his days herding sheep, caring for his father and brothers, and exhibiting true love for his adored friend, Yonatan.

Kabbalistic teachings tell us that the very particular spark of divinity we each encompass is exactly what we need to pursue. We are told that the young David refused to wear the rehal combat attire given to him by king Saul ; David stated, "'I cannot go with these; for I have not tried them.' And David put them off him." Some sages and commentators suggest that the regal attire was so becoming of David that from the king's gaze, he knew he had no business wearing it, and for the sake of peace and courtesy, removed them with the excuse of *feeling uncomfortable*.

The principal of pursuing your soul quest is embedded in the Kabbalistic views of soul elevation. We are here to pursue a specific purpose in our actions, our choices, and the overall lives that we lead. If one holds the potential to bring bliss or relief or great achievement to a certain location, goal, or another human being and does not pursue it with all his might, this spark is lost in the overall scheme of divine intervention and never reaches its goal. Moreover, the soul does not live up to its potential and may require reincarnating in another physical form in which the soul will be faced with yet bigger challenges in the same pursuit of its goal.

Following your own calling and remaining true to your nature is an important message in the story of King David, and just as much in our everyday lives. You may ponder, "Who am I, and what is my purpose? I'm definitely not destined for great things and achievements." You'd not only be mistaken, but you'd be doing your very soul an injustice.

We are intuitively drawn to certain activities and actions; at times, these sensations are placed within us in order to challenge us to overcome them. That is the makeup of an addiction or an "unkosher" pursuit. Nonetheless, by definition, we are given these intuitive quests and demands because we are the only ones who are able to achieve a particular result, a blessing, a solace, unto a place, a person, a cause.

Yes, the feeling of such a meager entity within a world populated by billions can be overwhelming on one hand and apply serenity on the other—or rather a removal of responsibility. Yet, Kabbalah tells us that our roles in this universal structure are unique, and as such, we are solemnly obligated to pursue and achieve what we were placed here to achieve.

## Saul and David: A Complex Relationship

Saul was "young and handsome, there being no one of the children of Israel handsomer than he; from his shoulders and upwards he was taller than any of the people." (Samuel I 9:2) Yet he had outstanding modesty and humility and an innate nobility of character.

Kabbalah teaches that Saul's soul was rooted in what is known as the "World of Concealment" ("World of the Male"), while that of David descended from the "Revealed World" (*yesod* of *Nukva*, the female world or female genitalia, to be exact). For this reason, Saul was modest, or hidden. This can also be related to the principal of transparency for the person who practices a sacred existence. We are told by Kabbalah that transparency means that one is stripped of any layers, and so any interaction with any other human or in any situation is free of masks or "garments."

Saul, as he was from the world of *Tohu*, of the concealed, his kingship, could not endure. Saul's soul root lay in the sixth of the Kings of Edom, relating to the sephira of Yesod, whose name was similar; this king was one of the Edomite Kings whose death is mentioned explicitly in Genesis 36:37, "And Shaul of Rehoboth by the River reigned in his stead" and then immediately in verse 38 we are told, "And Shaul died." David, on the other hand, is rooted in the world of *tikkun*, or "repair", and for this reason, his kingship endured. [40]

Since the house of royalty was destined to be from Judah, Saul, a descendent of Benjamin, deserved to be king in his own right, but wasn't destined to father a succession of royalty, unlike David.

---

40 "Likutei Moharan, Go See." 2019. Sefaria.Org. 2019. https://www.sefaria.org/Likutei_Moharan%2C_Go_See?lang=bi.

# Saul's Failings

Saul was rebuked for being "small in his own eyes" and not assertive enough in his mission as "the head of the tribes of Israel." This can also stand as disbelief in the divine to a degree, by Kabbalistic views, because self-trust is sacred as can be, given that the human soul is formed of divine sparks.

Side note here; the pursuit of David by King Saul, in quest of the former's demise, was solely based on jealousy and sourced in Saul's lack of self-appreciation. The Zohar tells us that the principle of jealousy is sourced in that lacking precisely. How, if so, can one fight jealousy? Kabbalah tells us that it is done by expanding and enhancing faith and belief. Offering love, compassion, or caring to another is the enhancement of belief. By practicing these actions, one signals to the Creator the realization that this life isn't only about the small selfish self.

According to some sources, Saul reigned for only two years. Samuel the prophet ceased to appear before him; instead, he sought David, his successor. Regarding this unbecoming behavior of Saul's self-mistrust, the Talmud states, "Be not overly righteous like Saul, who thought to be more righteous [than God Himself] and had mercy on the wicked," which referred to his "missed battle" with the Amaleckim.[41]

The Baal Shem Tov teaches us that when one comes before the Heavenly Tribunal upon his death, he is shown someone else who seemingly has sinned and is asked to voice his opinion on the case (just as the prophet Nathan asked David to pass judgment on "the poor man's lamb," referring to his misconduct of possessing Bat Sheba and arranging her spouse's demise[42]). Only after the newly deceased passes judgment is it demonstrated to him that his deeds were similar, and thus his sentence is his own verdict in the afterlife.

---

41 "Yoma 22b." n.d. Www.Sefaria.Org. Accessed September 11, 2020. https://www.sefaria.org/Yoma.22b?lang=bi.

42 "II Samuel 12." n.d. Www.Sefaria.Org. Accessed September 11, 2020. https://www.sefaria.org/II_Samuel.12?lang=bi.

Kabbalistic teaching tell us that although David's sins were rebuked by many losses in his family and decedents, one who sins and is does not make excuses for himself, all his sins are forgiven, as the verse states, "thou mayest remember, and be confounded, and never open thy mouth anymore, because of thy shame; when I have forgiven thee all that thou hast done, saith the Lord GOD."

Simply put, if one remembers and exhibits remorse for unfavorable actions and no longer holds an excuse by reason of humiliation, the Creator will forgive all that one has engaged in. Therefore, David, the paramount repentant, merited a royal line of kings to descend from him, whereas Saul's reign lasted a mere two years, his outstanding character traits notwithstanding.

## The Eroticism of Lurianic Kabbalah

We are familiar with many motifs of eroticism and sensuality with various esoteric doctrines; we are educated about the enchantment of kundalini, the enlightenment of yogic breathwork, and so on. In Kabbalistic teachings, nonetheless, the very core of creation is erotic and sensual, in its essence.

Let us look at how this manifests and try to connect it to our personal, tangible relationships.

Kabbalah tells us that the story of creation depicted in Genesis 1 is the source of it all. When the Creator embarked on what we refer to as tzimtzum, or contraction, he simply separated the top water from the bottom water, thus establishing a separation between seas and sky. In between, he enabled the creation of our world as we know it, the world of Assiyah, or action. Now, the word for sky in Hebrew, which, as stated earlier, sources the meaning of creation on a verbal and pronounced level, is *rakia* or *shamayim*. If we relate to the former, we will see that this word means to hammer out, to flatten, which refers to the fact that the upper water is hidden behind a flattened, hammered surface—a screen, if you will—that holds the upper water behind it. In Kabbalistic views, this is the source of the mystery of rain.

When we look at the latter term for sky, *shamayim*, it literally means "holding water."

Kabbalah tells us that the "dance" between the upper water and the bottom water holds the key to all of creation, and that this key is super erotic and arousing.

Let's go back to the sephirot.

We are told that the upper water, where the godly essence lies, is the sephirah of Binah (different Kabbalists may debate regrading different sephirot as the very one that may hold this notion most profoundly). The bottom water is represented by the sephirah of Malchut, where Shekinah resides, and where our earthly world of creation is embedded.

In this very intrinsic Kabbalistic rational, the source of abundance, wholesomeness, prosperity, luscious existence, fruitful, and lusty being is the nourishment of the bottom water of Malchut by the upper water of Binah.

"Is that it?" you may ask. Not quite. We are also told that the relationship between the receiver, bottom water, the femme, and the upper water, the homme, the *bestower* or giver, strictly lies in the hand of the receiver, the bottom, the feminine.

In other words, Kabbalah tells us that the dance of seduction is completely in our human hands, the world below, the world of action; we are exclusively responsible to draw the attention and lure the top water, the divine, into "bed" with us. Essentially, the Creator carved this universe in a way that, independent from our action below, there can be no action from above that vigorously invades the bottom entity. This means that if our actions are not sacred and divine but deprecating and harmful, the whole universe suffers from dying crops, no rain, deprived resources, loss, "natural" disasters, and so forth. We are told that if we do engage in righteous and meaningful, globally bestowing actions, we will yield God's *massive secretions* straight into the very core of us and fertilize our very being, the female wetness, with sensational gifts of existence. If that isn't a sexy, erotic scene, I don't know what is.

So, what does that have to do with us and our relationships? First, we must acknowledge how profound the source of life being drawn from below and propelling up to the divine unity really is. In the biblical stories of our forefathers and foremothers, we see the motif of wells as a receptacle of water from above. For reference, we are told the magical story of Rebecca, who is sent by divine intervention to her "local" well the very moment that Abraham asked for divine guidance in locating a suitable mate for his son, Isaac. The story of Jacob and Rachel begins at the well when Jacob exhibits both grand chivalry by helping Rachel with the heavy stone that covered the well in order to draw water for her sheep and goats, all along being laser focused on the incredible godly incident this occurrence commemorates, as we are told in Genesis 29:11: "And Jacob kissed Rachel, and lifted up his voice, and wept," which was his awe-stricken response and meditative prayer in light of this unequivocal incident.

Even in the modern era, in locations which modern Westernism left untouched, the only interaction between males and females could take place at the well, as a representation of an ancient tradition. Moreover, as we noted, the well acts as a reciprocal of the "water above," generating life by being drawn from below in order to nourish, fertilize, and sustain. This interaction enables humans to signal to the divine above of the infinite dyadic exchange that the Creator so craves and is moved by, if one allows for some form of personification of the divine source.

We stimulate and imitate the cosmic divine union between the Shekinah and the godly source. We are a micro cosmos, a small representant of the macro paramount of existence. In other words, the application of these tendencies toward our love lives, sex lives, and general sacred dyads, is impacted on a daily and hourly level by our very choices of action. This does not mean we are to become saints and relinquish our eclectic attire in favor of an orange toga; it does mean, nonetheless, that we take responsibility for our misbehaviors, our insults, our lack of communication, attention, effort, that impact our relational exchanges, as well as the state of our very existence, globally.

When you look at this picture and comprehend the massive global ramifications of our behavior, you cannot simply relate to sex or a relational exchange as casual or unimportant. You are simply obligated to give these aspects of life your very detailed attention and effort in order to fit in the luxurious piece of jigsaw puzzle that is you to help form the entire beautiful piece that is our universe.

# Quickstep Meditation

Take a quick look at the Tree of Life once more if you need to be reminded of its structure.

We will focus on the erotic connection between Binah and Malchut to form this divine nourishment we discussed.

Sit in a comfortable position and close your eyes. Inhale to the count of five and exhale to the same count. Repeat this breathing three to five times while placing your hands on your knees, palms facing up, for receiving mode.

When you feel relaxed, place your hand on your left eye and the other hand on your feet.

Start to imagine a trickling sound of water, first slow and quiet, starting from the bottom of your sitting body, quiet and slow, washing and tickling your feet and sitting area. Slowly and gradually start to imagine this water forming into a deeper pond, surrounding your genitals, your abdomen, and your thighs. The sound becomes a bit stronger as you allow it to wash over your lower body as if you're sitting inside the ocean with your bottom half covered. Start to imagine the slow sound of drops hovering on the top of your head, slowly seeping onto the left part of your face. The sound becomes stronger and more intense, like a forming rain. Now, begin to push the sea water from the bottom toward the rain water on the top by moving your hands, the one below slowly ascending while the one above slowly descending. Gradually start to imagine the sound of both the ocean from below and the rain from above, strengthening and becoming louder. Feel your entire body being washed by this intense collision of pleasurable, invigorating water. You're not troubled or uncomfortable, this feels rewarding and blissful, like an oasis within the desert.

Allow this sensation to take over and indulge in it. When you feel satisfied, slowly return your hands toward the left side of your face and feet and allow the water to retreat.

Allow your hands to lay casually on your knees facing down, and take a few more breaths to the count of five.

When you're ready, open your eyes.

# Chapter 29

*I took the one less traveled by, and that has made all the difference.* —Robert Frost

Kabballah tells us that a spiritual journey has no shortcuts, and we are given a tangible representation of this essential "long route" requirement by the physical body. Kabbalistic teachings tell us that just like the human body is built in the shape of a head on top, heart in the middle, and lower extremities at the bottom, so does our spiritual and soul growth start as an idea (head) progress into feelings and emotions (heart), and finally descend into actions (legs).

The state of *tikkun*, or "correction," a concept we mentioned earlier, is likened to a human being, where there is a harmonious and symbiotic relationship between all body parts. In Kabbalistic teachings, we are told about the sephirot being arranged either in "circles" (Igulim) or a single "straight" (Yashar). The terms "circles" and "straight" are synonymous with chaos (the source of timtzum) and correction (returning to our divine nature, tikkun). In chaos, the sephirot were arrayed in circles, one concentric circle within another, each circle having no physical contact with the other. In the straight condition, conversely, the sephirot are arrayed in the form of a human being, having a balanced relationship.

In the Zohar, we are told about the three elements that are essentially the blueprint of creation, and the goal to reunite with our divine nature.

We discussed the concept of tzimtzum (contraction) and the principle of tikkun (healing of the universe). But, in between, we are looking at the most imperative aspect of our human responsibility. Kabballah tells us that the divine light, upon the tzimtzum, was perfectly set in immaculate vessels of light. Yet, sourced in chaos, the vessels broke and shattered, leaving behind innumerable *klipot*, or shells, as mentioned prior,semi-empty vessels that are either devoid of the divine light, or lock it tightly inside them and act as a type of invader, or pandemic, if you will. Left untouched, these shells aim to bring the universe to its demise, but, by our acts of repentance, kindness, mutual responsibility, accountability, and respect, we can heal the vessels and repair the world; thus tikkun. This principle of the klipot is complex and intricate.

When the Vessels of Chaos shattered as a result of the principle of contraction, Kabbalah tells us that 288 sparks (yes, it advises a particular number, which stems from the four dimensions of seventy-two (Names of God), that descended from the four forms of the *unspoken name*), which "fell" and became embedded in the lower levels of creation. As they fell downward, they broke further into smaller particles.

As they continued to descend, they became more numerous and coarser due to their egotistic origin. The more refined sparks were assimilated into the world of emanation (Atzilut), while others, less refined, descended into the world of creation (Beriah) or formation (Yetzirah), constituting the "evil" (or independent) parts of those levels. The coarsest sparks landed into our world of action (*Assiyah*), and ultimately created these kelipot shells.

It should be noted that the Shattering (called *Shvirah*, in Hebrew) of the Vessels was not an accidental flaw in the divine plan. On the contrary, this process allowed for the creation of the evil inclination, thus providing man with the exercise of free choice and the challenge to create a tangible and "livable" existence (Kabbalah calls this *Dirah Betachtonim*). Furthermore, hidden sublimely within the kelipot are the original Lights of the World of Chaos. When a person transforms these kelipot through abolition of problematic choices or habits, or by repentance and the formation of kindness (*Teshuvah*), he unleashes those Lights. In everything material, Kabbalah tells us, there are sparks of holiness that are released when used for the sake of good. It could be that certain sparks wait hundreds or even thousands of years for someone to release them, very much like a divine and magical genie in a bottle. This task is called the "Refining of the Sparks."

Examples of this refinement can be found in all our habitual actions—relational and personal in particular. If we relate to our partners at a soul level, and strive to allow these dyads to be sacred and soul elevating, it will allow our bodies (the foot soldier of the soul) and our souls to release these divine sparks and enable the "correction" on a global scale. We can relate this to other habitual actions like food consumption.

Kabbalah tells us that since body and soul are held together by nourishment, every kosher food item contains sparks of holiness that are released when the food is consumed for the sake of good, such as maintaining great health in order to allow the body to pursue noble actions. The soul, which stems from the World of Correction, is nourished by these sparks, the roots of which are in the World of Chaos. Man is reliant on food because his soul is nourished by the light of the holy sparks that are packed nicely in the food that originated in the world of Chaos. Conversely, we are told that a lavish and non-mindful consumption, solely for the sake of ravenous indulgence (emphasis on solely, because food or sex should be enjoyed by definition, but not independently of value) forces the light to remain within the kelipah until the body utilizes the energy derived from the food for divine and legitimate purposes or pursuits.

## Armageddon and Why We Should Care

Many depictions of the principle of Armageddon have been attempted throughout the years. According to the book of Revelation in the New Testament of the Christian Bible, Armageddon, from Hebrew: הר מגידו , or Har Megiddo, is the prophesied location of a gathering of armies for a battle during the end of times, or as the launching of messianic times, and global peace on earth. The actual location is variously interpreted as either literal or symbolic.

In the Old Testament, at the very end of the Prophets section, the verse says "Behold, I will send you Elijah the prophet before the coming of the great and terrible day of the LORD."[43]

Whether we are advised regarding "the great and terrible day" or the aspect of messiah, we are told that once the return of the twelve tribes of Israel is completed, this serene period of complete resurrection and peace can emerge.

The global fascination with spiritual growth could be viewed as an advanced step toward these fantastic days. And as we are told in the Kabbalistic views, each of us holds a responsibility in the manifestation of this notion, which now in light of the current COVID-19 pandemic, could be viewed as sourced in the devoid shells (the klipot).

Now more than ever, our choices matter and our initiation toward a global healing is imperative, not on an esoteric level, but in the most practical and divine manner.

## The Principles of Bitul and Dvekut in Relationships

As discussed earlier, there are a number of differences, as well as similarities, between the wisdom of Kabbalah, in all its various Kabbalistic schools of thought, and other esoteric teachings, especially those that originated in Eastern cultures.

Let us look at yet another parity and disparity within the concept of Bitul within Kabbalistic teachings. If translated literally, Bitul means nullification of self. Now, when we relate to other esoteric teachings, we are immediately presented with the idea of humans being simply a receptacle for the universe, and as such, we are not a real entity but a vehicle that drives energy contained in a body of a meager significance, and aims to create divine unity by disregarding the vessel and connecting to the universal source.

Conversely, Kabbalah tells us that, although the concept of being a part of a whole, as in a container of the divine sparks and shells, is embraced here as well, the difference lies in the idea that it isn't simply

43 Malachi 3:23 KJV

energy that we are aiming to conjoin with on a global level, but rather an omnipresent Godly source that is very much existing, and is always striving to maintain a relationship with us.

From that particular place, the concept of Bitul, or nullification, does not mean disregarding the body and the relation to energy completely, but rather *counting* the body as this vessel that *must take tangible action*, in order to eliminate the selfish egotistical mannerism, so to devoid the human tendency for sole pleasure, and make "sacrifices" in comfort and indulgence, in order to unite with the divine. Here, in comes another concept, and that is the concept of Dvekut.

Dvekut can be translated to "cleaving." Again, obviously the goal of our godly sparked soul is to cleave to the divine creator and work daily to enhance our proximity to his divine warmth on emotional and spiritual levels. In order to become closer to divine emanation, and to strive for the godly light source that we so crave, one should aim for an ongoing relationship with the "true self." "What is this true self?" you might ask. The true self is, of course, our souls, and they speak in sentiments from within; how does that translate into an actual experience? The conversations that our souls engage in with us are much more clandestine and quieter than the subconscious mind. They rarely appear verbally and don't *nudge*, the way the mind does. The way the soul chooses to converse with us can manifest through different sensations and emotions—states that are very familiar, yet are rarely given the attention or contemplation they deserve. This can appear in a form of a joyful sensation for no apparent reason; you wake up in the morning and feel utter jubilation out of nowhere. The opposite feeling or sentiment can appear just as randomly (nothing is really random, naturally). You may feel a sudden frustration or the need to burst into tears for no apparent reason at the time of experience. These types of messages are soul sourced, and they are a form of compass to your true connection with your divine purpose.

Experiencing more unbeknownst blissful moments versus discomfort and dismay, unrelated to particular event, may signal that your path is correct and allow you to proceed in the assigned direction.

We discussed the four elements that reside in each one of us. Mostly, we exhibit more intense tendencies of one or two of the elements, and we are well aware (if connected to our inner voices and intuition) of our most prominent nature, most of the time. Then, we discussed the water element in the core of creation and the fact that our innate facet is to exude our interests in the sacred relationship with the divine, or "feminine wetness," in a form of actions and choices, in the quest to receive the abundance and blessings from the "upper water." Here, the imperative element of fire enters. The soul is essentially the fire within your body. When we leave this world, we may appear to physically look the same, but the spark within us is gone, like a light switch turned off. That is the soul, the spark, the fire, our "feminine luminary," if you will.

How does this translate into our relational choices? As with all other experiences of soul source, we are a microcosm in this relation, and as we strive to become one with our divine sparks, our relational choices and actions matter. Does this mean we should become conservative and demur in our erotic and intimate life? Not at all.

In fact, the Talmud (the Jewish body of civil and ceremonial law)[44] tells us that a man is welcome to indulge in any form of sexual exchange with his partner, not based on any tradition or prohibition, if they agree to it, and while the laws of family purity apply. In other words, we are not prompted to practice conservative and uninspiring sexual exchange, but we are encouraged to invest a sense of divinity in this act, as it is in fact divine. And not only can and should the act of love be enjoyable under these suggestions, but it should also elevate our souls to a higher realm if practiced with a sense of Bitul—the nullification of solely intrinsic, egotistical desires.

## Quickstep Meditation

For this unique meditation, we will choose the sequence אום, as it represents removing or reducing the ego and forming a bridge to upper worlds, as described before, provided that we occupy the lowest of

---

44 "Yevamot 44a:5." — — —. n.d. Www.Sefaria.Org. https://www.sefaria.org/Yevamot.44a.5?ven=William_Davidson_Edition_-_English&lang=bi.

worlds in this realm. The sound of this sequence should be pronounced *om*, very similarly to the Eastern *OM*.

You may use אום while scanning the sequence, chanting it, or seeing it in your mind's eye while keeping your eyes closed. Chanting and seeing with your eyes closed can obviously be conjoined in order to enhance the experience.

Sit comfortably and place your hands on your knees. Take five deep inhales and five deep exhales, to the count of five each.

Begin to visualize the sequence and apply whichever method that suits your choice for the purpose of this meditation.

Stay focused; go back and forth between the specific letters, their shapes, and their sounds.

Remain focused and start shifting your body, rocking it from side to side or back to front. The body is the receptacle that carries this energy and the connection to the divine, and thus should be utilized in this practice.

Remain here and keep breathing naturally for a few moments; we will practice a pranayama, a yogi breathing sequence, to get you focused on your goal. When you're ready, place your index finger on your right nostril and the thumb on your left nostril. Close the left nostril and inhale through the right nostril, then close it with your index finger, release the left nostril and exhale through it. Now, keep the left nostril open, inhale through it, then close it with your thumb, and open the right nostril for exhale. Repeat these alternating breaths, inhales, and exhales for five counts each.

When you feel relaxed and satisfied, slowly open your eyes.

## Manifestation and Divine Sparks

The principle of manifestation has become massively popular in the last decade. People from all walks of life, backgrounds, experiences, political stances, religions, races, and genders exhibit a draw toward the unfamiliar, mystical, and, most important, gratifying. So, when we look at the rationale of the principle of manifestation, regardless of which theory or tool we choose to employ, the main drive behind these choices is egotistical in nature. In other words, if I want the best body, partner, career, house, car, fill in the blank, all I need to do is visualize myself in these situations in order to manifest them in the physical realm since they already exist in a parallel reality. That can be very correct, and many testimonials will attest to the validity of these beliefs and will even provide proof of that manifestation in the physical life. Nonetheless, the main correlation between these faith-based quests and Kabbalistic teachings is indeed the concept of faith. The differences, however, are vast. In Kabbalah, we are prompted to pursue and told that we have a role in this world, in this body, in this existence. We are not able to achieve these by mere visualization of the practice of belief, because the core of Kabbalistic wisdom is the ongoing, infinite relationship between us as humans in a body form, and the divine, nature, and the cosmos.

Moreover, relating to the shells or sparks that were discussed earlier, we are told in Kabbalistic views that anywhere we are and anything we do appears in our lives in order for us to accomplish our designed goal of attaining the divine sparks that await for us in the very specific situation, or location, in order to release them; only *we*, each one of us individually, hold the ability to release these very sparks. That is quite a responsibility, and we are advised that pursuing this goal is the only way we can "serve" our purpose and complete our roles in this life, if we are to avoid reincarnation and a "do-over."

In this same realm of manifestation, we are often encountered with the concept of transcendence. In the global Eastern esoteric teachings, a transcendent human is one who discovered his purpose, who can lead a life of kindness and tranquility, and who is open to unfamiliar experiences with this reality that is our perception. Here as well, the message is a tad different; Kabbalah refers to both principles of transcendence and immanence. These teachings call the principle of transcendence *makif* and the concept of immanence *pnimi*. The former is external, not within, by definition surrounding, while the latter is internal, inside.

In our prior discussion, we mentioned the circles (igulim) and the straight (yashar) in the worlds of independent interaction between the worlds, versus a straight connection between the upper world of emanation all the way down to our world of action. The circles represent transcendence as an external, overall force, while the straight relates to the immanent. Every one of us holds both elements within. Transcendence can be related to our wishes, our desires, and so on, essentially an entity that doesn't have a "localized" presence, while the immanent is localized and centered. Here we can find our thoughts (mind), feelings (heart), and the manifestation of the senses.

In other words, our manifestations (immanence) are bound to the external (transcendence) and thus the body, in its actions, is essential to the principle of manifestation. When one integrates both, one arrives at the most profound complementation of both.

# Chapter 30
## How about That Body?

Conversely to many ritualistic and cultural practices, Kabbalah and Judaism do not condone the art of inking or tattooing per se. The religious reasonings behind this choice are plenty, but we will focus on the esoteric and spiritual realm of things for this purpose. The rationale is that this body of yours carries a mission, and this mission can be accomplished in the greatest and most efficient manner by using the exact tools it was given. The choice of altering the skin permanently by inking suggests that us humans believe we can *upgrade* the divine vessel that we were initially granted with. Nonetheless, the practices regarding this aspect have many leniencies based on different components. In one, it is suggested that the tattooing of defiled skin that was created by the lack of awareness of this "prohibition" or this rationale is not only accepted, but is a source of an even greater receptacle of light, a bigger light-containing shell, because it's aligned with a shattered container from which the klipot were created.

The soul is a flame, and fire has the tendency to rise up and high; it defies gravity. The soul's purpose, in its fiery form, is to push us up, to allow us to strive for dreams and wishes, while the body is grounding; the body exists in order to get the soul back in the "wick."

We were given our bodies to contain our souls, but not to deal solely with survival of the flesh—it's not what our purpose is here. Also, the body is here not randomly, and our specific bodies were given to be borrowed, to actualize our flickering, the soul, the search to go higher, and the illumination the soul provides. That said, we are not allowed to abuse our bodies on our own "selfish" quests, but to utilize it as a servant to the soul. It is quite enchanting to consider the element of fire as such that, as much as you give, you are never diminished. The flame is always getting stronger with additional flames, it doesn't subside, similar to your soul. "What do I need" versus "what am I needed for" makes all the difference in this context. When you're in a mode of being of service to a divine plan in all aspects of your life, you're serving your soul rather than your body.

## Why Does God Have Seventy-Two Names?

Kabbalistic teachings tell us that among the many outlets of meditative and spiritual cleaving to the divine, we can benefit from the seventy-two sequences that represent the essence of the Creator. How were these accumulated, and why seventy-two? Kabbalah connects this origin to the story of Exodus, as representative of *the* time of divine intervention, and the manifestation of miracles, both in Egypt, and once the children of Israel embarked on their journey, with the parting of the Sea of Reeds as its acme.

In the story of the exodus from Egypt, we encounter three consecutive verses describing God's power, just before splitting the sea, which allowed for the dry passing of the chosen people, and the drowning of their pursuers.

And the angel of God who had been going ahead of the camp of Israel now moved and went behind them, and the pillar of cloud went from in front of them and stood behind them. Thus [the pillar of cloud] came between the camp of Egypt and the camp of Israel, making it cloud and darkness [to the Egyptians], but it gave light by night [to the Israelites], so that the one came not near the other all the night. Then Moses stretched out his hand over the sea, and God drove the sea back with a strong east wind all that night, and made the sea dry land; thus the waters were divided.[45]

In the Hebrew text, each of these three verses contains seventy-two letters, remarkably. In the Zohar, it is stated that these three verses refer in sequence to the divine attributes of the "middle triangle of the sephirot"—loving-kindness (Chesed), strength (Gevurah), and beauty (Tiferet). The harmonious blending of these three emotive attributes forms the basic paradigm of how the Creator relates to this universe.

Thus, placed together they form a composite "name" of God, since a name is a means by which one is made known to others and manifests his attributes.

The fact that each verse contains seventy-two letters means that they can be aligned in parallel, forming seventy-two sequences (triplets) of letters. The Zohar takes this further and presents a relevance to Ezekiel's vision of the *merkava* (chariot). In Ezekiel 1, we are told that the four faces of the beasts carrying the divine throne, in Ezekiel's vision, were that of a man, a lion, an ox, and an eagle. The lion face signifies loving-kindness, the ox face signifies strength, the eagle face represents beauty, and the man face represents the sephirah of Malchut, or sovereignty. Kabbalistic commentary compares this to the "sin of the golden calf," as an unhitching of the four animals of the chariot, by this particular scene, referring to one of the animals presented, the ox.[46]

By this commentary, it was not proper for the Jewish people to invoke the power signified by the ox when they ended up misusing this manifestation, later on in the golden calf fiasco.

The Zohar relates to the zodiac aspect of this scene, as the Exodus took place during the month related to the Aires sign(ram) which precedes the Taurus (bull) sign. Since the Passover sacrifice was a ram,

45 Exodus 14:19-21 KJV

46 Shemot Rabbah 43:8

the Jewish people subdued the astrological power ascendant at that time and seeing that the sign of Aires had been overcome(i.e. offered as sacrifice), they thought they can get away with invoking the next icon, the bull, in the sin of the golden calf celebrations, mentioned in Exodus 32. This scene evolved into a great loss of faith and progressed into future suffering and a price the nonbelievers, had to pay. what triggered these unagreeable behavior to begin with?

Let us connect this to our own dyadic exchanges with one another.

# Uncertainty

The great enemy of any relationship, including our erotic exchanges, as well as our spiritual quests, is the "unknown." Just as the children of Israel were struggling with the invisible and unpredictable creator, so are we impacted by the lack of stability or the ability to see "where or when" things are heading. Kabbalistic teachings tell us, nonetheless, that in order to have a relationship with the divine, we first must form a trusting relationship in the "bottom water," our personal, romantic exchanges. This is attained by leniency toward the unknown, in the earthly relationships, in a shape of gratitude, more giving, and the avoidance of "counting scores" with our beloved, which is a very human thing to do, yet devoid of divine light.

# Quickstep Meditation

Take a quick look at the Tree of Life once more if you need to be reminded of its structure.

We will focus on the divine connection between Chesed/Gevurah/Tiferet (the middle triangle of emotions), and then add the connection to Malchut in order to form the scene of Ezekiel's chariot (*maaseh merkavah*, in Hebrew).

Sit in a comfortable position and close your eyes. Inhale to the count of five and exhale to the same count. Repeat this breathing sequence three to five times while placing your hands on your knees, palms facing up, for receiving mode.

When you feel relaxed, place your hand on your right shoulder for Chesed, and your other hand flat on the ground for attachment and grounding.

Start to imagine a strong light with a bluish accent hovering over your shoulder, pressing it and making it heavy. Remain there for a few moments, imagining the strength and roar of a lion embedded in this sensation. Gradually, utilize this strength and shift it slowly to the left shoulder, evoking a maroon shade, changing gradually from the prior blue.

Now, add the face of the ox (bull), hovering over and being provoked with a red flag, propelling it to soar forward. Remain there for a few moments taking it in, and then gradually shift your energy and hand, to your heart/chest. Begin to invoke the color purple, allowing it to shift from the prior red and invite the presence of the eagle. Gradually, feel yourself rising above and becoming light and airy, still maintaining the beam of purple light. When you're ready, start shoving the entire energetic field and your hand toward the bottom, in between your feet or thighs, based on your sitting position. Lift your other hand and push the energy between the two hands. This energy has a strong dark blue color and is human, yet divine. Remain there and stay laser focused on the sensation that you're in the bottom water, tempting the divine power to anoint you with his blessings and abundance. This feels rewarding and blissful, like an oasis within the desert.

Allow this sensation to take over and indulge in it. When you feel satisfied, allow your hands to lay casually on your knees facing down, and take a few more breaths to the count of five.

When you're ready, open your eyes.

## Do You Believe in Magic?

I mentioned this prior, yet its global familiarity is worth a second noting. The familiar term used by all magicians and illusion artists globally, abracadabra has an interesting background. It originated in Aramaic, a

Semitic language that shares many similarities to Hebrew, yet is quite extinct at this point in time. Many of the original Kabbalistic writings originated in Aramaic and were later translated into Hebrew and English for practicality. In fact, the Zohar is written in Aramaic in its entirety. Back to that magical spell, *abra* is the Aramaic equivalent of the Hebrew *evra*, which means, "I will create." While *cadabra* is the Aramaic equivalent of the Hebrew *kedoobar*, which means "as was spoken." So essentially, the principle of the divine creating this universe simply by the utterance of specific Hebrew sequences, is compartmentalized in this exactly: *I will create in my words.*

## No Light without Darkness

The teachings of Kabbalah proclaim that to reconstruct the Shekinah, the process of figuratively dying and rebirthing must take place. Under these terms, the image of the redeemed, rebirthed Shekinah is that of Keter, Chochma, and Binah, folded into their centers; Chesed and Gevurah, folded into themselves; Tiferet, Netzach, and Hod, folded into themselves; and Yesod and Malchut—all centered into the Tree of Life core. Now, it forms a central column of seven spheres, very similar in appearance as well as nature, to the chakra system we are all very familiar with, but also exactly what we referred to as a straight, rather than circles, in the divine manifestation form.

Gershom Scholem, in his myriad of Kabbalistic commentaries and analysis, states that even the Shekinah, the female counterpart of the divine, experiences a sense of void or lacking. Scholem states that all of the sephirot preceding Shekinah (Malchut) have a form of place or position in advancing the spiritual path, yet Shekinah (Malchut) is passive and receptive, and does not have much influence on the actions *leading* to it.

In relation to the placement and significance of the Tree of Life and the sephirot, we are further advised by the Kabbalistic views that each triad and sephirah holds a firm position in the tangible human body; that is, for the context of utilizing divine energy for the practice of sacred relations and kind acts in the world of action, or the world of tikkun (correction), where we spend our days. Regardless, it is essential to understand the logic of it. The upper triad of Chochma/Binah/Daat, the intellect, corresponds to the lobes of the brain.

The middle triad Chesed/Gevurah/Tiferet, and bottom triad Netzach/Hod/Yesod, are merged, and correspond to the right and left arms and torso, the right and left legs, and the male sexual organ, respectively. The final sephirah, Malchut, corresponds to the female sexual organ. The *partzufim*, translated as "faces," are the nature of each "circle" or group of sephirot that stand for the four different levels of soul existence. In the table below, you can observe the actual distribution of it.

| Partzuf | sefirah | world | body | Name HAVAYA |
|---|---|---|---|---|
| Arich anpin | Keter | Atzilut-emanation | skull | hey |
| Abba Imma | Chochma Binah | Briah-creatioon | Right lobe left lobe | vav |
| Zeir anpin | The midot | Yeztirah – formation | Legs, arms, torso, male sexual organ | hey |
| Nukva d'zeir anpin | Malchut | Asiyah – action(corecrtiuon) | Female sexual organ | vav |
| | | | | |

Under a similar value mentioned earlier, Leah and Rachel represent converse locations within the sacred name. Leah represents the upper Hey and Rachel represents the lower Hey as Binah and Malchut respectively.

We have discussed the array of rituals and intentions that the Kabbalistic teachings suggest when it comes to the sexual union and the sacred relationship. Another interesting ritual that is applicable in Jewish nuptials receives a broader scope of rationale by these teachings.

In Jewish tradition, the bride and groom are united under a form of a "pop up" canopy known as a *chupa*, and before their unity is official, the groom must break a glass by stepping on it to signify the fragility of the sacred unit.

By Kabbalistic teachings, we also understand that this shattering symbolizes the sexual union. The breaking of the glass prefigures the married couple's sexual exchange that is not only permitted now, but is obligatory, as we explained earlier in the laws of purity and conjugal rights. We are also advised that breaking of the glass symbolizes the "breaking of the hymen," even figuratively, which is a reason why any groom aims to get the job done in one initial shot, rather than repeatedly stepping on the elusive glass.

The groom can break any kind of glass: old, new, borrowed, or blue. Whatever one chooses, it should be well wrapped to prevent injury. A heavy cloth napkin is standard, but one can enhance the ritual with a satin pouch or a velvet bag.

The idea of a functional marriage represented in the aspect of sexual union thereof is applied by coupling of Z'eir Anpin (the male organ) and Nukva (the female genitles).

The Arizal refers to *face-to-face coupling* since in order for the world to exist, there has to be at least some type of coupling, however superficial, between Z'eir Anpin and Nukva.

By way of analogy, if a married couple is not attuned to each other (let's say because they are distracted by the exigencies of their careers/occupations) and their love for each other is very suppressed, they can still continue to keep their household running on "automatic pilot," communicating on only the most superficial level. But life in their home during this period will certainly be dull, dreary, and even somewhat oppressive. When their consciousness "matures" and they turn to each other in order to relate on a deeper level, the effect of this heightened type of relationship will spill over into all the elements that make up life.

The Kabbalists get even more specific and state that the presence of a "female" (i.e., recipient) to receive and reproduce the male seminal essence can only inspire a person to couple with that female if he is mature enough to sense the value of propagating himself (or his ideas) for the benefit of the outside world.

As we mentioned earlier regarding the dance of the "bottom wetness" and the "upper water," in order to couple, the male and female partzufim, within the Tree of Life, must mutually arouse each other. The Zoharic terms for these processes of arousal are "the descent of male water" and "the ascent of female water," respectively. The images evoked are that of rain for the male and the upwelling of spring water, for the female.

# Chapter 31
## Receptivity: How Technology Can Serve Us

Even connection on a soul level is enabled by technology today. How? Consider the universe as a large musical composition where each one of us plays a role of a single note. By utilizing these tools, one can pro-actively, rather than reactively, be part of a global result. One can either influence or be influenced, to be truly unified with others, on a positive and a majestic level.

Another interesting aspect of technology is that it essentially defies time and space by providing immediate and infinite accessibility to anyone, anywhere, at any time. By allowing this to occupy a significant part of our lives, to say the least, we are agreeably enrolled in the divine plan of creation, which the Kabbalists tell us is signified on a micro level by our modern "omnipresence."

## Light My Fire

The Arizal tells us that the male/female energies and our role as a micro luminary (the soul stands for the fire that ignites the external shell, the body, toward divine action) is manifested in the dynamic between the sun and moon.[47] In the beginning, commentators tell us, the moon, representing the female energy (female cycle and menstruation is calculated by the moon) *complained* to the Creator of the existence of two equally sized luminaries and their "roles." As we discussed earlier, this kind of "complaint" would be ego sourced, and thus, God diminished lady moon, leaving "a greater light to rule the day, and a smaller light to rule the night." Of course, this commentary isn't a proclamation regarding the moon's pettiness or jealousy, but rather this example is utilized here in order to present the dual nature of creation. The smaller luminary represents the receiver in this "celestial dance," while the sun represents the giver, as in all feminine/masculine radiant/reflective energies in the universe and between worlds.

Since both are necessary components of creation, there is no intrinsic superiority of one over the other; from the Creator's perspective, they are both "great luminaries."

This "sin" of the moon and its subsequent banishment from the daytime is seen as the precursor to the primordial sin of Adam and Eve; consumption of the forbidden fruit and the subsequent banishment from the Garden of Eden.

Kabbalistic teachings tell us that this luminary "dispute" could have been easily rectified had Adam honored God's single prohibition; alas, not only did this not advance in the desired direction, but the "primordial sin" placed us humans at an even greater disadvantage. We are in fact notified that Adam was prohibited from the "consumption" only for a number of hours prior to the launching of the Shabbat, the day of rest—yet he failed to heed.

## Tree Huggers

The ancient Kabbalists tell us that, primordially, all trees were fruit-bearing, and that this will also be the case in the messianic times ahead. Yet, we

---

47 Wisnefsky, Moshe, and Ben Šelomo. 2008. *Apples from the Orchard : Gleanings from the Mystical Teachings of Rabbi Yitzchak Luria.* Malibu: Thirty Seven Books.

are well familiar with fruitless trees; the commentary here adds that a fruitless tree represents an imperfect universe, for the ultimate function of a tree is to produce fruit. In this sense, Deuteronomy 20:19 tells us that "man is a tree of the field," and thus the fruitless relationship is an anomaly, not a common occurrence. It is imperative to state that this isn't claimed in regard to the fertility aspect of the sacred union, regardless of the notion of "be fruitful and multiply," but rather to the soul elevation factor of a fruitful dyadic exchange. Our failed and dysfunctional relationships are a "symptom" of a dysfunctional world, and our aim as walking and talking vessels of divine sparks is to bring a correction, a tikkun, into our very existence, one that holds the potential to ripple forward anywhere we go.

Kabbalistic teachings[48] tell we all possess two souls, or rather two sides of the same divine entity: an "animal soul," called *nefesh behemit* in Hebrew, which embodies our natural, self-oriented instincts; and a "divine soul" or *nefesh elohit*, which embodies our transcendent drives, our desire to escape the egocentric notion and relate to the bigger picture, anything outside of us or our selfish needs and wants.

As assumed, the animal soul constitutes that part of ourselves that is common to all living creatures: the instinct for self-preservation and self-perpetuation. But since we are more than a sophisticated animal, we can graduate from the self and its needs ("How do I survive?" "How do I obtain food, shelter, money, power, knowledge, sexual satisfaction?") to a divine perspective ("Why am I here?" "What purpose do I serve? What can I do to pursue this purpose?"). When we reach the point at which we cease to function on a basic animalistic level, we begin to realize our uniqueness as human beings.

This is not to say that the animal self is to be rejected in favor of the divine human self; both of these functions are indispensable to a life of fulfillment and purpose. Even as we stimulate the divine in us to rise above the merely animalistic, we should aim to curb and refine our animal selves, learning to cultivate the constructive elements of selfhood, such

---

48 "Tanya." n.d. Www.Sefaria.Org. Accessed September 11, 2020. https://www.sefaria.org/Tanya%2C_Letter_of_Holiness.1?lang=bi.

as self-awareness and worth, courage, perseverance, while weeding out the egotistic and profane.

# Involvement

We might be doing something fully and completely; we might even be doing it joyously. But are we there? Are we involved?

Involvement means more than doing something right, more than giving it our all. It means that we care, that we are invested in the task. It means that we are affected by what we are doing, and that we are fully invested in whatever the consequences of actions may be.

Shouldn't the fact that I'm "doing" be enough? Kabbalah tells us that it isn't. we are given the example of the pomegranate, which holds much significance in the world of the divine and esoteric. In the Song of Songs 4:3, we see the lover telling his beautiful beloved, "thy temples are like a pomegranate split open behind thy veil." As interpreted by the Talmud (the book of Jewish law), the pomegranate is not just a model for something that contains many particulars. It also addresses the paradox of how an individual may be "empty" and, at the same time, be "full of good deeds as a pomegranate." The emphasis here is on the emptiness, or the value of these deeds, not their recipient, but rather to the giver's soul.

The pomegranate is a highly compartmentalized fruit: each of its hundreds of seeds is wrapped in its own sac of flesh and is separated from its fellows by a tough membrane. In the same way, it is possible for a person to do good deeds—many good deeds—yet they remain isolated acts with little or no effect on his nature and character. He may possess many virtues, but they do not alter the person; he may be full of good deeds, yet remain a shell, morally and spiritually.

The pomegranate in this sense represents our capacity to overreach ourselves and act in a way that surpasses our internal spiritual state. It is our capacity to do and achieve things that are utterly incompatible with who and what we are at the present moment.

# Praying versus Blessing

In Genesis 21, we read that the matriarch Sarah finally gives birth to Isaac. Prior to this statement, we are told that she "was barren, without any children."[49] The emphasis on Sarah being barren and without children, multiplying that statement in different variations, hints that Sarah had no womb, which means that the fact that she gave birth was nothing short of a miracle.

Not only was Sarah barren, so were all the matriarchs. We are told of Rebecca, "For she was barren" in Genesis 25:21, and also, "Rachel was barren" in Genesis 29:31. Leah's situation is not mentioned explicitly, but it is derived from the verse, "And God saw that Leah was despised, and He opened her womb." Thus, Leah also would not have had children naturally, without divine intervention and as compensation for her relational disadvantage.

Why is the notion of infertility an emphasized and uniting factor across the board of our foremothers? Kabbalistic teachings provide various answers to the above question. The leading one being, "Why were the Matriarchs barren? It is because the Holy One had a desire for their prayers and a desire for their talk?"[50]

But does this make sense? Why would the divine source demand our pleading, and moreover, the pleading of the sacred foremothers? When you dig deeper into the commentary, you realize that this statement does not mean that the Creator literally needs our prayers, but rather that he *wants* us to pray because prayer can have a revolutionary and altering effect. Prayer holds the potential to alter one into a different person with a different destiny. It can elevate one to a higher spiritual level. Note that the concept of prayer relates to any form of connection to the divine, *hityachadut* in Hebrew, that enables a "conversation," verbal or internal, with the divine. It can be achieved via meditation, chanting, or yogi practices.

---

49 Genesis 11:30

50 Genesis Rabba 45:4

Kabbalistic teachings further explain that challenges are based on a person's righteousness. The greater a person is, the more difficult are the tests that he or she must go through. The Creator, according to this logic, examines nice looking pitchers, rather than pitchers in poor condition. Similarly, in order to become a Navy Seal, one is forced to go through a difficult process of toughening, in comparison to a simple draft.

The Midrash Rabba (the commentary of the five books of the Torah and the five scrolls [*megillot*]) offers a unique approach to this matter. The Matriarchs do not give birth "so that they will accompany their husbands in their beauty." That is, the objective is for them to remain as beautiful as a bride on her wedding day. Since the emphasis on physical beauty might be inspiring, yet does not fall into place with the traditional view of importance on a global scale, it is suggested that the emphasis might not be on physical beauty, but on the end result—the unifying factor of a joint destiny; difficulties and tests are liable to drive a couple apart and put a distance between them, yet adversity can also propel a couple to get closer to one another when the problem is viewed as a *mutual* challenge.

So this applies to the notion of different forms prayer and the part they play in both getting closer to the divine source as well as to our partners. We have stablished the idea that prayer can literally alter the course of action a certain individual should experience in the life course; what is the difference between this practical approach of prayer and blessing? We often pine for a blessing from above and at times might even seek that approval from a tangible entity, such as clergy or other official source of solace. But it is imperative to comprehend that the Kabbalistic interpretation of a blessing is profound, yet less powerful than a prayer, thus the global esoteric draw toward mindfulness and meditation. In acquiring a blessing, we can receive what *should be* given to us, perhaps in a speedy fashion or much earlier than it was coming; yet, a blessing given through a channel or a vessel in a tangible form, be it human or otherwise, cannot *create*, only *format*. In other words, our "destiny" cannot be altered by blessing, but it can be rerouted by prayer.

# Quickstep Meditation

We will return to the seventy-two sequences of the divine and choose the sequence יהו for this purpose as this should represent a priestly blessing for wellness, positivity, and the removal of any negative thought, given that we occupy the lowest of worlds in this realm. This sequence should be pronounced as *YAY*.

You may use יהו while scanning the sequence, chanting it, or seeing it in your mind's eye while keeping your eyes closed. Chanting and seeing with your eyes closed can obviously be conjoined in order to enhance the experience.

Sit comfortably and place your hands on your knees. Take five deep inhales and five deep exhales to the count of five each.

Begin to visualize the sequence and apply whichever method that suits your choice for the purpose of this meditation.

Stay focused; go back and forth onto the specific letters, their shapes, and their sounds.

Remain focused and start shifting your body, rocking it from side to side, or back to front. The body is your receptacle that carries this energy and the connection to the divine, and thus should be utilized in this practice.

Remain here and keep breathing naturally for a few moments. We will practice some pranayama. When you're ready, place your index finger on your right nostril and the thumb on your left nostril. Close the left nostril and inhale through the right nostril, then close it with your index finger, release the left nostril, and exhale through it. Now keep the left nostril open, inhale through it, then close it with your thumb, and open the right nostril to exhale. Repeat these altering breaths, inhales, and exhales for five counts each.

When you feel relaxed and satisfied, slowly open your eyes.

# Chapter 32

We all have all aspects of the Tree of Life within us, only some aspects are less developed than others. Malchut, or Shekinah, represents the egotistical, "earthly" sephirah of them all since it sits at the bottom, connecting to lower worlds under, and attaining the upper nine sephirot (sephirah from sapphire/luminous).

## Addiction According to Kabbalah

We all have our ticks and challenges; for some, these turn into a problematic habit, or can even be defined as an addiction. But what does it have to do with the spirit? Isn't addiction a physical struggle, whether it is alcoholism or another drug dependency, unhealthy food consumption, or abusive behavior that deprecates another? Kabbalistic teachings look at this very common challenge differently. Let's go back to the definition just to make sure we comprehend the core of it. We understand that the addict has a fundamental inability to live peacefully and contentedly, and thus uses his or her behavior (drug of choice, or other manifestations) in order to induce a temporary state of relief from his or her deep, incessant discomfort with life.

What is it that makes the addict unable to handle life like other individuals in the first place? If we were speaking of a physical ailment—say chronic migraines—we would not say that the problem is not the head pain or that the pain is only a symptom. Instead, we would define it as a complex neurological disease that affects 18 percent of women and 6 percent of men in the US alone.

OK, so how does understanding it help? The understanding of what the actual matter is, rather than referring to the symptoms as "the problem," allows the addict to stop escaping to the destructive behavior, and instead approach the source of the suffering.

Let us break it down even further, shall we? We are all very familiar with the the Twelve Steps program and the Alcoholics Anonymous foundation. This establishment formed a bridge that has since enabled millions of people struggling with malfunctional behavior to seek and find a solution. What most of us are not aware of is how all of it came to be. Briefly, the founder of this system was a nineteenth century business-man named Rowland Hazard who struggled with an alcohol addiction himself. As with most creative ideas, this one emerged from a personal need that wasn't yet met.

Hazard sought for a solution to his problem for decades until he finally ended up in one very unique clinic; that of Carl Jung. To make this saga shorter, Jung suggested to Hazard that the only way he believed a relief could be in the cards for him was through a spiritual quest, one that involved "a vital spiritual experience." What does that mean? Jung wasn't certain himself, but he did recognize that in the cases which found long-term relief from habitual destruction and addictions, the patients made a complete psychic and spiritual leap. This sounds fantastic, but from that "meager" point emerged Hazard's healing (different than curing; the former is infinite while the latter is short-lived) as well as the establishment of the Twelve Steps program. In Hazard's case, it was the Oxford Group, a popular religious movement of the day, that stressed rigorously honest self-reflection, prayer, and meditation.

Let us look at some of the AA principles:

- We recognize we have a challenge that requires solving.
- We are honest with ourselves.
- We talk it over with another person.
- We make amends to those we had harmed.

- We try to carry this message to others with no thought of reward.
- We pray to whatever godly or divine source we choose.

So how does this all relate to Kabbalah and our relationships? From these experiences, and the only solution that was found for the struggle of addiction and habitual pain, we can conclude that the source of relief being spiritual can only mean one thing: that addiction or malfunctional habits are maladies of the soul.

What does it mean to be spiritually ill? what is the root cause of the spiritual illness called addiction?

The infinite relief, achieved through the spiritual ground, across all boards on a global scale, regardless of any background, race, age, gender, or denomination, is that the person who is challenged in this realm is inflicted with the yearning for divine guidance and can become well only by having some contact with the Creator, whether within him, or externally.

Does that mean that everyone suffering from these challenges are really supersensitive, spiritually passionate seekers?

Not exactly.

More aptly stated: *all* human beings have a deep-seated need for spiritual contact. But most of us can manage through life without it. Kabbalistic teachings tell us that addicts, conversely, are challenged by the dissonance of this lacking, the sense of separation from the divine, the ache of loneliness that we have all encountered with the breaking of the vessels, what we referred to as Shevirah.

For people struggling with addictions, these challenges are sourced in the core. The very experience of separation manifests in seeking an external remedy when the only applicable solution is within, through spiritual consciousness.

Kabbalah tells us that the Song of Songs relates to the craving of the Creator's closeness, as this entire poetic creation is an allegory for humanity as the feminine voice, and the Creator as the masculine.[51]

---

51 Song of Songs 2:5 KJV

To make things more comprehensible, regardless of our situations and whether we are plagued with habitual tendencies that are disagreeable (aren't we all?), we do not really have an existence that is independent from the all-encompassing, all-pervasive Unity of All.

Humanity strives for creation through unity with the divine, because in all worlds in which the soul travels and elevates, starting from our tangible world of action and all the way up to the world of emanation, we are only *forming* NOT *creating*, because creation is solely divine. Creating something from nothing is divine, and thus the "addict's" struggle is with the remoteness from that essence, which is, due to internal sensitivity, much more bothersome and destructive than it is for the rest of us simple dwellers. As humans, we can change something into another thing. Whether we speak of the artist who turns paint and canvas into a masterpiece, or a builder who turns steel and glass into a skyscraper, we are talking about the manipulation of form, not the creation of new existence. Matter and energy cannot be created or destroyed; they can only be changed into different forms.

By this logic, if you exist, then you are a something. But that's only because God is creating you that way in this instant. Your essence is to be nothing. Or, should we say, your true and natural state is to have no existence of your own, and to exist only as the Creator exists, within the totality and oneness of God.

## Soul Stuff

The core of Kabbalistic teachings focuses on the soul. In this view, the soul of a person comprises its "image" (tzelem) and its triad of soul components: nefesh/ruach/neshamah.

As we know, the soul is comprised of five levels: nefesh, ruach, neshamah, chayah, and yechidah. The latter two are the soul's "image." In short, the nefesh is the animating soul that enlivens the body. The ruach is the emotions. The neshamah is the intellect. The chayah is the will and lifeforce. The yechidah is the unique divine spark.

The "image" (comprised of the upper chayah and yechidah) enters the human body at conception; the nefesh upon birth, the ruach when it turns thirteen, and the neshamah when it turns twenty, by Kabbalistic views.

Does it matter whether the soul needs "repair" or whether it has accomplished its goals? Kabbalah teaches us that it does matter. Aligned this way, the soul of the "less righteous" undergoes repeated reincarnations, in order to be refined. Therefore, the refinement process of these souls is completed relatively quickly, in only four "generations."

But the souls of those who are mostly good, righteous people, the inverse is true. Each time they are reincarnated, they become purer than they were the time before. But since, unavoidably, they must commit some new sin in each incarnation, they will be reincarnated again and again, until they fulfill all 613 commandments in Jewish law and correct all the sins they committed in their previous lifetimes. Therefore, the number of incarnations they must undergo gets drawn out, up to two thousand. By the end of the process, fortunately, they require no more rectification at all.

Kabbalah tells us that "evil" can never face holiness directly, for holiness is a sublime light, and thus "blinds evil."

Ancients teachings say "the wicked do not greet the Shekinah,"[52] meaning they cannot face it directly. Rather, they are attached to it from the back, facing the Shekinah's back, and this is how they derive their sustenance.

In Hebrew, the idiom for "to greet" is literally "to receive the face of" (*kabalat panim*). If we imagine the forces of evil as *cosmic leeches* or other such sucking creatures, the imagery of them sucking off the back of the body conveys the idea that they receive only minimal life force from holiness. The front of the body houses much more vitality and sources of higher-quality life force.

---

52 "Sotah 42a:8-16." n.d. Www.Sefaria.Org. Accessed September 11, 2020. https://www.sefaria.org/Sotah.42a.8-16?lang=bi.

# Spells and Whistles

The Hebrew letters are said to be the divine code for all existence. In fact, it is believed that the Creator manifested this entire universe by uttering specific sequences of the Hebrew letters. In that sense, the creation of the universe and everything in it was compounded by these mysterious combinations of these sequences, including the shape of the letters, what they precede or follow, and the meaning of the sequence, in definition. In that sense for instance, the choice of calling a dog its Hebrew name, כלב, was based on the definition of the first syllable כ, which means "like" or "similar to," and the two following syllables לב, which stand for heart; in essence, it means "like a heart," which relates to a dog's nature. Kabbalah tells us that upon Adam naming all that this universe encompasses, these divine codes were decided based on the nature of each and every energy of the prospectively named.

# Form Your Own Manifestation

For the sake of this exercise, we will establish our own view of manifestation and reform things (of course we cannot create, only "reshape") from inflicted to "righteous."

Grab a piece of paper and pencil. I encourage you to use a pencil rather than a pen so that you are able to employ an eraser for a future task. Sit peacefully and focus on the sheet in front of you. Write down a few "I am" statements that come to mind without rethinking or heavily evaluating. This is a private exercise for self-exploration, so be candid and speedy.

Now that you've written a number of statements, retreat to a quiet place, and sit comfortably. Take a few inhales and exhales to the count of five to seven, whatever is more comfortable. Keep your eyes closed and body relaxed. When you feel relaxed and refreshed, go back to the statement sheet. Read the statements to yourself, and evaluate which are reinforcing and helpful, and which are deprecating and demeaning.

Tackle the statements that are not satisfactory and cross them out with the pencil. From within these "crossed" statements, retrieve a number of letters that can comprise a positive statement, and erase the rest.

For example, if a less appealing statement is "I am self-absorbed," retrieve the letters "d," "o," and "b" from "absorbed" and add the letter "l" from "self" to create the statement, "I am bold."

Repeat this routine for all your statements; if you came across one that doesn't "pen out," leave it be, its purpose will come to you at the right time.

When you conclude, repeat the quick meditative and breathing technique offered in the beginning, and then return to your daily routine.

www.ingramcontent.com/pod-product-compliance
Lightning Source LLC
Chambersburg PA
CBHW021045090426
42738CB00006B/191